A YEAR OF LIVING SINFULLY

7 DEADLY SINS. 365 DAYS.

A SELF-SERVING GUIDE TO DOING WHATEVER THE HELL YOU WANT

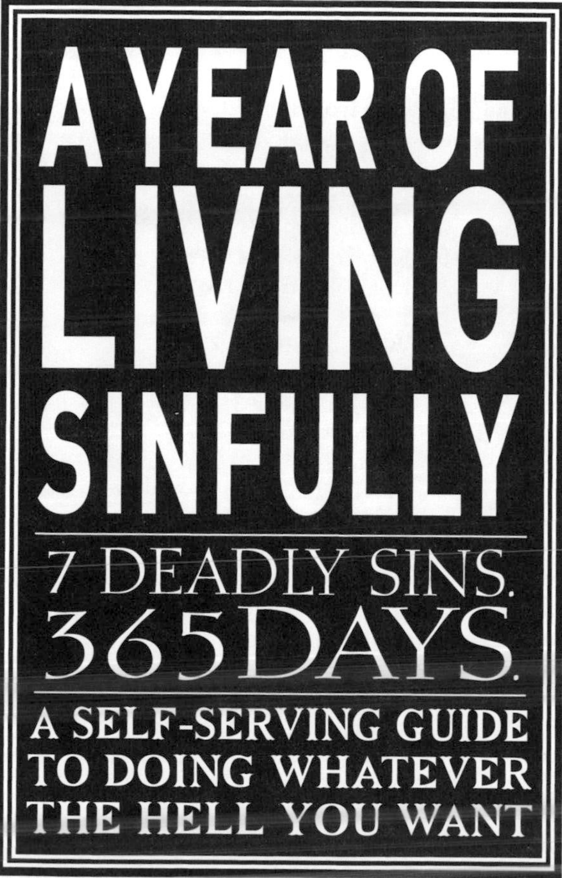

ERIC GRZYMKOWSKI
Full-Time Sinner

Published by
Adams Media, a division of F+W Media, Inc.
57 Littlefield Street, Avon, MA 02322. U.S.A.
www.adamsmedia.com

ISBN 10: 1-4405-1253-1
ISBN 13: 978-1-4405-1253-7
eISBN 10: 1-4405-3177-3
eISBN 13: 978-1-4405-3177-4

Printed in the United States of America.

10 9 8 7 6 5 4 3 2 1

Library of Congress Cataloging-in-Publication Data
is available from the publisher.

To my brother Brian, whose self-indulgent lifestyle provided ample inspiration whenever I ran out of fresh ideas.

Acknowledgments

After curating an entire year's worth of sinful activities, it's tempting to pretend I did it all without an ounce of help. That I single-handedly conceptualized, wrote, edited, printed, bound, shipped, and stocked this very book that you are holding in your hands. Alas, I was never a very good liar.

The truth is this book would never have come into existence without the help of some very talented writers and editors. Katie Corcoran Lytle and Peter Archer deftly guided me through the writing process from conception to finished manuscript, and the finished product is far superior thanks to your combined editorial prowess. Without my all-star contributing team of Sarah Gagnon, Scott Lieber, Amy Mortensen, Mary Kathryn Shannon, and Katie Walsh, this compendium would be more of a pamphlet. Their dedication to self-indulgence and hedonism is inspiring.

Creating a book is no simple task, but the editors at Adams Media continue to amaze me with the quality of the finished work that winds up on bookstore shelves. I hope you enjoy reading this one as much as we all enjoyed making it.

Introduction

Your entire life, you've done all the right things. You studied hard in school, stayed away from drugs and alcohol (for the most part), and spent countless hours volunteering your time and money to charity. Deep inside though, you can't deny the nagging feeling that you might be missing out on something. That the joy you get from all your philanthropy and general do-goodery pales in comparison to all the fun you could have should you choose to walk another path. One that's darker and more sinful. A little more self-indulgent.

Take a look around you. Society doesn't reward Eagle Scouts and those who head up the PTA with anything more than a pat on the back and maybe a free beer at the local watering hole. Instead, the hedonistic rock stars and smarmy politicians receive our endless praise and adoration. So if you want to really break out of your shell you'll have to act less like Mother Teresa or Nelson Mandela and more like Madonna or Charlie Sheen. After all you've done for everyone else, it's time you started to think about what really makes *you* happy for a change.

But transitioning from someone who spends most of the day worrying about other people to someone who focuses on making yourself deliriously happy takes more than just a weekend bender and a pack of unfiltered cigarettes. It takes dedication, patience, perseverance, and, most importantly, time—an entire year, to be exact.

In the following pages you'll find a comprehensive guide that outlines an entire year's worth of lavish, decadent, and sinful activities that, more likely than not, will make you ecstatic with happiness. In just twelve months, you'll spend, eat, waste, splurge, and sleep your way to a completely new person. You'll learn what it takes to ignore what's best for the world and focus your attentions on what's best for you, and to hell with the consequences.

Be forewarned though, kicking decorum to the curb and doing what makes you happy is not for everyone. But once you embrace your inner hedonist, you will find that there is no greater joy than doing precisely what you want, whenever you want to do it. But be careful. After tackling an entire year's worth of self-indulgent activities, you may uncover a dark, terrifying secret: It feels really good to be really bad.

JANUARY 1

Put the Focus Back on You

I am convinced that the majority of people would be generous from selfish motives, if they had the opportunity.

—Charles Dudley Warner, American author

On the first glorious day of the year, everybody focuses on ways to improve their lives. For some reason, they strive to achieve this by volunteering more, losing weight, and giving up some of their nasty habits.

That's ridiculous! Those activities will make your life worse, not better. Instead of striving to save the world, your New Year's resolution this year is to focus more on yourself. So, take the money you normally set aside for charities and roll it into your rainy day fund. Living a completely selfish and hedonistic lifestyle isn't cheap after all, and you're going to need plenty of cash to do it right.

While you're at it, cancel any volunteering you have lined up so you'll have time to plan your year of debauchery. The local nursing home will just have to find somebody else to pull the bingo balls on Sunday.

Unlike all the resolutions that you've failed to keep, you're going to make this one stick. Just be sure you don't lose sight of what's important. Yourself.

Rest for the Wicked Whenever you are tempted to do something selfless, go to the nearest store and buy something you don't need.

Backup New Year's Resolutions

- Gain twenty pounds
- Take up smoking
- Be less punctual

Order a Kid's Meal

Never eat more than you can lift.

—MISS. PIGGY

There's no denying it—fast food makes you fat. Unfortunately, it also happens to be delicious. Fortunately, there is a way to enjoy its wonderful, greasy goodness without all the guilt. Instead of ordering a milkshake, large fries, and a triple-decker bacon cheeseburger, turn your attention to the kid's menu. Sure you're decades past adolescence, but deep down you're still a kid.

So pick your favorite fast food option and order it up in kid's meal form. The portions are smaller, the taste is the same, and you get a fun toy to play with, too. Bonus points if you play in the indoor playground when you're done.

Rest for the Wicked Do not put the toy in your mouth. It's a choking hazard.

Most Unhealthy Kids Meals

- McDonald's Mighty Kids Meal: Double cheeseburger, fries, chocolate milk
- Wendy's Kids' Meal: Chicken sandwich, fries, chocolate Frosty
- KFC Kids Meal: Popcorn chicken, potato wedges, string cheese, soda

JANUARY 3

Drink Twenty-One Shots

Live as long as you may, the first twenty years are the longest half of your life.

—Robert Southey

On your twenty-first birthday, it is customary to drink twenty-one shots to commemorate your passage into adulthood. If twenty-one is a still-fresh memory, congratulations! This should be easier the second time around. But even if you're well past twenty-one now, it's still important to let loose. Not because you have something to prove. Not because it's going to make you forget your problems. Simply because it's going to be one hell of a good night.

So go ahead and do it: drink twenty-one shots like it's your twenty-first birthday. Pace it out throughout the day. Wake up early and have a shot an hour until night time. Eat meals in between, and most importantly, mark each shot with a tally on your forearm. Once you're done, no one will ever doubt your drinking ability again.

Rest for the Wicked A lot of people don't care for the taste of shots, but don't let that stop you. Have a beer nearby to use as a chaser.

Best Shots to Try

- Jaeger-bomb: Jaegermeister, Red Bull
- Soco and lime: Southern Comfort, lime juice
- Three Wise Men: Jim Beam, Jack Daniel's, Johnnie Walker
- Tequila

JANUARY 4

Read a Book on the Phone

The true art of memory is the art of attention.

—Samuel Johnson

When you hear the phone ring, there's always a moment of panic. Chances are it's that one friend or relative who is just calling to listen to him or herself talk. Yes, you love your grandma to death, but surely you have better things to do than listen to her drone on about her dry skin for two hours.

The good news is that nobody ever said that you actually had to pay attention. Instead of waiting anxiously for the phone to ring, make the call yourself. Instant brownie points. Once the gabbing commences, crack the spine of your favorite novel, snuggle into a comfy recliner, and get comfortable. You're going to be here for awhile.

Rest for the Wicked Throw in an occasional "hmm" or "you don't say" to feign interest.

Excuses to End the Conversation

- "I can't hear you anymore. I think your phone is broken."
- "Is it 7:30 already? Time for bed."
- "Shoot, I forgot I have jury duty. Got to go."

JANUARY 5

Take the Elevator One Floor

I have never taken any exercise except sleeping and resting.

—Mark Twain

Ever since the invention of the elevator, staircases have been demoted for use only during single-floor journeys. But why do we even bother using them then? There aren't any Elevator Police enforcing a minimum number of floors per elevator ride. Who cares if you're in a two-story building? You deserve that elevator ride just as much as someone riding to the observation deck on the 103rd floor of the Sears Tower—especially if you're carrying something heavy.

Some people might call it laziness, but it's really a way to preserve your energy. After all, if you're in a building with an elevator, you're probably about to do something strenuous like check Facebook at your desk or walk around a department store. Don't waste precious energy hoofing up the stairs when you can arrive at your destination perfectly cool and collected.

Rest for the Wicked If anybody glares at you, bring an empty box and pretend it's full of heavy office supplies.

Fun Things to Do on Elevators

- Face the wrong direction.
- Press all of the buttons.
- Sing along with the Muzak. Loudly.

JANUARY 6

Stage a Private Concert

A record is a concert without halls and a museum whose curator is the owner.

—Glenn Gould, Canadian pianist

There is no such thing as a good concert venue. Either you're wedged into a dingy bar, waist-deep in sweaty armpits, or you're in the back of an empty stadium struggling to hear. The only surefire way to enjoy yourself is to have your favorite artist come to you.

First, you need to decide on a band. Keep in mind that you may need to set your sights fairly low. You have a decent shot at scoring a local indie band, but chances are you're completely out of luck if you have your heart set on Billy Joel. So call some friends, set up a backyard stage, and hope the neighbors don't call the cops. Sure it's about 1,000 times more expensive than buying a CD, but it's at least 2,000 times more awesome. After all, you can defray the costs by charging admission. Even friends and family don't get a handout. There's no such thing as a free lunch, right?

Rest for the Wicked Hire a few bouncers to keep out the riffraff and keep the crowd under control.

World's Worst Concert Trends

- Moshing
- Charging for water
- Limiting one beer per customer
- Holding up cell phones instead of lighters

JANUARY 7

Play Video Games All Day

I never let any of my sons beat me at video games.

—Coolio

When you're not at work, you have a few options. You can either explore the world by visiting museums, eating out, engaging in the human experience. Or, if you are the type who is easily overwhelmed by such things, there's always the timeless, antisocial art of video gaming. Why waste your time mucking about in reality when the virtual world is so much more entertaining?

So blow the dust off your forgotten consoles and stretch out those thumbs. You're in for a rough afternoon of gaming. Rediscover your lost love of Zelda, steal a car in Grand Theft Auto, or find the golden gun in Goldeneye. You can use your day to replay old games or discover new ones, just as long as everything you do today revolves around a screen. Some people say video games help develop hand-eye coordination and problem solving skills. That's justification enough right there.

Rest for the Wicked Try to at least open a window and let some natural light in to get your daily intake of vitamin D.

Best Video Games of All Time

- Legend of Zelda: Ocarina of Time
- Donkey Kong
- Grand Theft Auto IV

Turn Winter Into Summer

Winter, a bad guest, sitteth with me at home; blue are my hands with his friendly handshaking.

—Friedrich Nietzsche

As the cold wind blows against your windows, you may wonder why you didn't settle down somewhere more tropical. All the blankets in the world can't warm you up when you're dealing with yet another snowmageddon. Fortunately, all you need to do to feel like you're living on the equator is crank up your thermostat. A lot. Sensible people keep their heat at a chilly 65°F in the winter, but tonight you're going to blast it to a balmy 80°F (or higher if you can).

Yes, wasting fossil fuels is bad for the environment. Yes, your heating bill is going to skyrocket this month. But you won't be worrying about either of those things when you can finally ditch the hat and gloves for the evening. To make your hot winter's night even better, invite a few friends over and throw a winter beach party. Trade in your oversized hoodies and thermal underwear for bikinis and swim trunks and cool off with some frozen daiquiris. Just because it's winter doesn't mean you can't still have a good time.

Rest for the Wicked Seal all windows and doorways to prevent excess heat from escaping.

Vodka-Infused Pineapple

1 pineapple, cored and cut into 1-inch chunks
1 750 ml bottle of vodka

1. Pour vodka into a large bowl and submerge the pineapple in the liquid. Cover with plastic wrap and let stand for 24 to 48 hours.
2. Pour the contents of the bowl through a large mesh strainer held over separate bowl. Arrange the pineapple chunks on a plate and serve.

JANUARY 9

Steal WiFi from Your Neighbor

The day I made that statement, about the inventing the Internet, I was tired because I'd been up all night inventing the camcorder.

—AL GORE

Having 24/7 access to the World Wide Web has improved your connection to both friends and strangers—but it's also one more monthly autodraft payment coming out of your bank account. If you aren't willing to pony up the cash to stay connected, don't be afraid to leech off your neighbors. Think of it as a logical extension of your neighborly give-and-take. You water their plants when they're on vacation; they give you free Internet.

It doesn't matter if they're donating their WiFi unwittingly or if you've never actually watered their plants. They'll never notice and you'd be happy to babysit the hanging baskets if they asked. It's the thought that counts. And besides, if they were so worried about protecting their network, they'd be smart enough to put a security password on it.

Rest for the Wicked Keep your Internet theft to low-profile stuff like checking e-mail. If you start downloading the entire Law and Order SVU series, they may notice the lag in service.

Excuses If You Get Caught

- "That's so funny. Someone's been using my Internet connection too!"
- "It wasn't me. I still use dial-up."
- "I'll water your plants! Please don't take away my Internet."
- "What is the Internet, anyway?"

JANUARY 10

Deep-Fry Everything

I was never unusually squeamish; I could sometimes eat a fried rat with a good relish, if it was necessary.

—Henry David Thoreau

Many people overlook the fact that deep-frying an item—regardless of its flavor profile—increases its deliciousness by a power of ten. Don't believe it? Think about the following gustatory delights:

- Macaroni & cheese: check.
- Pickles: check.
- Ice cream: double check.

Sadly, only a fraction of the average diet consists of fried food. Such a shame. All that flavor-enhancing power sacrificed in the name of a thin waistline.

Not you though. You're perfectly happy the way you are. And just imagine how happy you'll be once you deep-fry everything in your kitchen.

So, tie on your apron, heat a few quarts of oil in a dutch oven, prepare some batter, and throw in whatever you can find. Sweet foods like candy bars, fruit, cookies, and brownies work great, but don't forget more off-beat savory items like olives, eggs, and pizza.

Rest for the Wicked Cook sweet and savory foods in separate oil. Otherwise your deep-fried Oreos might taste like fish sticks.

Foods Not Enhanced by Deep-Frying

- N/A

JANUARY 11

Lounge in a Hammock All Day

How beautiful it is to do nothing, and then to rest afterward.

—Spanish Proverb

The mention of a hammock evokes images of swaying palm trees, cool island breezes, and endless piña coladas. Too bad you're stuck in a wintry wonderland. But lucky for you, hammocks needn't be limited to faraway tropical paradises; the sun doesn't have to be shining in order for you to lounge around all day.

Once you've procured your hammock, get busy doing nothing. Place a stack of magazines and books within reaching distance, along with a cooler full of lemonade, beer, or fruity cocktail creations. If you're just as content to lie there free of distractions, go ahead and let the soft swaying of your suspended bed lull you into a deep relaxing sleep.

You may have a lot to do today, but is any of that stuff as appealing as taking a tropical vacation in your living room?

Rest for the Wicked Go for a fabric hammock if you have a choice. The knots on traditional rope hammocks can leave uncomfortable marks on the skin.

How to Get into a Hammock

1. Stand with your back pointing toward the hammock's center.
2. Gently sit into the hammock like a chair and wait for it to level out.
3. Swing your legs up and stretch them out.
4. Lie back.
5. Relax!

Only Watch Reality TV

Anyone who relies exclusively on television for his or her knowledge of the world is making a serious mistake.

—Steve Powers, American artist

These days, television programs fall into one of three categories: news, crime dramas, and reality shows. And there's only one genre worth watching: reality shows.

Let's face it, your friends aren't going to be discussing actual breaking news next time you get together. They're going to be talking about the latest girlfight or love triangle on their favorite reality show, and you need to keep up.

So rebel against those who say reality television is a waste of time and brain cells. They're wrong. On the contrary, it's the best way to stay in the know. So watch reality shows. All of them. You'll be amazed at how quickly you start to feel great about yourself. After all, you've never eaten a twenty-pound burrito right before running a road race in South Africa before giving a rose to the partner of your dreams—at least not yet anyway. And if there's one thing to be learned from reality TV, it's that those that can't do, watch.

Rest for the Wicked Some people think reality TV is trash, but think of them more as sociological experiments or exercises in how not to live.

Most Sinful Reality Shows:

1. *Bad Girls' Club*
2. *The Jersey Shore*
3. *The Real Housewives* franchise

JANUARY 13

Eat Ice Cream for Breakfast

Ice cream is exquisite. What a pity it isn't illegal.

—VOLTAIRE

It's a busy morning, and somewhere between styling your hair and brushing your teeth you have to tame your ravenous stomach. A quick peek around reveals the usual boring suspects—cereal, bagels, or week-old toast. But when you spy a container of ice cream, it's love at first sight.

Sure, it's not a breakfast item by conventional thinking, but who the hell wants to be conventional? Ice cream equals deliciousness, pure and simple. Whether it's cookie dough, chocolate fudge, or coconut, your stomach will thank you for giving it something awesome. And if you really need to justify your indulgence, help yourself to strawberry ice cream for that serving of fruit or coffee ice cream to get your daily dose of caffeine. After all, you've already factored in your daily dose of dairy.

Rest for the Wicked Eat at least two scoops to avoid hunger pains later.

Starbucks-Inspired Sundae

coffee ice cream
chocolate syrup
whipped cream
chocolate sprinkles

- Scoop a generous portion of ice cream into a bowl and drizzle with chocolate syrup. Apply whipped cream until you can no longer see the ice cream underneath. Top with sprinkles and enjoy.

JANUARY 14

Leave All the Lights On

Middle age is when a guy keeps turning off lights for economical rather than romantic reasons.

—Lillian Carter, American nurse and mother to President Jimmy Carter

There's no denying that turning off lights saves money, and it's good for the environment. But that's little consolation when you slip on one of your dog's chew toys and break your wrist.

So what are you waiting for? Flick on every light in the house and bask in the warming glow of a dozen iridescent bulbs. Since 90 percent of a light bulb's energy output is emitted as heat, the bulbs will actually help warm up the chilly January evening. Plus you can wander around to your heart's content, confident in the knowledge that you can see every snag in the carpet and avoid every loose nail.

Best of all, since your house is lit up like the Fourth of July, no burglar in his right mind would get within 100 feet.

Rest for the Wicked Invest in a sleep mask to block out the blinding light while you sleep.

The Eternal Light Bulb

A fire department in Livermore, California, houses one of the world's oldest working light bulbs. The bulb is more than 100 years old and was still on and working as of 2011.

Score a Free Continental Breakfast

Happiness depends on a leisurely breakfast.

—John Gunther, American Writer

The concept of a free meal might be an oft-doubted notion, but you can make the myth a reality. All you need is an unguarded continental breakfast and a little clever thinking. Sure you can easily afford to pay for a top-notch breakfast, but it's far more satisfying to pilfer one from a hotel conglomerate. Besides, the staff's just going to throw out the leftovers anyway, so you're really doing them a favor.

As any heist movie will demonstrate, the most important thing for a successful score is to stake out your target. Assess any security measures you will need to overcome and make note of all the exits should you need to make an abrupt retreat. Once you are fully prepped, pretend to be a guest and proceed to nonchalantly stuff your face with unlimited scones, muffins, cereal, and bagels. Just be quick about it. Countless thieves, far more skilled than you, have gotten pinched because they lingered too long at the coffee bar.

Rest for the Wicked If someone asks for your room number, just look confused and start muttering in another language.

Perfect Tourist Disguise

- I ♥ [insert city name] T-shirt
- Binoculars and massive SLR camera hanging around your neck
- Sunglasses (regardless of the weather conditions or time of day)

Buy an Entire Row of Seats for Your Flight

A hundred years ago, it could take you the better part of a year to get from New York to California, whereas today, because of equipment problems at O'Hare, you can't get there at all.

—Dave Barry

Before you book your next flight, imagine that the doors to the plane are just about to close, and your entire row is somehow still empty. Then imagine your disappointment as two passengers the size of elephants plunk down on either side of you.

While you can't remove annoying fellow passengers through sheer force of will, you can make sure they never have the chance to exist. The next time you have a long flight, go ahead and splurge—buy the entire row of seats.

That's right, the entire row. And milk that luxury for all it's worth. Read a book with your back against the window and your legs across the entire row. Pack some noodle salads and watermelon and set up a picnic on the two spares. Curl up on all three and take a nap.

And if some poor soul squeezed into the center seat behind you asks to take one of yours, have a ready response. "I paid for these," you can say, "and they're all mine."

Rest for the Wicked Be sure to buckle up. You don't want turbulence raining on your luxury parade.

Tricks to Increase Your Air Space

- Request an aisle seat
- Cough a lot and wear a face mask
- Fake-vomit into the courtesy bags

JANUARY 17

Make the Opposite of an Anonymous Donation

The poor don't know that their function in life is to exercise our generosity.

—Jean-Paul Sartre

Pure philanthropy is a rare trait in a person. If they're going to do some good, most people want to get credit where credit is due. And you are no better.

Today you're going fork over a large chunk of money to the charity of your choice. And then you're going to publicize the crap out of it. After all, you are going through all the trouble to donate money. The least the charity could do is acknowledge your generosity. Besides, perhaps the publicity will encourage other selfish people to get in on the charity train.

First, pick a charity, preferably one that makes you look the most saint-like—anything related to saving animals, terminally ill children, or the homeless are always safe bets. Then, donate an absurd amount of money to that cause and promote the hell out of your generosity.

Make your "selfless" act of generosity known through every portal possible. Don't be subtle. Brag about it on your Facebook page or Twitter account. Create a web page devoted to your substantial gift. Or erect a billboard heralding your general awesomeness to anyone passing by.

Rest for the Wicked Don't donate to any perfectly upstanding but less "aw"-inspiring charities.

Weirdest Charities

- Tall Clubs International Foundation (charity for tall people)
- The Order of the Azure Rose (organization to revive chivalry)
- The Critter Connection (guinea pig rescue group)

Only Drink Milkshakes All Day

That's a pretty f#king good milkshake. I don't know if it's worth five dollars, but it's pretty f*#king good.*

—Vincent Vega, *Pulp Fiction*

Blend some milk, a little ice cream, and maybe a few strawberries or some chocolate syrup, and voilà, you have one of the best cold-liquid mash-ups of the twentieth century: the milkshake. So why do you only indulge in them once in a blue moon? Maybe you secretly love milkshakes, but you're one of those, "Oh, I couldn't possibly!" types. Three words for you: live a little.

Consider this: all milkshakes, all the time. What's for breakfast? Strawberry milkshake. Lunch? Peanut butter milkshake. Dinner? Chocolate milkshake. Dessert? That old standby, vanilla. A milkshake may not be the healthiest food in the world, but it sure does a great job of convincing your stomach it's had a full meal. The result? A diet that's sure to shed a few pounds that's also easy to stick to.

Rest for the Wicked Take it slow. Two words: brain freeze.

Unusual Milkshake Flavors

- Maple-Bacon
- Guinness
- Cap'n Crunch

Take Over the Office Thermostat

I get here early every morning so I can set the thermostat. I like it a little cooler, around sixty-six degrees. I'm more productive. Maybe some people don't like it as cold as I do. But I don't care.

—OSCAR, *THE OFFICE*

Ever since companies started cramming strangers together in small quarters, people have been arguing about a subject that transcends all genders, races, religions, and creeds: the temperature.

The marketing team hates the cold, and the accounting folks can't stand anything above sixty degrees. But let's not forgot about the most important person in the office. You.

Today is your day. You're tired of being uncomfortable, and it's time to take control. The secret is to be stealthy. Arrive early, and wait until any other early risers leave the room to make coffee or grab a bagel. After that, it's as simple as adjusting the needle and walking away. If anyone changes the temperature during the day, just pull the fire alarm and change it back during the evacuation.

Until they figure out how to enclose cubicles in individual climate-controlled bubbles, the battle will rage on. But today, the winner is you.

Rest for the Wicked Always keep a sweater and a small fan next to your desk, just in case.

It's a Trap!

Beware: Your efforts may be in vain. Some HVAC companies install dummy thermostats near every cube to give employees the illusion of control.

JANUARY 20

Pretend You Lost Your Voice

People have to talk about something just to keep their voice boxes in working order so they'll have good voice boxes in case there's ever anything really meaningful to say.

—Kurt Vonnegut

The weather. The traffic. The latest in disgraced celebrity gossip. These are all topics you may discuss on a daily basis, regardless of whether you give a damn about any of it.

Truth be told, some days you wish life came with a mute button. But since it doesn't, a well-timed case of laryngitis may be just what the doctor ordered. Sorry, lady on the subway who wants to talk about the humidity, but these apologetic gestures mean I've been stripped of my vocal abilities. What's that, Linda in Accounting? You want to monopolize my entire lunch hour analyzing last night's episode of *Glee*? Shame, but I can't today.

After all, a day of silence may be all you need to happily sustain another year of mindless small talk. Actually, better make it two days.

Rest for the Wicked Be careful not to stub your toe or slam your hand in a door. One cry of pain and your cover of silence is blown forever.

Cat Got Your Tongue?

Your fake laryngitis doesn't necessarily have to be caused by a fake infection. Common causes of the condition include vocal overuse, smoking, drinking, and allergies.

JANUARY 21

Sleep for Twenty-Four Hours

There is only one thing people like that is good for them; a good night's sleep
—Edgar Watson Howe, American editor

These days, nobody gets enough sleep. Most people are lucky if they snooze six hours a night, and plenty get by with even less. While it's impossible to make up for all that lost slumber in a single day, you can certainly make a dent.

Spending an entire twenty-four hours in bed might seem like a waste of time, but what else would you be doing with that time? Unlike going to the movies, paying bills, or driving to the beach, sleeping all day requires no money and burns zero fossil fuels. It's good for the environment and the soul.

This is going to be the single laziest, most relaxing day of your life so make sure you have plenty of pillows, warm blankets, and comfortable pajamas. Do your best to put all of your responsibilities out of your mind and focus on the task at hand—pure, unadulterated sleep.

Rest for the Wicked If you are a light sleeper, keep a fan running nearby to create white noise and block out any interruptions.

Best Sleep Aids

- Morgan Freeman recordings
- Civil War documentaries
- *War and Peace*

JANUARY 22

Buy a Robotic Vacuum

When your dreams turn to dust, vacuum.

—Author unknown

The vacuum cleaner is so 2002. In today's world you don't have to lug a big, cumbersome vacuum cleaner out of the closet when you want to clean. Instead you can solve the problem of a gross carpet with new age technology: your own cleaning robot.

Your purchase may seem a bit extravagant, but it's worth it to grab back some of your lost time. Just think, if you're wasting even just thirty minutes a week vacuuming, that's more than a whole day each year you could spend watching television or inventing a robot to do your laundry.

So head to the store and pick up one of those little disc-shaped robotic vacuum cleaners that looks more like a pet dog than a machine. Marvel as it detects when it hits a couch or table leg and heads in the opposite direction. It will cover every square inch of your floor in twenty minutes.

Congratulations, you're on the cutting edge of technology. Until something cooler comes along at any rate.

Rest for the Wicked Treat your new robot with care. You want it to think kindly of you after the machines become self-aware and enslave the human race.

How to Create Robot Art

1. Place your camera on a tripod
2. Turn off all the lights in a room
3. Lengthen the shutter speed of your camera to get more light to your sensor
4. Turn on your Roomba and let it clean. Its LED light will create a unique pattern.

JANUARY 23

Only Eat Things Containing Chocolate

What you see before you, my friend, is the result of a lifetime of chocolate.
—Katharine Hepburn

Since you likely eat at least three times a day, it's important to do it with style, class, and grace. It's also important to eat things that are really delicious.

If there's one thing uniting the world, it's our unending love affair with chocolate. So play your own game of Iron Chef for the day, and make chocolate the secret ingredient. It's decadent. It's delicious. And some dark chocolate is good for you. Studies have even shown that eating a small bar every day can lower both blood pressure and cholesterol. So, logically, eating the equivalent of 100 small bars must be 100 times better for you.

In the morning, you can start with a breakfast of chocolate cereal with chocolate milk. Then, instead of your regular morning coffee, order a mocha latte. For lunch, a Nutella sandwich. As for dinner, devour an entire chocolate cake. When you have your sugar hangover later that night, take two Advil and wash it down with a nice cup of hot cocoa. Rules are rules.

Rest for the Wicked Brush your teeth a few extra times during the day.

World's Biggest Chocoholics

According to the World Atlas of Chocolate, the following five countries consume the most chocolate per year per person.

1. Switzerland—22.36 lbs/yr
2. Austria—20.13 lbs/yr
3. Ireland—19.47 lbs/yr
4. Germany—18.04 lbs/yr
5. Norway—17.93 lbs/yr

Invent a Religious Holiday to Get Out of Work

I once wanted to become an atheist, but I gave up—they have no holidays.

—Henny Youngman

Every day, it seems somebody in your office is celebrating a different religious holiday—which wouldn't be a problem if you weren't so jealous that they get to leave the soul-sucking cube farm to do so. But what's stopping you from joining them?

Today you're going to fabricate a faith, as well as a nonexistent holiday, so you can pretend to fast and genuflect with the best of them. After all, secular people deserve time off, too. To begin, pull a religion out of thin air and invent a history of dogma (in case your boss quizzes you). Then invent a bogus-sounding holiday to go along with your equally bogus religion.

In an age where religious freedom is as important as breathing, there's no way your boss is going to deny your request for a day of religious celebration. Even if it is to celebrate "Super Awesome Day Off from Work Day."

Rest for the Wicked Don't mention anything to do with spells or human sacrifice. Your professional reputation is on the line here.

The Top 5 Lesser Known Religions

- Spiritism
- Pentecostalism
- Turtles and Tortoises
- The Dreaming
- Quimbanda

JANUARY 25

Move Your Dryer to Your Bathroom

Where there is no extravagance there is no love, and where there is no love there is no understanding.

—Oscar Wilde

When you take a warm shower, every moment you linger in the hot steam just delays the inevitable. Because once you turn that water off, you're trapped in the frozen wasteland that is your bathroom. A towel offers some relief, but it's hardly an adequate defense—unless, of course, you are willing to upgrade your bathroom hardware.

Granted, your clothes dryer is bulky, heavy, and awkward to move. But the trade-off of a warm, blissful embrace of a fresh hot towel far outweighs any inconvenience.

With the help of an unwitting partner, migrate your clothes dryer from its current location and wedge it in your washroom. Whenever you get in the shower, stuff your bath towel in and set it on high. Within a few minutes, you'll be treated to an experience that can only be described as "sublime."

Rest for the Wicked Take measurements of your bathroom before you attempt to move your dryer . . . and maybe purchase a hand truck. Why take unnecessary risks!

Alternative Uses for Dryer Sheets

- Hair static removers
- Insect and mouse repellents
- Car and locker air fresheners
- Disposable dust cloths

JANUARY 26

Take "Smoke" Breaks at Work

The time you enjoy wasting is not wasted time.

—Bertrand Russell, philosopher

It's always easy to spot the smokers at one's place of employment—they're the ones who are never at their desks. In fact, surveys have shown that the average smoker spends more than 100 hours a year on cigarette breaks. And if they can waste time in such colossal proportions, why can't you?

Since smokers are allowed outside multiple times a day to feed their addictions, it's only fair that normal people like you can take "smoke" breaks as well. Use your newly found free time to catch up with office coworkers, surf the Internet or just enjoy the fresh air. Chances are your boss will completely understand the need to take mental health breaks throughout the day (after all, who wants to stare at a computer screen for eight hours straight?). But if you have a real jerk of a boss, simply explain the rationale behind your "smoke" breaks. Even the meanest supervisor can't argue with that.

Rest for the Wicked Don't turn into an actual smoker when taking "smoke" breaks. Unless you want cancer, that is.

Optional Break Excuses

- Weak bladder
- Restless leg syndrome
- Allergy to toner

JANUARY 27

Send Naughty Pics to Your Significant Other

If somebody's looking at pictures of naked people and you go, "Oh I don't want to see that," you're lying. Cause naked people are always interesting. Always.

—Andy Richter, American actor and comedian

Digital cameras, cell phones, and the Internet have revolutionized the way we take and share pictures. At any time, we can take a picture and send it to someone on the other side of the world in a matter of seconds. And I do mean any time. But right now, nobody's watching, so now's the perfect time to grab your phone and slip away for a naughty bathroom photo session. It's time to prove you aren't always the little angel your significant other thought you were.

Lock the door and put on your sexiest striptease for the camera. Experiment with angles and different lighting to highlight your best assets. When it's time to send, fire them off in a series of increasingly explicit images to get your significant other really hot and bothered.

If you are worried about somebody else seeing the pictures, you can always crop out your head and Photoshop out any identifying birthmarks. But unless you're a famous celebrity or politician, chances are your naughty snapshots won't be circulating anytime soon.

Rest for the Wicked Don't use your company e-mail to send your naughty pics. IT workers are lonely, lonely people.

Celebrities Caught Sexting

- Lily Allen
- Senator Anthony Weiner
- Vanessa Hudgens
- Rihanna
- Brett Favre

JANUARY 28

Shave Your Head

I'm undaunted in my quest to amuse myself by constantly changing my hair.

—Hillary Clinton

Long, luscious, wavy hair is considered sexy in most of the world. Unfortunately, it also happens to be a royal pain in the ass to maintain. And for those not blessed with gorgeous locks, there's the never-ending battle with cow licks, widow's peaks, and split ends. It's enough to make you wonder if you wouldn't be better off without it.

Just imagine it for a moment, no more curlers, no more straightening irons, no more hair gel, no more scrambling with a towel when you get out of the shower. Just a smooth, sensual, bald head. It's what you've always wanted, but never had the nerve to do.

Trim your locks down with scissors first and then grab a fresh razor and head to the bathroom. Take one last look at that frustrating widow's peak and kiss your rat's nest goodbye.

Once you are fully shorn, head out for a drive and revel in the warm air whipping around your shiny new chrome dome. You'll be the envy of everyone you see. And if not, it's just hair. It'll grow back—eventually.

Rest for the Wicked Invest in a decent hat in case you aren't pleased with the results.

Notable Baldies

- Bruce Willis
- Sigourney Weaver
- Michael Jordan
- Natalie Portman
- Mr. Clean

Go Through the Express Line with More Than Twelve Items

Honesty is for the most part less profitable than dishonesty.

—Plato

During peak hours, grocery stores get so crowded that even the sweetest old ladies start throwing elbows. So when the checkout lanes get five-carts deep with grannies and loud-talkers on Bluetooths, skip the worst of the crowds and sneak into the express lane.

The sign says Twelve Items or Fewer, but does anyone really enforce that rule? Cashiers don't get paid enough to care and managers are too busy to worry about renegade express customers. The trick is to avoid detection from other customers.

Layer your basket to make it look like you have a small order. Hide your smaller groceries under large, lightweight items like leafy greens or paper towels. The next step is speed. Most registers let you swipe your credit card before the order is finished. Once the transaction has started and your card has been activated, it's way too much trouble to cancel it and ask you to leave the line.

Rest for the Wicked Shopping carts send off red flags to fellow express lane shoppers. Stick to baskets.

Supermarket Stats

- Average Price of Orders: $26.78
- Average Number of Trips Per Week: 1.7
- Average Number of Items Stocked: 38,718

Pretend to Be a Student

College is the best time of your life. When else are your parents going to spend several thousand dollars a year just for you to go to a strange town and get drunk every night?

—David Wood, English actor and writer

Remember college? Four years of keg stands, unlimited dining hall food, and Frisbee on the quad punctuated with the occasional philosophy class. Compared to your current daily itinerary of mindless cubicle work, pee-wee soccer games, family dinners, and reruns of *Seinfeld*, college was a veritable paradise.

Although you can't travel back in time to your glory days in college, you can travel to your nearest institution of higher learning to relive them. You may be several years (or decades) older than the average student, but that doesn't mean that you can't still keep up with them.

Once you are on campus, take this opportunity to sneak into a large lecture hall and actually pay attention—to make up for all the years you spent falling asleep in class. If the weather's nice, there's sure to be a protest or two going on that you can join. If you play the part right, everyone will just assume you're an aging grad student—and you might even get invited to a kegger.

Rest for the Wicked Be sure to bring along a backpack and $2 flip-flops to blend in.

Potential Activities to Relive

- Pull all-night study session
- Shower in community bathroom
- Steal dining hall trays
- Compete in beer pong tournament
- Attend an a capella concert

JANUARY 31

Shoot a Perfect Round of Golf (On Paper)

Golf is so popular simply because it is the best game in the world at which to be bad.

—A. A. MILNE

For a game that is supposed to be peaceful and tranquil, golf is about as relaxing as a trip to the dentist. But that doesn't stop millions of intrepid golfers from hitting the links every summer in pursuit of the single perfect round. It also doesn't stop 99.9 percent of them from failing miserably.

There's only one surefire way to shoot the ultimate round golf: cheat. You are the one holding the scorecard after all. Remember that downward spiral on the back nine? Nothing some creative math can't fix. And why not? Cheating at golf is a sacred pastime as old as the game itself. Who hasn't "accidentally" kicked their ball out of the rough or taken a mulligan or two?

With eraser in hand, go through your scorecard and make a few corrections. A birdie here, an eagle there. Nothing too crazy, just be sure you don't dip below the current record of 55. Otherwise you might have some explaining to do.

Rest for the Wicked Tip your caddie an extra $20 to buy his silence.

World's Toughest Courses

- Bethpage—Farmingdale, NY
- Jade Dragon—Lijiang City, China
- Pebble Beach—Pebble Beach, CA
- The Old Course—St. Andrews, Scotland
- The Kabul Club—Kabul Afghanistan

FEBRUARY 1

Drink Away Your Sorrows

I went on a diet, swore off drinking and heavy eating, and in fourteen days I lost two weeks.

—Joe E. Lewis

Most of the time, a single glass of wine is enough to take the edge off. Some nights, however, you may require a few dozen to achieve the same effect. Whether it's because you lost your job to someone half your age, or because your car was towed while you were filing divorce papers at the courthouse, there's no shame in drinking your problems away. But if you are going to drown your sorrows in alcohol, you might as well do it right. Instead of knocking a few back and calling it a night, you're going to drink until you can't feel feelings. And then you're going to drink some more.

Find a nice comfy stool at the bar and order up two shots of tequila—one for each hand. Wash it down with a few IPAs and maybe a whiskey sour or two. If the bartender gives you a hard time, tell him to mind his own business and pour you up another.

Rest for the Wicked Call a cab at the beginning of the night. You might not be able to dial a phone by the end.

Drinks to Avoid

- Cement Mixer: Bailey's and lime juice (curdles in your mouth)
- Motor Oil: Jagermeister, coconut rum, peppermint schnapps, and cinnamon schnapps
- Nyquil: Sambuca, triple sec, and grenadine

FEBRUARY 2

Don't Refill the Coffee Pot

I have measured out my life with coffee spoons.

—T. S. Eliot

As you trudge into the office and collapse on your desk, there is one saving grace to an otherwise miserable morning. A nice, hot cup of coffee. But once you finish topping off your mug with the last drops from the pot, you are presented with the ultimate office dilemma. To refill, or not to refill.

As long as nobody's watching, the answer is obvious. Bail.

Once you've gotten your fill—and checked to make sure the coast is clear—nonchalantly place the pot back in the machine and saunter off. Find a secluded area to enjoy your tasty beverage before anyone realizes the pot is empty. Once you are done, head back to the kitchen and join the witch hunt to track down the culprit. In reality, you're doing your coworkers a favor by leaving the pot empty. Perhaps instead of hyper-caffeinated brown sludge they'll turn to healthier options, like orange juice or soy milk.

Rest for the Wicked Destroy any security camera footage highlighting your lack of human decency.

Penance Should You Be Caught

- Wear a scarlet "C" on your shirt.
- Be forced to drink decaf for a month.
- Buy Frappuccinos for the whole office.

FEBRUARY 3

Start a Snowball Fight

The aging process has you firmly in its grasp if you never get the urge to throw a snowball.

—Doug Larson

During your entire childhood, you were constantly kept from starting a snowball fight. "Put the snowball down!" you were told. "Don't you dare!" Well, you're an adult now. And if there's one thing that persists even after you've entered adulthood, it's that little devil on your shoulder telling you to do the opposite of what you're told. So go on and start the snowball fight you never got to initiate when you were a kid.

It's important to establish yourself as a force to be reckoned with early on. So take risks: Do a sniper roll to get behind that tree. Expose yourself from behind that snowdrift if it means getting a better shot at your opponent.

Sure, you should probably be shoveling the snow instead of packing it into balls. But where's the fun in that? After all, the best part of being an adult is acting like a kid.

Rest for the Wicked Don't pull the old "rock in the snowball" trick. Remember that you're an adult now—and you'll be tried as one.

Best Hiding Places in a Snowball Fight

1. In a tree
2. Behind a civilian
3. Under a (parked) car
4. In a snowman
5. On top of a building (sniper style)

FEBRUARY 4

Order the Most Expensive Menu Item on a First Date

You should order the most expensive thing on the menu, so he knows you're worth it.

—PHYLLIS, *THE OFFICE*

The candles are glowing, the wine glasses are brimming and the conversation is punctuated by awkward pauses that can only mean one thing: a terrible first date.

Normally you would stick to a reasonably priced, yet mildly dull entrée like roasted chicken or lasagna. But since your date is as dull as an old knife, you might as well venture into more expensive territory.

Whether you've got a craving for crab legs or a passion for prime rib, go ahead and order up. If the date takes a turn for the better, your companion will know you're a sophisticated gourmet who enjoys the finer things in life. And if things continue to go less than swimmingly, at least a delicious $50 entrée will give you something to tell your friends about.

So sit back, relax, and enjoy another bite of filet mignon. You can always get lasagna next time. When it's your turn to pay.

Rest for the Wicked Pretend to be at least moderately interested in your date. Otherwise you might find yourself paying for the coq au vin.

A few of world's most expensive foods:

- The Zillion Dollar Frittata, Le Parker Meridien, $1,000
- Frozen Haute Chocolate, Serendipity 3, $25,000
- Bagel with white truffle cream cheese, The Westin New York, $1,000

Order Delivery from Closest Restaurant

And I don't cook, either. Not as long as they still deliver pizza.

—Tiger Woods

More likely than not you have a go-to restaurant for those times where you want a delicious fresh-cooked meal, but don't have the energy to turn on the oven. But what about when you are not only too lazy to cook, but you're too lazy to even make it out the door? Sure a pizzeria or Chinese restaurant will deliver right to your door, but you shouldn't have to settle for greasy pizza or gloppy mystery meat. You may be lazy, but you're not broke.

Call up your restaurant of choice and ask if you can reserve a table for one. Then politely request they set up that table in a special location—your living room. Before they hang up on you, insist that you will make it worth the waiter's while. Offer to pay double, or even triple the menu price and promise a generous tip on top. You may meet with some resistance at first, but they should eventually cave to the power of the almighty dollar.

Rest for the Wicked Answer the door carrying crutches to justify the 100-foot delivery request.

World's Longest Pizza Delivery

In 2006, Paul Fenech traveled 12,347 miles to hand-deliver a pizza from Opera Pizza in Madrid, Spain, to a customer in Wellington, New Zealand.

Use the Carpool Lane Alone

Americans will put up with anything provided it doesn't block traffic.

—Dan Rather

It's bad enough that you have to sit in traffic, but watching fellow motorists zoom by because they had the foresight to carpool is unbearable. Just this once, don't hesitate to sneak into the HOV lane.

You'd like to carpool—it's good for the environment and saves gas—but none of your coworkers live nearby. But just because you can't find a warm body to fill the passenger seat doesn't mean you have to suffer. Rummage around your car for stray clothes, grocery bags, sporting equipment, and anything else you can use to craft a makeshift passenger. It doesn't have to be perfect, just enough to fool a cop at a glance.

Once you've constructed your dummy, slowly merge into the carpool lane and enjoy the rest of your speedy, uneventful commute. Be sure to wave at your fellow solo commuters as you leave them in the dust.

Rest for the Wicked Adjust your passenger vanity mirror so it obstructs your dummy passenger.

Slugs Invade Carpool Lanes

In some urban areas, a symbiotic relationship known as "slugging" has developed where drivers offer free rides to car-less commuters to utilize carpool lanes.

FEBRUARY 7

Abuse the Student Discount

Living in the past has one thing in its favor—it's cheaper.

—Unknown

Students sure do have the life. They can sleep until noon, eat pizza for every meal, drink like a fish—and get discounts using their student IDs. Time may have taken its toll, but you still slightly resemble the picture on your old student ID. Why not use it to get the same perks you did as an undergrad? Passing as an undergrad will not only help you save a few bucks to put toward your college loans, but it'll also convince people that you're younger than you are.

Next time you're at a movie or museum, whip out the college ID and put on your best "I survive solely on ramen noodles" face. Chances are, the person ringing you up won't give it a second thought.

You spent thousands to go to college—why not stretch it a little further?

Rest for the Wicked Don't lose your ID. Once you're years removed from the school, it's virtually impossible to order a new one.

Best Places to Use a Student ID

1. Movies
2. Museums
3. Amusement parks
4. Bars and nightclubs
5. Restaurants

FEBRUARY 8

Be Late for Everything

The trouble with being punctual is that nobody's there to appreciate it.

—FRANKLIN P. JONES

In our task-oriented society, it seems that punctuality is heralded above all other virtues. But if you stop to think about it, perhaps you spend a little too much time worrying about being on time. Here's a new motto: You'll get there when you get there.

If your friend says, "Meet me for coffee at 2:00," give yourself permission to get there at 2:30. Roll into work at 10:00 and promise to stay late to make up the difference. Skip the apologetic glances when you show up to a movie after the opening credits. Eventually the people around you will adjust.

And after all, chances are you'll be a lot happier if you feel free to linger over that cup of coffee instead of just rushing out the door.

Rest for the Wicked Three exceptions to the rule: job interviews, funerals, weekend visits with your grandmother.

The Expectation of Lateness

In Mexico City, locals advise showing up at least an hour late for dinner. A guest who arrives any earlier risks surprising an unprepared host.

Dress Up for No Reason

The more you'll dress up the more fun you'll have.

—Brian Molko, lead singer of the band Placebo

Hanging in your closet, hidden behind your drab weekly wardrobe, you'll probably find a handful of fancy duds you only save for "special" events. Unfortunately there hasn't been such an event since the turn of the century.

But just because there's nothing special about today, doesn't mean you can't create your own excuse to dress up. After all, you spent a lot of money on those fancy clothes, so you might as well get some use out of them for a change.

Get out your most elaborate, expensive outfit and get ready to show yourself off. Go about your day the same way you would if you weren't dressed to the nines. Activities as simple as going to the grocery store or getting the mail can be "fancy" if you want them to be.

Rest for the Wicked Avoid places where your expensive clothes won't cause a scene. You want to stand out, after all.

Most Underutilized Clothes

- Wedding gowns
- Three-piece suits
- Kilts
- Prom dresses
- Oversized hats

FEBRUARY 10

Take a Limo to Starbucks

The limousine is the ultimate ego trip, the supreme sign of success. It shouts: "Hey, this guy is really and truly Mr Big."

—William Proxmire, American Senator

Unless you happen to be a rock star or a professional athlete, chances are the last time you rode in a limousine was on the way to your senior prom or your wedding. And if you wait around for another opportunity to present itself, chances are you never will again. But who says you need a good reason to ride in a limo?

While you could certainly catch a cab to your local coffee house—or even hoof it—a double caramel macchiato tastes that much sweeter when you can pick it up in style. Sure taking a limo raises the price of your coffee by 2,000 percent, but you deserve to spoil yourself—and the added boost to your ego will be well worth the extra cash.

Rest for the Wicked Invest in a pair of dark sunglasses to give the illusion you are an important celebrity.

Other Potential Destinations

- Local bar on open mic night
- Gym
- Movie theater
- Ice cream parlor
- Ex-boyfriend/girlfriend's house

FEBRUARY 11

Avoid the Mirror All Day

Never believe in mirrors or newspapers.

—JOHN OSBORNE, BRITISH PLAYWRIGHT AND PRODUCER

In our appearance-centric society, we are slaves to the mirror. It's the first thing we look at when we wake up, it stares us down every time we use the bathroom, and many of us even carry around pocket-sized versions.

Why do we even bother looking in the mirror? If it's early, you're not going to like what you see. The middle of the day? Too busy to fix anything anyway. And if it's at night, eh, you'll just fix it in the morning. Perhaps it would be better to just steer clear of them entirely.

When you wake up this morning, put all your concerns about your appearance out of your mind and walk confidently past any reflective surfaces. Nobody is going to care if you miss a cowlick while brushing your hair, or if your tie is slightly askew. And if somebody does say something, just pretend you're starting a new trend.

Rest for the Wicked Avoid seeing your reflection in unsuspecting places like store windows or puddles.

Zero Years Bad Luck

It was once believed that burying the pieces of a shattered mirror would counteract any associated bad luck.

FEBRUARY 12

Catch a Free Double Feature

Stealing, you'll go far in life. Actually, there is something funny about getting away with it.

—Mike Judge, American film director

Not that long ago, it was possible to go to the movies with a few dollars you found in your old coat pocket. But thanks to 100-ounce sodas, flimsy 3D glasses, and bathtub-size popcorns, you're lucky if you can make it out of the theater without taking out a second mortgage on your house.

Stick around for a second showing, however, and you magically cut the price of your ticket in half. And regardless of whether you stay for one movie or ten, the theater is still going to show the same number of films that day, so nobody loses.

Once the first movie ends, follow the rest of the crowd until you have an opportunity to slip into another theater. If that film has already started, the chances are pretty slim anybody is going to come by asking questions. No harm, no foul, right?

Rest for the Wicked Stuff your pockets with snacks from home to avoid concession-stand price-gouging.

Other Price-Reducing Tips

- Wear a gray wig to claim senior discount
- Sneak in children in oversized handbags
- Pass off old stubs as new

FEBRUARY 13

Go Off the Grid for the Day

Solitude is painful when one is young, but delightful when one is more mature.
—Albert Einstein

Thanks to e-mail, cell phones, text messaging, and laptops, it is now physically impossible to fall out of touch with the ones we love. Sadly, the same is true for everyone we'd rather avoid.

Today you are going to return to a simpler time, when ignoring your mother-in-law was as simple as letting the phone keep ringing. When calling in sick to work meant actually taking the day off—not Skyping into the weekly meeting from bed. It's true that some important things may fall through the cracks, but you're entitled to a little "me" time.

Go ahead and turn off your phone, unplug your laptop, and set your Facebook status to "MIA." Now that nobody can get a hold of you, the world is your oyster. Go for a long walk, read a good book, or just sit and meditate on how peaceful your life would be if you never heard a computerized chime, beep, or ring again.

Rest for the Wicked Lock your electronics in a safe to remove temptation. Alert important family members to your plans to prevent mass panic.

Alternative Means of Communication

- Can phone
- Smoke signals
- Scent marking
- Telegram
- Face-to-face interaction

FEBRUARY 14

Send Yourself Flowers

The last time I saw him he was walking down lover's lane holding his own hand.

—FRED ALLEN, AMERICAN COMEDIAN

For single people, there are few things worse than the endless parade of flowers, chocolates, and stuffed animals carried through the office by their lovestruck coworkers on February 14th. That goes double for anybody with a careless partner who couldn't be bothered to send anything.

While you could cross your fingers and hope this is the year you finally get flowers at work, why not just cut out the middleman and send them yourself? Like they always say, if you want something done right, do it yourself. Besides, unlike your forgetful partner, you actually know which type of flower is your favorite.

Instead of the standard dozen red roses, go for broke and send yourself an entire floral arrangement. Get creative with the attached card and claim they are from a secret admirer who can't stop thinking about you. At the end of the day, you can even bring your surprise gift home to make your significant other jealous. Serves them right.

Rest for the Wicked Disguise your handwriting or have a friend write the attached love note.

Alternatives to Flowers

- Singing telegram
- Giant chocolate heart
- Stripper gram
- Skywriting

Pimp Your Library Collection

"Classic." A book which people praise and don't read.

—Mark Twain

One of the best ways to impress guests is to decorate your home with rows and rows of intelligent, thought-provoking books. Too bad all you actually read are comic books and trashy romance novels. Luckily there is a way to look cool without having to do the work of actual reading. Just buy a bunch of smarty pants books and fake it.

Go to a used book store and pick up all the smart-sounding books you can find. Shakespeare, Dickens, Emily Dickenson, Jane Austen, Poe, Fitzgerald, Freud, Jung, Nietzsche, and Kierkegaard are a good start. The wearier and more broken in they look, the better. It'll look like you actually read them.

Best of all, the chances that anybody will call you out on your ruse are slim. A 2005 poll conducted by the Associated Press found that the average person only reads four books a year, and 25 percent didn't read a single one.

Rest for the Wicked Elevate your bookshelves' front two pegs so your bookcase doesn't fall forward.

World's Largest Library

The Library of Congress is the largest library in the world, with more than 147 million items on approximately 838 miles of bookshelves.

FEBRUARY 16

Treat Yourself to a Romantic Dinner for One

I want to start a chain of restaurants for other people who are like me called ANDYMATS—the restaurant for the lonely person. You get your food and then you take your tray into a booth and watch television.

—ANDY WARHOL, ARTIST

Romantic dinners are always a treat, but dinner for two is an expensive proposition. Instead of grumbling about how the last nice dinner date you went on happened during the Clinton era, why not step up and take yourself out?

The benefits of taking yourself out for a romantic evening are enormous—you can pick the restaurant, the time, your wardrobe, your drinks, and your meal without having to consider anyone else's preferences. Plus, you can order a decadent dessert without having to share with anyone.

At first, you might feel awkward at the thought of sitting at a table for one in a beautiful candlelit restaurant. But leave your inhibitions at the door. You're pretty awesome, and you deserve a night on the town.

Rest for the Wicked Sitting at the bar is a great way to take yourself out and still have a chance to interact with other restaurant patrons.

Dining Alone Tips

- Bring along a book
- Ask for a seat in the back, so nobody bothers you
- Tip more generously, as you are taking up a table for two alone

FEBRUARY 17

Cancel Plans to Stay in and Veg

Weekends don't count unless you spend them doing something completely pointless.

—Bill Watterson, cartoonist

You work long hours and sometimes nothing sounds worse than meeting up with your friends for a long night of drinks, dinner, and barhopping. Going out requires getting ready, looking good, and socializing for hours on end, whereas if you stay in, your night will be filled with sweatpants, movies, and delicious treats. The answer is clear: cancel your plans and just stay in.

You may have to endure some disappointed groans and childish name-calling from your friends, but their jeering will be easy to stomach when you're hunkered down in your PJs for the start of a much-needed reality TV marathon.

So order a pizza, clear a cozy space on the couch, and settle in for a long night of relaxing bliss. Your friends can waste their money on watered-down shots if they want to. All you need is a bottle of wine and a good book.

Rest for the Wicked Make sure your kitchen is stocked with delicious goodies for your evening marathon of laziness.

On Your Night In, Challenge Yourself To . . .

- Watch an entire season of your favorite television show
- Blow through that novel you haven't gotten around to reading
- Don't turn on the oven. Subsist solely on chips and cookies.

FEBRUARY 18

Sit Around in Your Underwear

I wasn't really naked. I simply didn't have any clothes on.

—Josephine Baker, dancer, singer, and actress

Back in your bygone childhood years, the majority of your time was likely spent in nothing more than Mickey Mouse or Barbie underpants. But now that you're an adult, modesty (and often the law) compels you to cover up for daily activities. But imagine your normal activities without the excess clothes: no collars or sleeves to restrict you, no fabric to adjust, no tight waist to battle; just you, the open air, and your skivvies. Sounds great, right?

Bring back the underwear mode and spend your time at home sans clothing. Try whipping up some pasta carbonara while sipping a glass of wine, or spend some hours sprawled on the couch for a movie marathon, all in your underoos. If anyone stops by for an unexpected visit, resist the urge to cover up. Instead, greet your friend with the stiffest poker face you can muster and ask him or her to join you. They'll either find it really liberating—or really weird.

Rest for the Wicked When cooking in the kitchen, throw on an apron to protect all that bare skin from splattering grease.

No Underwear Under There

The first form of underwear began in the Middle Ages. Similar to shorts, they were called braies and were worn solely by men. Women didn't start to wear underwear until the nineteenth century.

"Borrow" a Coworker's Lunch

What's mine is mine, and what's yours is mine too.

—UNKNOWN

If your office is like the rest of corporate America, the break room has plenty of coffee to boost your energy and an endless supply of oversized water jugs. But if you want real food, you're out of luck.

Fortunately for you, there's a free supply of real food hidden away—you just have to walk into the communal kitchen and crack open the refrigerator door.

Sure the scattered homemade lunches aren't technically open for public consumption, but your coworkers really can't expect a brown paper bag to deter someone as hungry—and as selfish—as yourself. Besides, based on the garbage they're bringing to work everyday, you're doing them a favor by forcing them to splurge on takeout.

So while everybody is plugging away at their spreadsheets and progress reports, sneak away from your desk and swipe an unattended brown bag from the kitchen. Since you are dealing with stolen goods, just scarf down the contents right there and dispose of any incriminating evidence.

Finders keepers, losers weepers.

Rest for the Wicked Check yourself for stray crumbs before you return to your desk. The devil is in the details.

Excuses If You Get Caught

- "It's National Bring a Friend a Lunch Day, and I thought you'd brought one for me!"
- "This is my favorite meal! It was so sweet of you to bring me your leftovers."
- "I brought in donuts last week. I thought today was your day to bring in snacks."
- "I brought the exact same thing today. I guess someone must have eaten mine."
- "The devil made me do it."

FEBRUARY 20

Adopt a Sexy Accent and Pretend to Be from a Foreign Country

Use what language you will, you can never say anything but what you are.
—RALPH WALDO EMERSON

Right now, at hundreds of bars around the world, countless unattractive men and women are going home with hotties way out of their league. And all because they can speak with an exotic accent. Well, two can play at this game.

First, settle on an accent that's both sexy and easy to mimic. The more obscure the origin, the better. Once you've had some practice, take your new sexy accent out on the town. Chat up a few unsuspecting locals and watch them swoon at your feet and offer to buy your drinks. Consistency is key. You can be way off, as long as you don't switch between your accent and your real voice.

Sure it's childish, but so's dating.

Rest for the Wicked Beware of long-term relationships. You can't keep up the accent forever.

Top Five Sexiest Accents

- Australian
- Irish
- Italian
- French
- Scottish

FEBRUARY 21

Cut in Line

If they gave me four dollars, I'd wait in line.

—David Williams

You are an important person with important things to do. You can't waste your time standing around. So don't! If the only thing standing between you and the counter is a line of your peers, feel free to jump in.

Make sure that you're mentally ready to dodge the queue. When you arrive at the line, stand next to the person who's waiting in front of you rather than behind him or her. Check out any magazines or candy bars in the aisle so you appear distracted. Edge up to the counter and quickly move to the front. Do not look back.

Remember, you've been jumped in line plenty of times. Think of this small act of defiance as evening out the cosmic balance.

Rest for the Wicked Watch out for flying objects thrown by the pissed-off people behind you.

People to Avoid Pissing Off

- Pregnant women
- The elderly
- Anyone with multiple body piercings

FEBRUARY 22

Give Yourself a Snow Day

Getting an inch of snow is like winning 10 cents in the lottery.

—Bill Watterson, cartoonist

For children, flakes of snow mean the promise of a day off from school to frolic in a winter wonderland. Sadly, all it means for you is an extra hour to get into the office and back-breaking shoveling when you return. Luckily, there's an easy way to recapture that youthful excitement: Take a snow day.

It doesn't matter if it snowed two feet last night, or if there's just a thin dusting leftover from last Tuesday, putting in some face time at the office is not worth risking your personal safety.

Instead of putting on your suit and tie, dig out your old winter coat for a day of slushy merriment. Build a snowman with some local schoolchildren, start a snowball fight with your neighbor, or sled down your empty street. Just resist the urge to head to work—not that that will be too hard.

Rest for the Wicked Stock up on tomato soup and hot chocolate in case you get cold.

Homemade Snow Day Equipment

- Hollowed out tennis ball—snowball maker
- Large garbage bags—sleds
- Bread pans—molds for snow fort blocks

Skip the Gym and Go to Krispy Kreme

Exercise is a dirty word. Every time I hear it, I wash my mouth out with chocolate.
—Unknown

Whether you work out religiously or have an exercise regimen primarily consisting of broken promises, don't give your sweat-filled gym a second thought. Instead, hop in the car and head for the bright lights and sickeningly sweet smell that can only mean one thing: Krispy Kreme.

With glazed doughnuts to die for, Krispy Kreme is the ultimate in indulgent, gooey deliciousness. If you get there at just the right time, you'll be treated to a freshly baked, sugar-filled treat still warm from the oven. And don't be afraid to lick your fingers so you don't miss a morsel of this one-of-a-kind snack. The gym will still be there next week, and besides, your muscles need a day to rest in order to repair the damage from a workout—but no one needs to know how often your off-days are.

Rest for the Wicked Don't look at the calorie count before buying. Just don't.

Best Accompaniments to a Krispy Kreme Doughnut

- A glass of chocolate milk
- A fresh cup of black coffee
- Another Krispy Kreme doughnut

FEBRUARY 24

Buy a Hot Tub for Your Living Room

Oh, that sound? I'm in the hot tub, reading a novel.

—Jane Smiley, American novelist

Millionaires have tons of cool, extravagant things in their mansions, like home movie theaters, ping pong tables, indoor pools, and trampolines. Why let them have all the fun?

Today you're going to buy a hot tub. And then you're going to put it in your living room. Just think, all the relaxing, indulgent benefits of a hot without having to expose yourself to the neighbors every time you use it—plus there's TV!

It's easier—and safer—if you hire someone to install it, so go that route. Once the hot tub is in place, it's time to set the mood. Surround your hot tub with scented candles and turn on some nice, mellow jazz music for a night of relaxation.

Rest for the Wicked Try not to spend too much time in your hot tub or you could get dehydrated, dizzy, or really, really hot.

Hot Tubs of the Ages

Archeological evidence shows that as much as 4,000 years ago, hot therapeutic baths were enjoyed by the early Egyptians.

FEBRUARY 25

BYOB to a Bar

A bartender is just a pharmacist with limited inventory.

—Unknown author

Bars can be great places to unwind and meet new people, but unless you plan to sit and nurse a glass of tap water all night they're also super-pricey. The average bar charges around a 300 percent markup for drinks, which is hard-earned money out of your pocket every time you take a sip.

Luckily, there's a simple solution to the problem. Instead of spending your life savings at the neighborhood pub, invest in a flask and BYOB. Is it illegal? Perhaps. Is it frowned upon? Most certainly. But can you get away with it? Definitely.

The bar is packed, so nobody is going to notice if you top of your glass of Coke with a little whiskey. If you're nervous, just play bartender in the bathroom. Let those other suckers squander their money as they wish—you know how to beat the system.

Rest for the Wicked Keep your pals in the dark about your little secret—otherwise everyone will want in on your hooch.

Easy Drinks to Mix Discreetly

- Screwdriver
- Gin and tonic
- Rum and coke

FEBRUARY 26

Lie to Get Out of a Ticket

Never tell a lie, except for practice.

—MARK TWAIN

Lying to get out of a ticket is nothing out of the ordinary. People try it every time they get pulled over, and almost all of them fail. While you could argue this proves that honesty really is the best policy, perhaps their lies just weren't big enough.

Next time you see those flashing red and blue lights on your tail, prepare for the biggest lie you've ever conjured in your life. When the cop walks up to your car, squirm around uncontrollably and start speaking in tongues. Channel scenes from *The Exorcist* and convince the officer you've been possessed by demons that forced your foot on the accelerator.

If he's still not convinced, just give it another go. Change gears and admit that you are actually a secret government agent on a mission to save humanity from a catastrophe of biblical proportions. You'd love to tell him what it is, but then you'd have to kill him.

While it's true that the officer may throw you in a psych ward, it still beats having to show up in traffic court.

Rest for the Wicked Remember, it's not a lie if you believe it's true.

Other Methods to Avoid Tickets

- Offer the cop a doughnut
- Good old-fashioned flattery
- Stop doing illegal things

FEBRUARY 27

Throw a Temper Tantrum

There's no point in being grown up if you can't be childish sometimes.

—THE DOCTOR, *DOCTOR WHO*

Being civilized is overrated; sometimes you just need to let all your emotions out. Children have been aware of the healing benefits of a good scream for eons, but now even science is catching on. One study conducted by child psychologist Dr. David Lewis found that individuals who engaged in short screaming sessions experienced rapid drops in stress levels and increased strength and stamina.

Pick a small and insignificant situation, like someone stealing your parking space or the barista messing up your coffee order. Drop down to the ground and roll around like you're on fire and you need to put yourself out. Shout bloody murder and then hold your breath until you turn purple.

If anyone asks you what's wrong, simply continue to thrash about and yell at the top of your lungs, breaking only for intermittent sobs. Let out all of your negativity and frustration before standing up, dusting off your coat, and leaving the shop. Don't you feel better now?

Rest for the Wicked Don't throw this tantrum in a place you'd like to return to within the next few years.

Unacceptable Tantrum Locales

- During a transcontinental flight
- Your boss's office
- The middle of the highway

FEBRUARY 28

"Work" from Home

One of the symptoms of an approaching nervous breakdown is the belief that one's work is terribly important.

—Bertrand Russell, English philosopher

The alarm rings for work in the morning and your first thought is, "Hell no. Not today." Sadly, you blew through your sick days and vacation time months ago. Never fear, all hope is not lost.

Call up your boss and insist that you need to work out of the house for the day. Perhaps your car won't start, or your heat is busted and you have to wait for the repairman. Sure you are technically on the clock, but without your boss breathing down your neck you can take it a little easy for the day. Leave the TV on while you reconcile expense reports, take a two-hour break to reorganize your closet, or just avoid doing anything. After all, what's the fun in "working from home" if you're actually working?

If you feel bad about lying, just remember that about one-third of employed U.S. adults do not take all of the vacation days they receive each year. So, in reality, you're just taking a vacation day that you might have otherwise given up.

Rest for the Wicked E-mail your boss at random intervals throughout the day. That way you'll appear busy.

Excuses to Work from Home

- Threw your back out
- Caring for a sick child/spouse
- Dog ate your car keys

MARCH 1

Spike the Punch

If you don't drink, then all of your stories suck and end with, "And then I got home."

—JIM JEFFERIES, AUSTRALIAN COMEDIAN

Everyone agrees that forced office gatherings suck. Whether it's an awkward holiday party, somebody's birthday, or a mandated teambuilding workshop, no one wants to be there and everyone wishes they were drunk.

So rather than allow everyone there to waste their lives, do what everyone is begging someone would do anyway: Bust out that bottle of vodka and spike the punch.

Ten minutes ago everyone was standing around silent and bored. Now suddenly "Welcome to the Jungle" is blaring, Rick from accounting has a lampshade on his head, and a couple is making out on the copier.

Now take out your camera and enjoy the scene.

Rest for the Wicked Only tell your most trusted friends that you've spiked the punch, in case things get out of hand.

Signs It's Time to Spike the Punch

- Pin the Tail On the Donkey commences
- Everybody's checking their watches
- Conversation focuses on the weather

MARCH 2

Sneak Into a Fancy Country Club

I don't want to belong to any club that will accept me as a member.

—Groucho Marx

Country clubs are nothing more than opulent adult playgrounds where pretentious jerks gather to congratulate each other on being masters of the universe. Why would anybody want to subject themselves to such awfulness? Three things: unlimited expensive booze, teams of servants attending to your every whim, and super-cool smoking jackets. Enough said.

Unfortunately, you can't just walk through the door in your thrift-store pants and expect to be welcomed with open arms. You'll need to blend in. This involves copying the carefully cultivated look of a prep school student, otherwise known as yacht couture. The more self-centered you look, the better.

If all else fails, pass yourself off as a caterer. Obtain a metal cart with a white tablecloth draped over it and swiftly wheel it past the front desk and into the belly of the yuppie beast. Now that you're in, you can play the part of the club member and have a few drinks, play a round of golf, chat up that cute employee, and generally take advantage of your ill-gotten status. Wasn't the danger worth it?

Rest for the Wicked If sneaking across the golf green, avoid any stray balls, and try not to get any grass stains on your spotless clothes.

What to Do Once You're In

- Drink expensive brandy
- Pretend you don't care about money
- Laugh at poor people

Waste the Day Browsing the Internet

I like the word "indolence." It makes my laziness seem classy.

—Bern Williams

The Internet is big. Vastly, hugely, mind-bogglingly big. With the entirety of human knowledge at your fingertips, don't you owe it to yourself to spend some serious time mucking around in it?

The average person only spends thirteen hours per week browsing the Internet. That's barely enough time to scratch the surface on the wealth of silly cat pictures there are out in cyberspace. To make any serious progress, you're going to need to devote an entire day to web surfing.

Start by browsing through Wikipedia for at least five hours, then move onto mindless videos of people hurting themselves in amusing ways. Laugh out loud at the latest Internet memes while you sift through celebrities' Twitter posts in a separate window. Before you know it, all those pent-up Internet-browsing urges will be satisfied. So satisfied, in fact, that you may actually feel like working come Monday. But probably not.

Rest for the Wicked Don't forget to clear your browser history when you're done. No one needs to know you clicked through thirty-six pages of LOLcats today.

Best Sites for Wasting Time

- *Reddit.com*
- *Cracked.com*
- *textsfromlastnight.com*
- *fmylife.com*

MARCH 4

Join a Marathon in the Last Mile

It's unnatural for people to run around the city streets unless they are thieves or victims. It makes people nervous to see someone running.

—Mike Royko, newspaper columnist

When you tell people you've run a marathon, there's no denying the instant increase in admiration and respect that follows. In their eyes, you've achieved something that mere mortals simply aren't capable of. If only you could achieve that same glory without punishing your body for twenty-six grueling miles.

Lucky for you, nobody pays any attention to the first twenty-five.

Before the race starts, station yourself a mile from the finish line and strap a random number to your back. Once runners start to arrive, throw a cup of water on your face (to mimic sweat) and duck under the yellow tape to join the pack.

After you cross the finish line, feign lightheadedness and offer your fellow runners your heartfelt congratulations. And be sure to hit up the free massage tent. It's a nice perk after a long run.

Rest for the Wicked Have an accomplice create a diversion so nobody notices when you sidle into the pack.

Best Marathon Costumes

- Wedding Dress
- Chicken Suit
- Elvis
- Spider-Man

MARCH 5

Start a Charity for Yourself

Charity degrades those who receive it and hardens those who dispense it.

—George Sand, French novelist

If you've lived your life like a typical upstanding citizen up to this point, chances are that you give to various charities. But perhaps it's time to start factoring yourself into that equation. It's high time you set some of your hard-earned money aside for the [your name here] Fund.

So grab that checkbook and cut yourself a nice fat check to start yourself off. No need to bother with a mission statement: this charity is all about you. After all that hard work and selfless donating, you deserve it, after all. Whenever you are feeling charitable, drop a few bucks into your new "foundation." Once you've built up a nice chunk of change, spend the funds on whatever you'd like. That's not to say you should stop giving to charities all together. Just consider this a little side project.

Rest for the Wicked Never solicit donations from others for your selfish charity, as that's almost certainly illegal.

Potential Charity Names

- The Human Fund
- The Me, Myself, and I Society
- The Greed Group
- Hands Off My Moola

Drive at Your Own Speed

You're only here for a short visit. Don't hurry, don't worry. And be sure to smell the flowers along the way.

—Walter Hagen, American professional golfer

Whether you're touring a national park or admiring that lovely field of poppies on the way home from work, go ahead and slow down—and don't apologize for it either.

Why? Because in a world that moves faster than the speed of light, sometimes the only moment of zen you can hope for is a glimpse of grazing deer along the road or a stunning sunset on a Tuesday night commute. Besides, according to the EPA, you may conserve as much as 25 percent more gas while you slow down to enjoy the view—which is good for the environment, and your wallet.

So slow down, take it in, and don't worry about the number on the street sign or the honking horns. Don't waste your time feeling bad for anyone behind you either. Turns out there's a simple solution—it's called "going around."

Rest for the Wicked Flash any irritated drivers a big smile and a wave as they pass. Save the finger for when they're out of eyeshot.

Top Five Scenic Drives in America

1. Hana Highway, Maui, Hawaii: 38 miles from Pauwela to Hana
2. Turquoise Trail, New Mexico: 45 miles from Albuquerque to Santa Fe
3. Columbia River Highway, Oregon: 74 miles from Troutdale to The Dalles
4. Pig Trail Byway, Arkansas: 80 miles from Ozark to Eureka Springs
5. Highway 12, Utah: 107 miles from Torrey to Bryce Canyon National Park

MARCH 7

Walk Around Your House Naked

My ideal is to wake up in the morning and run around the meadow naked.

—Daryl Hannah

When you get home from work, the first thing you probably do is slip into something more comfortable. But when you think about it, what could possibly be more comfortable than nothing at all?

When you finish off a hard day, instead of changing into constricting sweatpants, just unzip and let loose. Nobody's watching, so you're free to walk around your house naked as a jaybird. But don't stop at just strutting around. Clean the place naked, watch TV naked, or even eat a sandwich naked. It's your house after all, you can do what you want.

It's not even about being sexy, it's just about being comfortable and relaxed. You were born naked, so it's only natural to wander around that way.

Rest for the Wicked Don't lose sight of your nakedness. If you forget and grab the mail in your birthday suit, you might offend a neighbor or two.

Emergency Clothing Options

- Potted plants
- Lampshade
- A black piece of rectangular construction paper
- Hands

MARCH 8

Sprawl Out on the Subway

A nickel will get you on the subway, but garlic will get you a seat.

—Unknown

After an eight-hour workday, nothing feels better than easing your overworked bum into the plastic seat of the subway.

Sure you're not pregnant, and all your limbs are in general working order, but physical fitness should not disqualify you from commuting comfortably. You're just as tired as everybody else (probably more so) and you deserve a seat just as much as they do.

Push yourself to the front of the platform and snag the first seat you see—and lay claim to it. Spread your legs as wide as possible and barricade yourself in with your briefcase to your right and your laptop to your left. If anyone complains, just avert eye contact and ignore them. When you see how uncomfortable everyone else looks as they struggle to stay upright when the train leaves the station, you'll be glad you did.

Rest for the Wicked Only piss off one passenger at a time to prevent an uprising.

Commuters Not to Mess With

- Mothers with more than two children
- Anyone talking to him or herself
- Passengers wearing anything cammo

MARCH 9

Take a Mutual Twenty-Four-Hour Break from Your Significant Other

It's better to have loved and lost than to have never loved at all.

—Alfred Lord Tennyson

As much as you may love your significant other, it can get a little dull doing the same things with the same person day after day. But just because things are getting a little stale, doesn't mean your relationship is doomed to failure. Sometimes the best way to spice up your waning love life is to take a little break—if only for twenty-four hours.

Just think, a one-day free pass to do whatever you want with whomever you want with zero consequences. At the end of the day, you can return to your loving committed relationship as if nothing every happened.

To begin, be straightforward. Present your no-strings attached idea as a way to explore your deepest desires without regret. Just remember, boundaries are essential. No twenty-four-hour tryst is worth ruining your relationship over. Unless of course said tryst is really, really cute.

Rest for the Wicked Despite what you may have heard on the playground, the pill does not protect against STDs.

Most Famous Open Relationships

- Charlie Sheen
- Hugh Hefner
- Tilda Swinton
- Abraham

MARCH 10

Splurge on High Thread-Count Sheets

Take care of the luxuries and the necessities will take care of themselves.

—Dorothy Parker

You're an adult, you deserve some adult sheets. And after a lifetime of sleeping on sub-par linens, you owe it to yourself to march over to Bed, Bath & Beyond, test out all the high thread-count sheet samples they have, and buy the softest, most luxurious ones you can find. Thread count refers to the number of threads present in a one-inch square of fabric, and conventional wisdom holds that more threads = more comfort.

Sure, whipping out your credit card at checkout may require an iron will, but good sheets will last you at least a few years, making this more of an investment than a purchase. Besides, if you're like one third of adults, you get less than six hours of sleep a night. Anything you can do to make your bed more comfortable could mean a few extra Zzs.

So don't settle for meager 400 to 500 thread-count sets. Splurge on 1,000+ Egyptian Cotton sheets. You're worth it.

Rest for the Wicked If the thread count is lower than 400, keep looking.

It's All about Thread Count

- 1,500 Thread-Count Egyptian Cotton, $400
- King-Size Silk Sheet Set, $390
- King-Size Organic Cotton Sheets, $400

MARCH 11

Bake and Eat an Entire Batch of Cookies by Yourself

In love, as in gluttony, pleasure is a matter of the utmost precision.

—Italo Calvino

Making cookies for friends is a labor of love. You spend hours carefully measuring, sifting, beating, mixing, and baking up tray after tray of delicious cookies, all for the pleasure of watching other people enjoy your creations. If you're lucky, you may get to sample a single cookie before the vultures devour them all.

Well, not this time. Today you're going to be a little selfish and eat every single last cookie all by yourself. Down to the last crumb.

Weight Watchers be damned. There's nothing shameful in consuming twice your weight in baked goods every once in a blue moon. And all that measuring, stirring, and baking burns off a couple of calories, anyway.

First, don stretch pants—or anything with an elastic waistband—and an apron. Then choose your favorite type of cookie—be it oatmeal raisin, chocolate chip, or gingerbread—set the oven to the necessary temperature, and get measuring.

Eating the batter as you go along, of course, is encouraged. If you start feeling sick, just power through. You aren't a quitter.

Rest for the Wicked Don't make any plans to leave the house within twelve hours of completing your task.

Other Formidable Eating Challenges

- A whole gallon of milk
- An entire chocolate cake
- A tablespoon of cinnamon

MARCH 12

Ignore Your E-mail

I often work by avoidance.

—Brian Eno, Musician

Think of all the time you spend on your work computer, constantly being distracted by that small ping signifying yet another pointless e-mail. You don't need to look at yet another forward from the coworker you avoid in the lunchroom and you don't need yet another update on your office's wellness goals from HR. In fact, if it weren't for email, think of all the work you'd get done. Alas, office etiquette forces you to reply, forward, and carbon-copy all day long. But sometimes you need a vacation from your inbox too.

Don't bother setting up an automated response. Just close out your inbox and leave it closed. Without having to respond to inane e-mails, you'll have the entire day to catch up on your expense reports and maybe even brainstorm a new project idea. You'd be amazed at what you can accomplish when you aren't pulled away every five minutes.

Your coworkers may be a little peeved that you're ignoring them, but the unexplained shunning may just force them to fix their own problems for a change.

Rest for the Wicked Avoid the wrath of your boss by setting up shop in a vacant conference room. Just make sure no big meetings are scheduled there that day.

Out-of-the-Office Auto-Response Ideas

- Day trip to visit your grandmother
- Pet emergency at the vet
- Volunteering at the local shelter
- 24-hour flu

MARCH 13

Steal a Magazine from the Doctor's Office

The more you read the more things you'll know. The more you learn, the more places you'll go.

—Dr. Seuss

For years, you've endured pokes, prods, and pricks at the hand of your cruel GP. But the worst part about going to the doctor's office is not being able to finish that article you were reading when you were called into the exam room. Today is the day you strike back against the unfairness of a place that makes you both sit in a cold room in a paper robe *and* doesn't allow you find out what exactly happened on the season finale of *Keeping Up with the Kardashians.* Perhaps it's time you swiped a little something extra for your trouble.

On your way out of the office, nonchalantly wander passed the magazine shelf and pick up the magazine you were reading before the nurse so rudely interrupted you. Before anyone notices, just roll it up, tuck it under your arm, and head for the exit. Now you can finish that article whenever you want—without worrying about impending needles.

Rest for the Wicked Be prepared to find a new doctor if anybody catches on.

Best Magazines to Swipe

- *Time*
- *Sports Illustrated*
- *Bon Appétit*
- *Rolling Stone*
- *The New Yorker*

MARCH 14

Take Advantage of Your Lunch Break

Ask not what you can do for your country. Ask what's for lunch.

—Orson Welles

This may not come as a surprise, but *your* lunch hour is valuable time that should be used for *your* benefit. Not as an opportunity to finish collating spreadsheets or listening to the twenty-five neglected voicemails on your work phone. Despite that, nearly half of all employees take less than thirty minutes to eat their lunch each day, and many do so while working at their desks. So today, you're going to damn The Man and take back what is rightfully yours.

When the clock strikes noon, get the hell out of Dodge and don't look back. Enjoy a hot meal at a nice restaurant, or just take a siesta on a park bench. You could even use the time to sneak in a few sets at the gym or run a few errands.

Whatever you do with your time, it will be infinitely better than staring at a computer screen.

Rest for the Wicked Check your watch before you leave so you keep it to about an hour.

Other Things to Reclaim

- Coffee Breaks
- Water Cooler Chats
- Half-Day Fridays

MARCH 15

Hang Out All Day at a Coffee Shop Without Buying Anything

Television is not real life. In real life people actually have to leave the coffee shop and go to jobs.

—Bill Gates

Coffee shops are great for so many things—picking up a last-minute breakfast sandwich before work, revitalizing yourself with an overpriced latte, or curing a hangover with a jet-black cup of joe. But there's one thing they're even better for: lounging around, wasting the day away.

Alas, nourishing your body with an endless flow of caffeine can be pricey. So why not just go to a coffee shop and do something novel—don't buy a damn thing. You'll probably want to grab a secluded corner spot so the baristas don't notice you. And feel free to keep your face buried in a book so no one will bother you even if they do realize you've been sitting there for five hours without ordering a single latte or fat-free muffin. But even if they do notice you, so what. You'll just be one of a dozen other bums who have nothing better to do than spend their day sniffing coffee—and what a happy bum you'll be!

Rest for the Wicked Get your daily dose of caffeine before heading to your local coffee house—that way, you won't be tempted to whip out your wallet.

Largest Coffee Shop Chains in the United States

- Starbucks—more than 11,000 stores
- Dunkin' Donuts—more than 6,700 stores
- Caribou Coffee—more than 400 stores

MARCH 16

Sneak Dinner Into a Movie

I'm gonna sneak you into the movies in my tummy!

—PATTON OSWALT

When a single candy bar or tub of movie theater popcorn costs more than the price of admission, something has gone terribly wrong. Instead of ponying up the cash and grumbling under your breath, it's time you took a stand.

But why stop at a concealed bag of M&M's and a can of soda? Why not go for broke and smuggle in an entire meal? Movies can last upwards of three hours these days, and you need your viewing fuel.

Don your baggiest attire (the more pockets the better) and stuff your person with the contents of your refrigerator. Leftover pasta, cheese and crackers, deli meat, and whatever else you have on hand. If you have trouble getting past the ticket taker, just bribe him with a salami.

Now sit back and enjoy the show with all the comforts of your home kitchen. Now you can spend more time enjoying the movie instead of complaining about concession-stand price-gouging.

Rest for the Wicked Leave the ice cream at home. A melted puddle of ice cream soup will surely give you away.

Easiest Meals to Sneak In

- Burritos
- Sandwiches
- Chicken Wings
- Sushi

Organize a Game of Strip Poker

People would be surprised to know how much I learned about prayer from playing poker.

—Mary Austin

There's that point in every lame party where the six people who actually showed up have to face reality. Nobody else is coming. But don't throw in the towel just yet though. There's still a chance to transform your lame gathering into a risqué event that you'll all remember for years to come. All you need is a deck of cards and a bunch of uninhibited party guests.

Wrangle up your small group of partiers and toss your inhibitions to the wind for an impromptu game of strip poker. If your guests were uptight before, you'll be amazed how quickly they loosen up once everyone's half naked and throwing their underwear onto the table. To make it even more interesting, you can add some wild cards to the game that force players to perform tasks like streaking around the house.

It may make a few of your more conservative guests uncomfortable, but at least it's infinitely more exciting than standing in an awkward circle sipping cheap wine.

Rest for the Wicked Going commando, while sexy, gives you a distinct disadvantage here.

People Not to Invite to Strip Poker Night

- Family members
- Any morbidly obese people
- Your boss

Don't Bring Anything to a Potluck

Have something to bring to the table, because that will make you more welcome.

—Randy Pausch

With the advent of the dreaded potluck, the onus of the meal was lifted off the host and placed like a yoke onto the shoulders of the event's poor guests. While you probably want to spend time with your friends, you probably don't want to spend a whole bunch of time making a huge dish that you have to transport hot to someone else's home. In this case it's not like you even get to keep the leftovers! It's time to shrug off the yoke and show up empty-handed.

The next time you find yourself invited to a potluck, simply show up at the door with nothing but a broad smile and a big appetite. There are plenty of excuses to use for your lack of contribution, but you shouldn't have to explain yourself. You didn't bring anything because you're the guest. Plain and simple.

Rest for the Wicked Be prepared for a lot of no-shows the next time you throw a dinner party.

Reasons Potlucks Suck

- You never get back your Tupperware
- It's hard to transport food without ruining it
- One casserole is delicious. Ten are disgusting.

Do a Second Job on Company Time

You will never "find" time for anything. If you want time, you must make it.
—Charles Bruxton, British parliamentarian

Everyone wants to find a way to earn a little extra money and many people have spent years dreaming of opening their own business. Unfortunately, self-employment is expensive. It's not likely that you just have a photocopier sitting around at home, after all.

If you're feeling really ambitious, don't hesitate to start your own business on the company dime. You have everything you could possibly need right at your disposal: copiers, fax machines, computers—even a water cooler. And just think of all you could accomplish if you stopped messing around at work and actually focused. Not for your company, of course, but for you.

While it's true your little side projects could get you fired, at least you'll have something to fall back on if you do get canned.

Rest for the Wicked Never use work e-mail for freelance correspondence, and save any incriminating files as "Definitely_Not_Freelance.doc."

Where to Look for Second Jobs

- Craigslist
- Monster
- HotJobs
- LinkedIn
- SimplyHired

MARCH 20

Take Your Neighbor's Newspaper

It's amazing that the amount of news that happens in the world every day always just exactly fits the newspaper.

—Jerry Seinfeld

Keeping up with the day's news is an important part of being an active member of the community and an informed citizen of the world, but who wants to pay to read all about everything bad that goes on in the world? Well the good news is that there's a simple way to get your news for free: steal your neighbor's paper.

The key to getting your news is getting to it before your neighbor does; after all, the news waits for no man, and neither should you. So rise early and snatch it up before his feet even hit the floor.

Rest for the Wicked Avoid getting caught by keeping the papers out of your own recycling bin. Instead, find another use for them or drop your already-read newspapers into your neighbor's bin. They were his originally, after all.

Reusing a Newspaper After You've Read It

- Line the bottom of a birdcage
- Fold it into a fun paper hat
- Dip strips into a flour and water mixture for papier-mâché
- Soak in vinegar and wash your windows
- Stuff into boots to preserve shape in summer storage

Selectively Obey Traffic Laws

I believe in rules. Sure I do. If there weren't any rules, how could you break them?
—Leo Durocher

Bicyclists have it good. When they want to move fast, they can take up the entire lane and act like a car. But the moment there's a red light, they just zoom on through and nobody gives them a second glance.

Their rampant disregard for certain traffic laws may be illegal, but it's certainly enticing. Imagine how much less stressful your commute would be if you could also pick and choose which laws you follow.

When you drive around today, use your judgment when it comes to the rules of the road. If you're the only person on the highway, perhaps you shouldn't bother hitting your turn signal. If there's nobody approaching at a four way stop, it's safe to assume you can roll through without coming to a complete stop.

You are a busy person with places to go and people to see. If bending a few rules gets you on your way a little faster, perhaps it's worth the risk of a ticket.

Rest for the Wicked Space your violations a few miles apart. If you get stopped, you don't want the cop to string several tickets together.

What to Do If You Get Pulled Over

- Never admit guilt. You have no idea why you got pulled over.
- Promptly produce identification and utilize your right to remain silent.
- Wait patiently in the car for the officer to determine your fate.

MARCH 22

Take the Largest Slice of Pizza

There's no better feeling in the world than a warm pizza box on your lap.

—Kevin James, American comedian

No matter how hard you try, it's physically impossible to carve a pizza into nice even slices. There's always going to be a few baby slices dwarfed by their mammoth counterparts.

Proper etiquette suggests you settle for the puny slices and offer up the more substantial pieces to your hungry guests, but why should you suffer just because your friends are too cheap to buy their own pie? It's your pizza, and you should get the biggest piece.

When you cut the pie, make sure you serve yourself first and head straight for the biggest slice. If you are feeling particularly greedy, you can pull a Garfield and cut a small sliver for your guests and take the rest of the pie for yourself.

You may have to deal with a few dirty looks and some irritated grumbling, but at least you won't be hungry.

Rest for the Wicked If you are worried about losing friends, cut the pizza away from prying eyes so your greediness won't be as obvious.

Hardest Foods to Share

- Sandwiches
- Soups
- All restaurant desserts

MARCH 23

Switch to Supermarket Tabloids

Being pretty crazy while being chased by the National Enquirer *is not good.*

—Margot Kidder, actress

You read the *New York Times* and watch CNN. You consider yourself a critically thinking, civically engaged member of society.

What's the fun in that?

Start reading the supermarket tabloids. That's where the real news is, the kind of news people actually care about, talk about, and find interesting. You'll learn really important things like which celebrity cheated, which celebrity has put on weight, and which celebrity is addicted to pills. It's a great way to collect culture gossip. And, who knows, it might actually be true every once in a while.

Rest for the Wicked Read the tabloids inside the pages of a real newspaper, like you're reading a comic book inside an algebra textbook, so that you can continue to look sophisticated while indulging your gossipy side.

Awesome Tabloid Headlines

- Woman Delivers Own Baby While Skydiving!
- Fatal Farts!
- What Car Would Jesus Drive?
- Honesty Falls to 3rd as 'Best Policy'
- Belief in Elves Reaches All-Time High!

MARCH 24

Throw Your Own "Surprise" Party

If you want anything done well, do it yourself.

—Bob Edwards

Have you ever been disappointed when someone forgot your birthday? Or forgot that on your birthday you like to do things a certain way? Well, take matters into your own hands and plan your own surprise party.

Start by creating a fake identity. The persona you need to assume should purport to be a long-lost friend of yours, preferably from childhood so that your current friends won't get suspicious. Next, e-mail everyone you know, then delegate. Have someone make you a cake, assign someone else to decorate, and put someone else on food and drink detail.

When you walk into your personally selected venue, put on your best "Oh my god, I can't believe you all did this" face. It doesn't even matter if today is your real birthday. It's not like your self-centered friends are going to notice.

Rest for the Wicked Create an alibi for the absent party planner.

Ultimate Surprise Party Elements

- Fog and bubble machines
- Live band
- Piñatas
- Open bar

MARCH 25

Just Lie There

Sex: the thing that takes up the least amount of time and causes the most amount of trouble.

—John Barrymore, American actor

There are those days where you have enough vivacity to be a sex acrobat, other days you just want it to be all about you. The problem is that no one wants to be considered an inadequate or inconsiderate partner.

It's time to put aside the guilt and give in to the languor. Next time the mood strikes and that special someone has you lying on the bed, keep lying there. If he or she tries to craftily turn the tango then hold your ground and let them do all the work. No need to even come up with excuses; you can make it known that today is your day and you want to be selfish. There's no doubt that giving into the selfishness will really pay off.

Rest for the Wicked Make sure to return the favor on a rainy day, or your partner will be a very unhappy camper.

The Upside to Not Just Lying There

Having sex three times a week burns about 7,500 calories a year — the equivalent of jogging 75 miles.

MARCH 26

Blast Awful Music in Traffic

There are two kinds of music; German music and bad music.

—Henry Louis Mencken, American journalist

Aside from running on a treadmill, sitting in traffic may very well be the most dreadful experience known to man. Nothing but you, your brake peddle, and a sea of angry motorists as far as the eye can see.

A little guilty pleasure music should help pass the time. Normally you'd play it at a whisper to spare your fellow motorists from your awful taste in music, but not this time. Today, you're going to crank your crappy tunes as loud as they'll go and everyone else will just have to deal with it.

If they didn't want to listen to Justin Bieber's greatest Christmas hits, they shouldn't have taken the expressway.

Rest for the Wicked Be prepared to roll up the windows to deflect flying coffee cups and tomatoes.

Most Irritating Songs

- "Friday," Rebecca Black
- "Mmm Bop," Hanson
- "La Macarena," Los Del Rio
- "The Song That Never Ends," Norman Martin
- "Who Let the Dogs Out?," Baha Men

MARCH 27

Get Out Your Aggression at a Shooting Range

Guns don't kill people, people kill people, and monkeys do too (if they have a gun).

—EDDIE IZZARD

Yes, guns are dangerous and the world might be a better place without them. But not half as dangerous as you're going to be if you don't let out your pent-up frustration.

You could try traditional methods like counting to ten or punching a pillow, but there's really no substitute for the raw power of a fully loaded semi-automatic stress reliever.

While it may be tempting to just head out to the backyard and start shooting anything that moves, it's far safer to get your aggression out at your friendly neighborhood firing range. There you'll be able to squeeze off round after round without worrying about when the cops are going to show up.

While you're shooting, imagine the cause of your frustration is the target and your bullets are the solution. Each time you hit a bull's eye, you'll be one step closer to serenity.

Rest for the Wicked Resist the urge to take the gun with you away from the range. Better to be unarmed when you try to solve the problem in real life.

Other Aggression Outlets

- Eat until you can't feel feelings
- Run until you pass out
- Break all your dinner plates
- Start a Fight Club

MARCH 28

Haze the New Guy at Work

We really did have a club whose members jumped from the branch of a very high tree into the river as initiation.

—John Knowles

Let's face it, nobody likes the new guy at the office. He's smug, standoffish, and far too full of himself for somebody who's only been there a week. Perhaps it's time to knock him down a few pegs with some good-old fashioned hazing.

Since fraternity-style hazing is a little too intense for the office—and a little too illegal—settle for smaller pranks like encasing the newbie's stapler in Jell-O or gluing his mouse to the desk. Tell him about how much the boss likes it when his employees call him T-Bone, or how Wednesday is "dress like your favorite superhero" day.

You can even enlist the rest of your office and come in early to cover his cubicle with sticky notes. Think of it as a team-building exercise that will bring everyone closer together. Everyone except for the new guy, that is.

Rest for the Wicked It's best to do most hazing while your boss is out of the office.

Rules for Hazing

- If he starts crying, you've gone too far
- Don't damage anything irreparably
- If caught, deny, deny, deny

Force a Friend to Skydive

If at first you don't succeed . . . So much for skydiving.

—Henny Youngman

Jumping out of a plane can be a thrilling, life-changing adventure, but it just isn't as fun if you don't have someone to do it with. And let's face it, your friends aren't exactly in a rush to defy death.

Unless you want to fly solo on this one, you may have to bend the truth a little.

Start by inviting your friend out for an afternoon of bargain hunting, video gaming, or whatever is most likely to get him or her to hop in your car. You've got a solid twenty minutes before your buddy realizes your true destination, and by then it will be too late.

It may be wildly dishonest, but once you are both back on solid ground your friend will have had too much fun to stay mad for long.

Rest for the Wicked In the following weeks, watch your back. The retaliation will be both swift and deserved.

Alternate Adrenaline Rush Activities

- Running with Bulls
- Street Luging
- Cliff Diving
- Heliskiing

MARCH 30

Watch a Movie at Work

The brain is a wonderful organ. It starts working the moment you get up in the morning and does not stop until you get into the office.

—Robert Frost

Rather than fake a sick day—again—go into the office and give off the impression that you're actually hard at work. But instead of polishing off those TPS reports, spend the day catching up on some new releases. Websites like hulu.com or even the iTunes store offer a wide selection that is just a mouse click away.

Make some popcorn in the office microwave and take advantage of that huge computer monitor. Every so often, you'll have to feign some typing or mouse clicking so that your coworkers don't suspect anything. Good headphones are important to pull this off—especially the small earbud ones that are less obvious and can be worn in just one ear.

Rest for the Wicked Always keep a spreadsheet open, one that's dense with numbers and formulas, so you can quickly click on it and appear to be doing work when your supervisor walks by.

Movies about Work to Watch at Work

- *Office Space,* 1999
- *Horrible Bosses,* 2011
- *Nine to Five,* 1980
- *Desk Set,* 1957
- *The Devil Wears Prada,* 2006

MARCH 31

Get Lunch for Free at a Grocery Store Sample Day

I am not a glutton—I am an explorer of food.

—Erma Bombeck, American humorist

On this special day of the week, the grocery store opens its arms to the hungry masses. For them, it's a marketing scheme to increase sales. For you, it's free snacks that you have no obligation to buy.

This isn't like a usual Tuesday night when you fake curiosity to get a free slice of deli meat before ordering a half-pound of the usual. On Sample Day, you can walk up to each department with your head held high, nibble your sample, and then move on without adding a single item to your cart. And walking out of the grocery store with a full belly and full wallet? It's a uniquely satisfying feeling that sure beats the guilty realization that you have a cart full of cheese doodles and frozen pizzas.

Rest for the Wicked Skip the shopping list and leave the carts at the front door. You'll be better able to weave through the crowds and butt your way to the front of the lines if you're not bogged down.

America's Favorite Grocery Stores

- Wegman's
- Publix
- ShopRite
- Trader Joe's
- Meijer

APRIL 1

Prank Your Family

There's an old saying in Tennessee—I know it's in Texas, it's probably in Tennessee—that says, fool me once (long pause) shame on, shame on you. Fool me, you can't get fooled again.

—George W. Bush

It may seem cruel and ruthless to prank your family, but it would actually be cruel not to. Imagine if they have to go the entire day without so much as sitting on a whoopie cushion; they'll think nobody cares enough to go to the trouble.

Make note of your subjects' daily habits and coordinate your pranking efforts accordingly. If he or she is an early riser, set all the clocks in the house forward two hours and watch as your subject scrambles to get to work on time. Is your mark a coffee fiend? Pour salt in the sugar bowl or sabotage the sink to produce a spray of water when he or she fills up the pot.

Whatever you decide, be sure to set up a camera to capture the shenanigans.

Rest for the Wicked Setup an ironclad alibi for yourself to avoid retribution.

Best Simple Pranks

- Super-glue eggs to the carton
- Coat their toothbrush with salt
- Balance a cup of water on an ajar door

APRIL 2

Space Out All Day at Work

Doing nothing is very hard to do . . . you never know when you're finished.

—Leslie Nielsen

Sure you want to make a good impression at work, but is it really worth it?

You hate your job, and you shouldn't be ashamed to admit it. And to prove it, today you are going to do the exact opposite of work. Nothing. Absolutely, positively nothing.

It may seem lazy, but the reality is that you deserve this. Think of all the times you've stayed late to finish a project, skipped your lunch hour to sit through a pointless meeting, or did somebody else's work because they were too incompetent to do it themselves. For everything you do for your company, they can deal with a single day of less than stellar productivity.

When you get to the office, simply sit down in your chair and stare into space. Don't answer the phone, don't even turn on your computer. Just sit there and be. Use the time to meditate or doze off, but avoid the temptation to do work of any kind. You'll probably walk out with a promotion at the end of the day.

Rest for the Wicked Paint a picture of an iris and pupil on the back of your eyelids, in case you fall asleep.

Koans to Clear Your Mind

- Does a dog have Buddha nature?
- What moves, the flag or the wind?
- What did you look like before your parents were born?

Beat Your Current Sex Record

If things go well I might be showing her my O-face. "Oh, Oh, Oh!" You know what I'm talkin' about.

—DREW, *OFFICE SPACE*

Sex is like track and field: everyone knows their own personal career record. When you were young and wild, it was standard for you and your significant other to do it twice in the morning right off, once in the afternoon, then three times before bed just to get some shut-eye. Now, what with a busier schedule, it's a bit tougher.

Of course, unlike track and field, training for a new sex daily high will require some days off. But that's what'll make the day of the competition that much better. Sit your partner down and explain what you want to accomplish. Not only will you get a day of fun and excitement, you'll probably find that your partner is nicer, more considerate, and listens to you more, too.

Rest for the Wicked Be sure to take some time out of the bedroom to stretch and move around.

Most Disconcerting Things to Hear During Sex

- "Are you sure that's a good idea?"
- "Does it always look like that?"
- "I don't think you're doing it right."
- Any name that isn't your own

Cheat at Trivia Night

Why is it trivia? People call it trivia because they know nothing and they are embarrassed about it.

—Robbie Coltrane

Everyone loves the excitement of Trivia Night—until their team loses week after week after week. Surely the opposing teams can't really know off the top of their head what color George Washington's eyes were, or what the capital of Namibia is. They must be cheating!

Maybe they are and maybe they aren't, but obviously there is only one way for you to win a damn Trivia Night—whip out the smartphone. Yes, it's against the rules, but it's Trivia Night, not the Olympic figure skating competition.

You probably don't want to get everything right on the night you "win"—be sure to leave one or two wrong answers. Above all, be discreet so no one else will be the wiser. But if you do get caught, just laugh it off and find a new Trivia Night—after all, a slap on the wrist is a small price to pay for self-esteem.

Rest for the Wicked Choose a table in a dark corner of the bar to decrease the chances of getting caught.

Best Trivia Websites

- *www.sporcle.com*
- *www.funtrivia.com*
- *www.factacular.com*

APRIL 5

Jump in Puddles

You can't tell how deep a puddle is until you step into it.

—Unknown

April showers bring May flowers. But they also bring out a bad attitude in everyone and turn the sidewalks into rushing rivers.

Instead of spending the month of April glowering under an umbrella or hiding in your damp apartment building, embrace both the weather and your inner child. Go puddle jumping.

You're not supposed to do this past the age of ten, but where's the logic in that? Sure, it looks a little childlike. But if you're trudging through a Nor'easter or a spring storm, you're going to end up soaked anyway. You might as well have some fun on your walk. And just try jumping in a puddle without smiling. It's impossible. You'll be loving life as you stomp in one puddle after another, sending rain showers up and onto the unsuspecting passersby power-walking past you.

Rest for the Wicked Jumping in puddles is a lot like jumping into a leaf pile—it's a childhood activity that's still a lot of fun and virtually injury-free. Shake off your uptight adult fears of stained clothes or soggy shoes and just have some fun.

Puddle Jumping Playlist

- "Umbrella," Rihanna
- "Singin' in the Rain," *Singin' in the Rain* movie soundtrack
- "Blame It on the Rain," Milli Vanilli
- "Purple Rain," Prince
- "Red Rain," Peter Gabriel

APRIL 6

Play with Your Child's Toys

In every real man a child is hidden that wants to play.

—Friedrich Nietzsche

You see them lying there, dozens of your kid's mini hot-rod cars with their super cool twisty racetrack, basically just taking up space. What a waste. Especially when here you are, waiting for him to get home from preschool, feeling a little bored and unmotivated to start that next load of laundry.

Time to put those toys to good use. Pick up those cars and race them across the kitchen floor. Grab those Transformers and declare war on the G.I. Joes. Dress Barbie in the outfits you totally would have loved as a ten-year-old. (Okay, maybe you still love them.) If your son or daughter happens to stumble on your play session, chances are they'll be thrilled to join in.

Think about it: Your kid's got about ninety-seven different types of toys. What's the harm in playing with one? Especially when no one's looking.

Rest for the Wicked Careful not to get so carried away that your child starts questioning your commitment to the principle of sharing.

Barbie's Real Name

Barbara Millicent Roberts is the full name of the original Barbie Doll.

APRIL 7

Fake an Impressive Life

I'd like to live as a poor man with lots of money.

—Pablo Picasso

It's date night, and there's only one thing standing between you and some wild post-date hanky panky. The messy, cluttered hole in the wall that you call home. While you can't change your station in life overnight, you can at least fake it for a few hours.

Check your local real-estate listing and track down an upscale loft in the trendy, hip part of town. Bonus points if it has a hot tub, dance floor, indoor basketball hoop, or access to a rooftop pool. Explain to the real estate agent that you're interested in buying, but you'd like to spend the night to get a feel for the place.

Now all that's left is to bring your date back to your swinging pad and watch as his or her jaw drops to the floor. Which is made out of rare canary wood, by the way.

Rest for the Wicked If you'll be drinking, hire a chauffeur to drive you and your date home. It will complete the illusion.

Most Expensive Real Estate

- Monaco – $6,550 per square foot
- London – $3,670 per square foot
- New York City – $2,160 per square foot
- Moscow – $2,210 per square foot

APRIL 8

Outsource Your Chores to Neighborhood Children

My second favorite household chore is ironing. The first being hitting my head on the top bunk bed until I faint.

—Erma Bombeck, American humorist

On a 90-degree day, nothing is more unappealing than going outside to do yard work. You'd much rather be lounging inside with a cold glass of lemonade than sweating your butt off for hours on end. Happily, the world has been kind enough to provide us with a plethora of people who will gladly do your work, often for minimal payment: children.

Neighborhood kids are perfect for taking care of any and all chores you simply don't want to do yourself, from raking the leaves to repainting the backyard shed. Between the ages of ten and fifteen, kids don't really have any other employment opportunities, so they're usually glad to do anything that will earn them a few bucks for candy, video games, or whatever the hell kids buy these days.

At first you might feel lazy outsourcing your chores to the little tykes. But look at it this way—you're encouraging kids to have a responsible work ethic from a young age, which has to help improve the economy sooner or later.

Rest for the Wicked Clear everything with the kids' parents before offering them a job—that way people are less inclined to think you're running some sort of weird children's sweatshop in your backyard.

Easy Chores for Kids

- Raking leaves
- Washing the car
- Mowing the lawn

APRIL 9

Get a Full Spa Treatment

It's a good thing that beauty is only skin deep, or I'd be rotten to the core.

—Phyllis Diller

To look the part at your 9-to-5 and make an impression at the bar after work, every inch of your body must be perfectly groomed and smelling like roses. And that, quite frankly, is one hell of a chore.

You can shave hours off your daily beauty routine if you get a jump-start on the process. How? Treat yourself to a full spa treatment.

Even if you stroll into the spa at your most slovenly, you will emerge fresh as a daisy—hair perfectly coifed, nails trimmed and painted, body hair groomed, and skin soft and blemish-free. At this point, you'll be fit for the cover of *Vogue* without having lifted a finger . . . except to sip from your complimentary wine. And after a 90-minute Swedish massage and half an hour in the steam room, you'll look and feel like your best self. With your morning routine cut in half and your confidence boosted, you'll feel ready to ask your boss for that promotion. And just like that, you can justify your spa day. You're not spoiling yourself. You're advancing your professional career.

Rest for the Wicked Unless you want to look like a lobster, avoid the chemical peels and stick to simple massage-style facials.

Music Most Likely to be Playing at the Spa

- Norah Jones
- Enya
- Sarah McLachlan
- Recordings of ocean waves and whale mating calls

Rediscover Prank Calling

Cell phones are the latest invention in rudeness.

—Terri Guillemets

Cell phones have changed the way we live, bringing the world to our fingertips on their shiny and beautiful screens. It's too bad their caller ID feature made prank calling impossible.

And what a shame it is. Think back to high school, and how therapeutic it was to prank-call your best frenemy. Back then, you could spend hours lying on your bed with your best friends, thinking up witty questions and then slamming down the rotary phone in a fit of giggles. A few hours later, you'd burned off all the stress from that morning's Algebra II pop quiz and had phone-to-phone contact with the most crush-worthy kid in school.

Well, prank calling isn't impossible. You just need to dial *67 to block your number from appearing. And once you do, you can indulge in the baddest bout of prank calling since 1996. You deserve it. You've got bigger stress now and you need a way to relax. So assemble your closest pals, order up a large pizza, crack open a few beers (after all, you're legal now), and work your way through your contacts list.

Rest for the Wicked For those who really want to kick it old-school, grab a roll of quarters and seek out the one remaining pay phone in town.

The Prank Call Hall of Fame

- Bart Simpson (calling Moe's Tavern for Seymour Butts)
- Canadian DJ Pierre Brassard (called Elizabeth II and pretended to be the Canadian Prime Minister)
- Miami radio station El Zol (called Hugo Chavez and pretended to be Fidel Castro, then did the reverse)

APRIL 11

Hire a Chauffeur to Ferry Your Kids Around

Children aren't happy without something to ignore, and that's what parents were created for.

—Ogden Nash

Kids are the source of much joy and pride, but let's be honest: The little suckers are demanding. Between driving them to the mall, movies, and friends' houses, when are you supposed to have time for yourself? That's why you should hire someone to do it for you.

This is especially important once they hit the age where they're embarrassed to be seen with you. It doesn't matter how cool you are (or how cool you once were—try to convince them of that; they'll never believe you), they'll insist you drop them off around the corner so their friends don't have to see your minivan or "This Car Climbed Mt. Washington" bumper sticker.

All they need is a ride—they don't care who they get it from. So hire a chauffeur and take a few minutes to yourself.

Rest for the Wicked Conduct an extensive background check on your chauffeur. These are your kids after all. You can't trust them with just anyone.

What to Do with All of Your New Free Time

- Sleep
- Take up a new hobby
- Catch up on your television shows
- Sleep some more
- Think of other ways to pawn your kids off on other people

APRIL 12

Buy Expensive Clothes, Wear Them Once, Return Them

Our minds want clothes as much as our bodies.

—Samuel Butler

Everyone's been there: You stop to admire the clothes in an expensive department store and realize you couldn't even afford the sunglasses on the mannequin—let alone the whole ensemble.

But just because you can't afford to buy them, doesn't mean you can't take them for a little test drive. You don't really want to keep them anyway, just flaunt them for a few hours.

Simply break out the credit card and head to the expensive part of town to pick up some classy threads. Now's your chance to impress that first date, Make your ex's jaw drop to the floor, and pretend like you are rolling in cash. As long as you keep everything in mint condition and don't remove the tags, you're good to go.

When you're done parading around town, return your fancy duds to the store and put the money back in your account like it never happened.

Rest for the Wicked Read through the store's return policy very carefully to avoid any store-credit-only loopholes.

Helpful Hints

- Clear deodorant won't leave incriminating white marks on clothes.
- Masking tape prevents scuff marks on the soles of shoes.
- Retail workers aren't paid enough to rat you out.

APRIL 13

Chew an Entire Pack of Gum in Ten Minutes

Well, there are some things you should know. You see gum on the street, you leave it there. It isn't free candy.

—SANTA, *ELF*

It's super sweet, incredibly cheap, and vaguely reminiscent of childhood. Bubble gum is the perfect candy. Or it would be if it didn't lose its flavor after twenty-seven seconds.

It's the same sweet song and dance every time. You spring for a pack of Watermelon Bubble Yum at the gas station and gleefully unwrap a sticky little block, your mouth watering at the smell. But by the time you've pulled onto the street, the flavor is gone and you're left chomping on a piece of pink rubber.

Say goodbye to that weird sense of loyalty to your bubblegum. Pop a piece in your mouth and enjoy the sweet rush of concentrated flavor. But the second it starts tasting flat, spit it out and unwrap another. At this rate, you're going to work through an entire pack in about ten minutes—but at a dollar a pack, you can afford to turn 'em and burn 'em.

Rest for the Wicked Remember to remove each piece before you pop in another one. Otherwise you risk giving yourself a case of bubblegum-induced TMJ.

The Best Bubble Gum to Chew in a Hurry

- Bubble Yum
- Dubble Bubble
- Hubba Bubba
- Bubblicious

APRIL 14

Scope People Out Unapologetically

It pays to be obvious, especially if you have a reputation for subtlety.
—Isaac Asimov

When you encounter a particularly smoking hot individual among a sea of ordinary bland faces, you can't help but sneak a tiny peak at the eye candy as it passes you by. But alas, that tiny glimpse is all you get, and it goes by so fast you've forgotten all the subtle details minutes later.

When you think about it though, aside from general human decency (which you threw out the window months ago) there's nothing stopping you from feasting your eyes to your heart's content. People that gorgeous require more than a mere glance to fully appreciate, and today you're going to give them the careful consideration they deserve.

Your goal is to be as obvious as possible in your oogling. This means checking people out until it's just as uncomfortable for you as it is for them. Think of it as a staring contest where the rules are reversed. The only way to lose is to actually look the opponent in the eye.

Don't worry about offending anyone. If anything, they should be flattered by your unwavering gaze. It means they've still got what it takes to get some attention—however unwelcome.

Rest for the Wicked Catcalls of any kind are strongly discouraged. You're creepy, but you aren't a creep. There's a difference.

Essential Oogling Gear

- Mirrored sunglasses
- Wide-brimmed baseball cap
- Cell phone (to pretend to play with)

Cheat on Your Taxes

When there's a single thief, it's robbery. When there are a thousand thieves, it's taxation.

—Vanya Cohen

Every year we do the same song and dance with the government. We make money, and they want some of it. Naturally, we don't want to give it to them. What's a law-abiding American citizen to do?

This year do what you've always wanted to do. Cheat on your taxes. Actually, cheat is a strong word. Massage your taxes. Luckily the government gives us all a chance to hide our money. First, open a PO box in Bermuda. We're not sure how this will help exactly, but it can't hurt. Also, that dining room table you just bought? Work expense. You've thought about work while sitting there, right? No? Doesn't matter, it's tax-deductible. Also, your pet dog can technically be considered a dependent since it relies on you for food, drink, and love. Actually, by that metric, so is the stray cat in the alleyway. All of a sudden, cha-ching. You've got a big tax refund coming your way. And you're only risking a multi-year prison sentence to get it!

Rest for the Wicked If caught, just claim it was your tax preparer's fault.

IRS Criminal Investigation Data

Fiscal Year	2010	2009	2008
Investigations initiated	1818	1778	1603
Prosecution recommendations	1090	1115	1129
Indictments/informations	1011	966	1038
Sentenced	867	810	734
Incarceration rate	79.6	78.1	78.6
Avg. Months to serve	33	27	28

Hit the Snooze

Blessings on him who invented sleep, the mantle that covers all human thoughts.

—Miguel de Cervantes Saavedra, Spanish writer

The best moment of your day is when you wake up at 6 A.M., look at the clock, and realize you still have another hour and a half to sleep. The worst moment of your day is when what feels like two minutes later you look at the clock and it reads 7:30 A.M. Your alarm is going off. Time to get up. Or is it?

Do what feels good. Drag that lazy arm out from your side and slam the snooze button. Get your nine additional minutes of sleep. Then when the alarm goes off again, hit the snooze button again. Repeat until you get tired of waking up every nine minutes and just unplug the thing altogether. Collapse effortlessly into your pillows and blankets. It's about time you feel good and refreshed when you wake up. You're not a farmer. Sleep in.

Rest for the Wicked Keep one eye open to make sure you actually make contact with the snooze button.

Greatest Movie Alarm Clocks

1. *Vanilla Sky:* "Abre los ojos."
2. *Groundhog Day:* the hotel alarm clock
3. *Ferris Bueller's Day Off:* the mother coming in to wake up Ferris
4. *Synechdoche, New York:* the opening scene
5. *Minority Report:* the wristwatch

And the winner is .... *Groundhog Day,* for it consistently working at 6 A.M.

APRIL 17

Invent a Vacation

The real voyage of discovery consists not in seeking new landscapes but in having new eyes.

—Marcel Proust

Tired of seeing everybody gloat about their exotic travels while you can hardly pay the rent each month? Don't get mad, get even.

Today you're going to give those smug bastards a taste of their own medicine and invent the vacation of a lifetime.

First, choose your dream destination. The sky's the limit here—since you won't actually be leaving your chair. A quick Google search and some Photoshop magic later, and you've suddenly got an entire slideshow's worth of memories.

Fake pictures in hand, create an online album with an obnoxious title—Jet-Setting to Paris!!!—and post it to all of your smug, travel-happy friends. With any luck, they'll be so busy planning their counter trip that they won't notice you're wearing the same clothes in every picture.

Rest for the Wicked Make sure your trip is humanly possible. You can't have a photo in London at noon and another in Sydney three hours later.

Best Vacations to Invent

- Backpacking in Nepal
- African safari
- Sailing in the Greek Islands
- Bike tour of France

Crack an Expensive Bottle of Wine to Celebrate a Mundane Achievement

Life is too short to drink bad wine.

—Unknown

Wouldn't it be nice if you felt as though you accomplished something magnificent every day? Like that time you successfully passed the CPA exam, or the day you got engaged. Unfortunately you're not going to do something fantastic every day, but that doesn't mean you can't kick up your heels anyway.

Everyone knows life is more fun when you have something to celebrate, so go ahead and turn one of your most mundane "achievements" into a splurge-worthy occasion. Filed your taxes on time? Crack open that $300 bottle of Dom Perignon stashed behind your cheap vodka. Took your dog to the vet for her check-up? Treat yourself to the vintage bottle of Barolo that Grandma gave you as a college graduation present.

Let's face it—not all of us are going to win the Nobel Prize or invent the next Facebook. So we might as well just break open a bottle of bubbly to celebrate a mundane achievement that says, "I'm here and I'm not a failure."

Rest for the Wicked Be careful not to hit yourself in the face if uncorking a bottle of champagne.

Consider These Wine-Worthy Occasions

- Doing your laundry before you run out of clean underwear
- Mailing mom's birthday card on time
- Finishing reading *The Lord of the Rings* trilogy

Do a Half-Assed Cleaning Job

I'm not going to vacuum until Sears makes one you can ride on.

—Roseanne Barr

You've overlooked the dirty dishes, mountains of dust bunnies, and curiously sticky floors for far too long. If you don't clean up soon, whatever is growing in the fridge might become self-aware and stage a coup.

But let's not get ahead of ourselves here. You certainly do have to tidy up a bit, but nobody ever said you had to go crazy. After all, is there really a difference between something that looks clean and something that is clean?

Instead of vacuuming the carpet—which wasn't really that dirty to begin with—just spray some deodorizer on the ground. That strange smell emanating from the vegetable drawer? Nothing a little baking soda can't fix. And you'd be amazed how quickly you can mop if you strap sponges to your feet while you walk around.

With the time you've saved cutting corners, you can focus on more important things—like finishing last week's Sunday crossword or watching reruns of *The Bachelorette.*

Rest for the Wicked Keep your house messy whenever possible. That way, small improvements will appear more dramatic.

Waste of Time

Each year, the average person spends 657 hours tending to household chores.

APRIL 20

Give Zero Weeks' Notice

The best way to appreciate your job is to imagine yourself without one.
—Oscar Wilde

Have you ever sat behind your desk at a job where you're underpaid and underappreciated and imagined re-enacting job-quitting scenes like those in movies such as *American Beauty, Fight Club,* and *Office Space?* If so, it's time you made your daydream a reality.

There's no need to think about your post-quitting plans. The only thing to consider is how to make your kiss-off the most memorable your office has ever seen—though neglecting to give the requisite two weeks is in itself probably going to earn you firm standing in the company's quitting history.

Giving your boss a two-week cushion is for suckers. You've been a subordinate for as long as you've had the job. Now it's time to become the boss of your biggest work project yet: quitting.

You wanted to do something, so you went and did it. When you get home, make sure to add "go-getter" to your resume.

Rest for the Wicked On your way out, don't do anything illegal like break a computer or hurt a coworker. Those things are only fun in the movies, when there are no consequences.

Five Movies with the Best "I Quit!" Scene

1. *Fight Club*
2. *American Beauty*
3. *Office Space*
4. *Jerry Maguire*
5. *Joe vs. the Volcano*

APRIL 21

Try On Expensive Jewelry Just for Fun

I have always felt a gift diamond shines so much better than one you buy for yourself.

—Mae West

Diamonds and emeralds and sapphires and rubies—these are a few of your favorite things. Too bad the most impressive piece in your collection is a big chunk of turquoise you bartered away from a street vendor.

Even if your only hope for a lavish piece of jewelry involves convincing a man to get down on one knee, that doesn't mean you can't model some pricey baubles just for fun. So head on down to your favorite jewelry store and tell them you're shopping for your sister who looks just like you. Or better yet, tell them the truth. Women do it every day.

Then go ahead—try on that ruby-encrusted bracelet, the diamond solitaire earrings, the emerald-drop necklace. Revel in it. And then walk away. After spying the price tags, the selections on the street might not look so bad after all.

Rest for the Wicked If you do decide to make a purchase, be sure to compare prices at another store. Some experts say buying from the upscale brands in the business could mean paying up to 80 percent more.

Movie Gem

The iconic scene from the 1990 film *Pretty Woman,* where Richard Gere snaps the necklace case down on Julia Roberts's fingers, was improvised. Roberts's laughter was her natural reaction.

APRIL 22

Stay in Bed All Day

You can't teach people to be lazy—either they have it, or they don't.

—Dagwood Bumstead, "Blondie"

As the sun slowly creeps its way through the curtains, you think through all of the possible ways to spend this beautiful day. You could head to the beach, go for a nice bike ride, or putter around in the garden. Then again, who says you have to do anything at all?

It may be fun to go frolicking out in the warm rays of the sun, but it can be just as gratifying to tell that burning ball of fire to bugger off while you watch cartoons. Sure you could wait for a rainy day to sit around in your underwear, but complete and utter sloth is infinitely more satisfying when there are actually better things to do.

So unplug the alarm, wrap yourself in an extra blanket, grab a bag of chips, and see if you can make it through the entire day without leaving your bed. If you get bored, set important goals for your afternoon, like watching the entire *Arrested Development* series, or beating every level of Angry Birds.

Rest for the Wicked Rent at least seven movies.

Movies to Watch in Bed

GIRLS:

- *Sleepless in Seattle*
- *Somewhere in Time*
- *Casablanca*

GUYS:

- *Terminator 1,2,3*
- *Tomb Raider*
- The entire *Star Wars* series

Drive 100 MPH

Remember folks, street lights timed for 35 mph are also timed for 70 mph.

—Jim Samuels, American comedian

For the most part, nobody adheres to speed limits. Traveling five to ten miles per hour over is pretty much standard. But for some reason we all stop there. Everyone has the urge to gun it and let her rip now and then, yet we never indulge that urge.

Sure it's dangerous, and you have to pay a fine if you get caught, but so what? Live a little. Besides, you'll be a safer driver once you know what your car is really capable of.

Find a long stretch of highway and do a preliminary pass, keeping an eye out for speed traps. Once you are sure the cost is clear, double back and get ready for your speed run. Open the windows and feel the rush of air as you hit 100 mph and zoom past hordes of law-abiding motorists. Once you've enjoyed the rush of adrenaline for a bit, ease back down to a reasonable speed before Smokey gets on your tail.

Rest for the Wicked Turn off your cell phone to avoid distracting text messages or calls.

Fastest Car

In September 2010, Charles E. Nearburg drove the Spirit of Rett streamliner 414 mph across Utah's Boneville Salt Flats, beating the wheel-driven land speed record.

APRIL 24

Stage a Fashion Show at an Expensive Clothing Store

Women usually love what they buy, yet hate two-thirds of what is in their closets.
—Mignon McLaughlin

You know those swanky clothing stores you pass occasionally—the ones with the windows full of glamorous gowns and tailored basics that look impossibly chic?

Sure, you're not one to buy a dress that costs the equivalent of six months' rent. But if you're just dying to know how you'd look in that shimmery, floor-length evening gown, remember there's no charge to try it on. So round up a couple of girlfriends, put on your Sunday best, and walk in there like you own the place. Breeze through, grabbing every beautiful dress and ensemble your heart desires. Request to be shown to the fitting rooms. Try on everything. Buy nothing.

Because in clothes like that, just for a few minutes, you get to be a different person. You're wealthy! You're glamorous! You're Julia Roberts in *Pretty Woman*! Just, you know, without Richard Gere's credit card.

Rest for the Wicked Careful not to accidentally tear or stain any of that posh clothing. You could end up with a brand-new silk gown—and a hefty amount of debt.

Style By the Hour

Want to wow with the perfect dress but don't have the cash? Try *www.RentTheRunway.com*, where you can "rent" clothing from luxury brands at a fraction of the cost.

APRIL 25

Take a Three-Hour Lunch Break

The three-martini lunch is the epitome of American efficiency. Where else can you get an earful, a bellyful and a snootful at the same time?

—Gerald R. Ford

With noon rapidly approaching, your brain starts spinning with possible answers to the question that flummoxes workers from Maine to Montana every day: where should I eat lunch? You had Chipotle yesterday, Pret the day before and can't stand the thought of setting foot in Quizno's again. If only you could stretch your hour-long lunch break to an hour and a half…

Well, who the hell says you can't? Sure, maybe it's not "encouraged" at your place of business, but then again, neither is Facebook stalking, and you don't let that stop you. To keep it semi-legit, just sneak out of the office while your boss is in a meeting—that way, they'll never know how long you've actually been gone.

And while you're at it, turn that hour and a half lunch into two, or even three hours. Have multiple courses and a few glasses of wine at the most leisurely restaurant you can think of. Go try on that cute outfit you've been oogling in the Bloomingdale's window for weeks. Or take a stroll in the park to clear your head. Just don't return to work until you've wasted three solid hours of your day. After all, if you're going to do something, you might as well do it right.

Rest for the Wicked Take along a hat and a large pair of sunglasses to disguise yourself in case you spy the company president at the next table.

After "Lunch," Check For . . .

- Red wine-stained teeth
- Post-sex hair
- Suspiciously red eyes

Buy an Expensive Painting

Look, it's my misery that I have to paint this kind of painting, it's your misery that you have to love it, and the price of the misery is thirteen hundred and fifty dollars.

—Mark Rothko

If there's one rule of adult decorating we should all heed, it's this: All posters need frames. But it's more than that. Even if you tore down that "Starry Night" poster and accompanying thumbtacks years ago, it might be time to consider taking the next step toward a more refined adulthood: buy a real painting. And what makes art more "real" than a hefty price tag?

When we say "painting," we don't mean prints or reproductions. In terms of a unique display for your home, nothing beats an original work of art with textured brushstrokes and that new painting smell. And don't worry, original paintings can be found lots of places—galleries, on the web, or directly from the artist.

So browse the selections in person or online, find something you love, and display it above your fireplace like the cultured adult that you are. Leave the mass-produced paintings of generic flowers where they belong — in dorms and hotel rooms.

Rest for the Wicked The art business is rampant with scam artists who misrepresent their inventory. Be sure to research the gallery or artist you're dealing with before writing a check.

Most Expensive Paintings Ever Sold

- "No. 5, 1948," Jackson Pollock ($155.3 million)
- "Woman III," Willem de Kooning ($152.5 million)
- "Portrait of Adele Bloch-Bauer I," Gustav Klimt ($148.7 million)
- "Portrait of Dr. Gachet," Vincent van Gogh ($142.7 million)
- "Bal du moulin de la Galette," Pierre-Auguste Renoir ($135.1 million)

APRIL 27

Disorganize Your Desk

If a cluttered desk is the sign of a cluttered mind, what is the significance of a clean desk?

—Dr. Laurence J. Peter, American educator and hierarchiologist

There's a lot to be said for a clean work space. It shows your coworkers that you are organized, efficient, and ready to take on whatever tasks come your way. But if spotless living isn't really your strong suit, it can be a difficult front to maintain.

As long as you get your work done on time, it shouldn't matter if you have a few stray candy wrappers floating around and haven't rinsed your coffee mug since March. If anything, a messy desk reflects how hard you've been working. A busy worker doesn't have time to straighten up.

This afternoon, instead of organizing your paperclips according to size and color, you're going to make it look like a tornado hit your cubicle. Unroll the tape dispenser and throw a few wads of tape around your computer. Empty the contents of your junk drawer and scatter them about your work space. A few empty coffee cups, some random printouts, and a collection of sticky notes later and you'll look like the busiest (albeit grossest) person in the company.

Finally, after years of pretending to be an anal-retentive neat freak, you can embrace the slob you were born to be. Feels good to be yourself, doesn't it?

Rest for the Wicked Don't do any permanent damage to your space. You still have to work there tomorrow.

Half-Assed Cleaning Techniques

- Use Windex on everything (monitors, chair, phone, coffee mug)
- Throw away overly soiled Tupperware
- Can't find a place for something? Under the desk it goes.

APRIL 28

Hog the Bathroom

How long a minute is depends on what side of the bathroom door you're on.

—Unknown

At first glance, there really isn't much to enjoy about your morning routine. Especially when it is interrupted every five minutes by an impatient spouse or roommate anxious for their turn. But you'd be surprised how much more pleasant it can be when you simply ignore the irritated bangs on the door and enjoy yourself.

Instead of rushing through your shower to preserve hot water, crank it up as high as it will go and bask in the warmth. Since you've gotten the bathroom nice and steamy, now might be the ideal time to lounge around in your towel and catch up on some reading. At the very least, it's a chance to mentally prepare yourself for the day ahead.

Sure, your partner may be a little peeved after the first half hour or so, but that's a small price to pay for your own personal day spa. If his or her whining becomes too much of a nuisance, you can always drown it out by singing in the shower. The more irritating the tune, the better.

Rest for the Wicked Check the locks beforehand to prevent unwanted intrusion.

Viable Excuses

- "I forgot how to turn the shower off."
- "Aliens abducted me for an hour."
- "I didn't know I couldn't do that."

Sell Your Family Heirlooms

We are not cisterns made for hoarding, we are channels made for sharing.

—Billy Graham, American minister and evangelist

Among all your relatives, you have been selected to care for a cherished rocking chair or handcrafted pocket watch that once belonged to your great great great great grandfather. What an honor. If only the watch actually worked and the chair wasn't caving in on itself.

Would your great aunt Jinny really mind if you pawned her beloved silverware instead of keeping it in a box in the basement? Of course not. If she were still alive, she'd want you to let go of the past and look forward to the future. With a nice wad of cash in your pocket.

Wipe the dust off your old books, tea sets, jewelry, and any other valuables that have gone untouched for decades. Once they look presentable, take them to a local antique dealer. Hopefully somebody will pick them up who actually wants to display them, instead of shoving them between forgotten gym equipment and broken power tools.

Rest for the Wicked Check prices online to avoid getting swindled by unscrupulous antique dealers.

Junk That's Actually Junk

- Snow globes
- 99.9 percent of all baseball cards
- Board games
- Tea cozies
- Cigar boxes

APRIL 30

Stage a Food Fight

Food should be enjoyed rather than endured.

—Steve Hamilton, American author

As you sit down to another boring egg salad sandwich, you realize lunchtime as an adult is exponentially less fun than it was when you were a kid. There's no cool-kids table, hardly anyone trades snacks, and there's nary a PB&J sandwich in sight.

To liven things up, it's going to take more than a few stray armpit farts. What this situation calls for is a good old-fashioned food fight.

Without warning, duck behind the nearest chair and hurl pieces of your sandwich at unsuspecting coworkers. Chances are they will be too shocked to retaliate at first, which will give you a tactical advantage in the battle. As others join in, duck and weave your way around the office, launching food bombs as you go. When everyone runs out of food, dust yourselves off and return to to your desks as if nothing happened. Sound silly? Perhaps. But you'll be amazed at how easily a few macaroni and cheese bombs can improve office morale, and solidify you as the office "cool kid."

Rest for the Wicked Don't wear your best suit on food fight day. It's just common sense.

Best Foods for a Food Fight

- Mashed potatoes
- Macaroni and cheese
- Chili
- Tuna casserole
- Anything with peas

MAY 1

Blow a Whole Paycheck in One Night

Whoever said money can't buy happiness simply didn't know where to go shopping.
—Bo Derek, American actress

Hallelujah, the most glorious day of days is upon you. Payday. Time to be a responsible adult and take care of all those lingering bills and tuck a few extra bucks away for retirement.

. . . Or you could blow your hard-earned cash in a single night.

It's not like this is the last paycheck you'll ever receive. You'll have plenty of time to save money later. For now, enjoy yourself.

Head to the nearest bank and cash out your entire paycheck in full. Head out on the town and gorge yourself on expensive food, fancy clothes, overpriced drinks, and endless cab rides. Live like royalty for the evening until you collapse from exhaustion or run out of funds—whichever comes first.

Rest for the Wicked If you don't want to carry around a giant wad of cash, purchase a prepaid debit card for the value of your paycheck.

Proper Financial Planning

What percent of your paycheck should you spend on essentials?

- Food – 15 percent
- Housing – 30 percent
- Car – 10 percent
- Health care – 10 percent
- Entertainment – 10 percent
- Pension – 10 percent
- Savings – 15 percent

Improper Financial Planning

What entails an improper use of your money? The list is infinite, but surely includes the following.

- Hot Pockets – 20 percent
- Stamps – 45 percent
- Hairpins – 35 percent

MAY 2

Hitchhike to the Office

There's a frood who really knows where his towel is.

—Douglas Adams, *The Hitchhiker's Guide to the Galaxy*

Sure, you could drive, bike, or take the bus to work. But all of those methods require some amount of effort, or money. It's infinitely easier to just stick out your thumb and hope for the best.

Hitchhiking may be illegal, but it's a great American pastime as old as the car itself. It's also perfectly safe as long as you know what you're doing.

To start, position yourself on a busy stretch of road where you're sure to attract attention. Wear something flashy to make yourself more visible, and craft a funny sign to show potential rides that you're both funny and not crazy. Perhaps something like, "Come on, do I look like a serial killer?" or "Will give hugs in exchange for rides."

If nobody seems to be biting, resist the urge to show some skin to score a ride, as that will only attract the type of creep you are trying to avoid. Just be patient, somebody will show up eventually. You may even make a new friend out of the experience.

Rest for the Wicked Just to be safe, carry some pepper spray to ward off any potential serial killers.

The Hitchhiker's Guide to Hitchhiking

- Travel alone or with a partner. You'll never get a ride with three or more.
- Make yourself presentable. Ask yourself, would I pick me up?
- Please and thank you go a long, long way.

MAY 3

Stand Up Your Ex

Friendship often ends in love; but love in friendship—never.

—Charles Caleb Colton

After a painful breakup that left you eating takeout alone and routinely polishing off a pint of Ben and Jerry's in a single sitting, it's safe to say you hit a low point. So you got dumped. And it sucked. It happens to everyone. Now it's time to get the revenge you deserve.

Whether it's been three years or three months since you last saw your ex, reach out by sending an innocuous text or e-mail. Keep it light. Insist you'd like to make good on that "let's be friends" one-liner he/she so brilliantly declared the last time you were together.

Invite your ex to a very fancy, very public restaurant where they're bound to see people they know. Put the reservation under your name and confirm the date and time with your ex. Then go see a movie across town instead. Revenge may be sweet but humiliation is sweeter.

Rest for the Wicked Turn your phone off during the movie so you can successfully ignore the multiple phone calls and text messages your ex is bound to leave you.

The Five Stages of Being Stood Up

1. "Oh look, I'm the first one here!"
2. "They must be running late."
3. "It's probably car trouble—I'll try calling."
4. "No answer on the phone, that's strange."
5. "Whatever. I prefer eating alone anyway."

MAY 4

Eat with Your Hands

Whenever a man does a thoroughly stupid thing, it is always from the noblest motives.

—Oscar Wilde

Though eating is usually a pleasurable experience, it can be rather predictable. If a bowl of cereal for breakfast, sandwich for lunch, and protein-packed dinner sounds familiar, it's time for you to give a break to the monotony.

Why not shake things up by digging into your platter, fork-free? You'll be forced to savor the texture of your food as most of it will end up stuck to your fingers. You'll no longer have to curl noodles around your fork while eating spaghetti. Plus, think of the time you'll be saving by not washing any silverware. It's economical and "green."

If you're worried what others will think of your new eating habit, indulge in private. This way, you can live out your food fantasy in peace and focus on the finger-licking goodness in front of you.

Rest for the Wicked Wash your hands so you can enjoy food from bacteria-free fingers.

Best Utensil-Free Foods

- Steak (tear that meat apart)
- Salad (dip the greens in the dressing)
- Pudding (lick the goodness from your fingers)

MAY 5

Sneak Into a Hotel Pool

Free is the best. Anything free is good.

—Sandra Bullock

Swimming pools offer some of life's greatest summertime pleasures: hot sun, comfy lounge chairs, and refreshing water. But unless you fork out for a country club membership or hang with the teenyboppers at the super-chlorinated community center pool, they're off-limits to you.

That is, unless you pretend to be a guest at the nearest hotel. These days, every decent hotel has a pool. The good ones even have a hot tub and baskets of fluffy terrycloth towels. With a constant stream of guests in and out of the hotel lobby, it's impossible for the concierges to keep track of who belongs and who doesn't.

Remember to act like you belong. Skip over the front desk and walk straight to the elevators, where you'll be sure to find a gold plaque directing you to the swimming pool. Once you're there, unwind by soaking up some rays and perfecting your swan dive. While you're congratulating yourself on having gotten the best of the country club with none of the membership fees, remember to slip out a side exit.

Rest for the Wicked You don't want to look like you're coming to the hotel just to go swimming, so leave the pool noodles and inner tube at home.

Pool Games for One Person

- Practice your underwater somersault
- Do a handstand and walk around on your hands
- Hold your breath underwater as long as you can
- Play dead
- Jump up and flop down headfirst like in *Free Willy*

Use Cheats to Beat a Video Game

Video games are bad for you? That's what they said about rock and roll.

—SHIGERU MIYAMOTO, VIDEO GAME DESIGNER

Video games are a potential source of hours of entertainment. They're also a potential source of hours of frustration. Sometimes, despite our best intentions, we just aren't good enough to accomplish something. You have recently run into this problem with the castle in World 7 of Super Mario Brothers 3. And the theme music is so ingrained in your head now you're starting to sing old Beatles songs to the beat.

Luckily for you, there is a solution. Just type in a cheat into the game. They wouldn't put it there if it wasn't supposed to be used. They're as close as a Google search away. Up down left right B A B A up . . . or something. Suddenly you have unlimited lives and automatic flying power. That'll make jumping on the boss's head three times a cinch. Unfortunately, there are eight worlds in Super Mario Brothers 3, and you have an entire new world of frustration awaiting you.

Rest for the Wicked Stretch your hand muscles every hour for about ten minutes to avoid carpal tunnel syndrome.

The Origin of Cheats

Cheat codes have been in place since video games began. The first cheat codes were implemented for play testing purposes: play testers had to test the game and the cheats were made available to make the game easier if need be.

Take Full Credit for Mother's Day

When you feel neglected, think of the female salmon, who lays 3,000,000 eggs but no one remembers her on Mother's Day,

—Sam Ewing, Major League baseball player

Every family has two types of the children. There are the good ones who remember to send flowers and take their mothers to brunch on Mother's Day. Then there are the bastard children who can't remember what they had for breakfast, let alone that it's a holiday.

Good soul that you are, you almost certainly fall into the former category. So why, year after year, do you let your derelict siblings take credit for a gift you bought?

This year, instead of dutifully signing everyone's name to your handcrafted Mother's Day card, let your self-centered brothers and sisters fend for themselves. When Mother's Day rolls around and it's time to shower mom with gifts, make it a point to say that you picked it out by yourself, without any help whatsoever.

Your siblings may look like selfish ingrates, but at least this will be the last year they forget Mother's Day—and the year you're remembered as the Golden Child (and rewarded accordingly on holidays and your birthday).

Rest for the Wicked Don't let the card out of your sight for a second, or else your siblings may try to sneak their names in it.

Gifts All Mothers Secretly Hate

- Scented candles
- Aprons
- Half-dead PTO flowers
- Body lotion

Blow Your Savings on the Lottery

I've done the calculation and your chances of winning the lottery are identical whether you play or not.

—FRAN LEBOWITZ, AMERICAN WRITER AND HUMORIST

There are literally dozens of ways to invest your money. You can buy bonds, stick your money in a CD, open an IRA, or simply stuff it in a mattress. Sadly, regardless of which method you choose, it'll be years before you see any significant returns.

If you want instant gratification, there's only one thing to do: invest in the lottery.

While it's true the odds of winning the lottery with a single ticket are minuscule, this is precisely why you have to buy thousands of them. Besides, it's not really that much worse than playing the stock market. The only difference is that with the lottery, you actually know where your money is going.

Cash out your savings account and bring your stacks of cash straight to the local convenience store. Diversify your investment by buying local, state, and national lottery tickets as well as a few scratch-offs for good measure. Rather than brainstorming thousands of meaningful number combinations, it's best to generate them randomly at the store. That way you'll be able to blame the cashier if all your numbers miss.

Rest for the Wicked Buy your ticket at the location of the last winner. Clearly it's lucky.

Popular Lottery Strategies

- Picking previous winning numbers
- Using birthdays of loved ones
- Consulting a Ouiji board
- Praying to every deity simultanously

MAY 9

Drink Ten Cups of Coffee

If it weren't for the coffee, I'd have no identifiable personality whatsoever.

—DAVID LETTERMAN

When you've been drinking coffee as long as you have, the body builds up a resistance to the caffeine. Sometimes that one cup in the morning just doesn't do it. Sometimes even the second cup doesn't do it. Sometimes the third, fourth, and fifth cups don't even get the job done. So, screw it, just drink ten cups of coffee.

It's time you show your body who's boss. If you want to wake up, dammit, it's gonna happen. And if your body doesn't respond to the first five cups of coffee, well, body, we'll just see who wins this battle of the wills. The coffee machine at work is free, you're not going anywhere. You've got all day. And, now that you've drunk ten cups of coffee, all night too. And all of the next day as well. You may end up with a splitting headache and crash all at once, but at least you woke yourself up when you needed to.

Rest for the Wicked Have enough gum to cover the post-bender coffee breath.

A Nation of Addicts

The average person in the United States consumes 1.6 cups of coffee per day.

MAY 10

Pretend to Be Single for the Day

When they are alone they want to be with others, and when they are with others they want to be alone. After all, human beings are like that.

—Gertrude Stein

When you were single, you claimed to love every minute of it. The freedom! The possibilities! The opportunity to pee with the door open! Of course, now that you're in a relationship, you can finally stop worrying about dying alone. Really, you're happier this way. So why is it starting to seem like so much . . . work?

You know what you need? A single day. Take a day and don't do anything except what you want to do. Don't take any calls from your significant other—admit it's not on your list of priorities to hear about their work conflicts or how long they waited for the train. Go for a two-hour run, or sit on the couch and take in a marathon of the trashy reality shows your loved one refuses to watch. Make dinner plans with your friends, or devour an entire box of Kraft macaroni and cheese without fear of judgment.

Because just as taking a vacation day makes work more bearable, a single day gives you the energy you need to be in a relationship—happily.

Rest for the Wicked Make sure you've informed your significant other that you're taking a single day. Otherwise, twenty-four hours of radio silence may make returning to your relationship more difficult than you thought.

Other Things to Do on a Single Day

- Leave all the dirty dishes in the sink
- Listen to the music your significant other hates, loudly
- Talk to your friends for hours on the phone—or better yet, have them over
- Eat all the garlic and onions you desire
- Take up the whole couch

MAY 11

Read Your Significant Other's Diary

I do not keep a diary. Never have. To write a diary every day is like returning to one's own vomit.

—John Enoch Powell, British politician

It's sitting there starting at you. The small leather-bound book with a gold sash at the most recently written page. Inside it contains the unfiltered peek into your significant other's mind. It's scary, and the thought passes through your mind: Do I betray the trust I've spent months building up and read it? Or let this opportunity pass me by?

Of course you know the answer. Dive in, head first.

If your partner didn't want you to read it they'd do a better job of hiding it. Plus, you're dating, you shouldn't have any secrets from each other (except for the fact that you think their best friend is really hot—that can stay a secret). What the diary contains could blow your mind. Who does your significant other really want to sleep with? What do they hate most about you? What's the worst thing they think? Finally, you'll have a chance to know everything.

Too bad all it contains is a vision of your future together, picking out furniture and baby names and some details of a fight they had with their parents. The scariest thing you find out: your partner is lame.

Rest for the Wicked Memorize the exact position, angle, and direction of the diary before you pick it up so you can return it to its original position.

Worst Hiding Places for a Diary

- Sock drawer
- Under the bed
- On the bookshelf
- Backpack
- Microsoft Word doc called "Not Diary"

Sneak Into a Hotel and Sleep on the Community Couch

At my hotel room, my friend came over and asked to use the phone. I said certainly. He said, "Do I need to dial 9?" I said, "Yeah, especially if it's in the number."

—Mitch Hedberg

Traditionally, going on vacation allows you the opportunity to get away from your home life. Sure, you enjoy the sights and sounds, but more importantly you escape from work, chores, responsibilities, and bills and can finally relax. But why break the bank to get away? Any local hotel can accommodate your need to break out of your routine. Just walk in, pretend you belong, find the community couch, curl up, and fall asleep.

This is an especially useful tactic should you find yourself without a place to stay while traveling or if you get thrown out of your significant other's bed after you say someone else's name during lovemaking. The staff doesn't walk the halls at night, so you'll likely sleep completely undisturbed. And it's not like the hotel is losing any clientele: they're probably sold out anyway. Most importantly, you'll wake up fresh as a spring chicken. When you do wake up, don't stop indulging yourself, treat yourself to a free continental breakfast. They just throw out the leftovers anyway.

Rest for the Wicked Enter the hotel late enough that you don't have to sit inconspicuously for hours before you get to sleep.

Other Popular Places to Sleep Should the Hotel Not Work Out

- Park bench
- Park grass
- Backseat of a car
- Homeless shelter

MAY 13

Treat a Bookstore Like a Library

Where is human nature so weak as in the bookstore?

—Henry Ward Beecher

When you're in the right mood, there's nothing better than spending the entire afternoon with your nose stuck in a book. Now if only there were a way to read a brand-new book without paying a dime.

Oh, there are libraries for that, but you haven't stepped across the threshold of a library since you graduated college and you're not about to start now. You're going to do one better: You're going to use a bookstore as your own personal library.

Bookstores are practically begging you to read their books without paying. Clusters of overstuffed armchairs offer a reading spot far more comfortable than your furniture at home, while the attached coffee shop provides fancy lattes and cookies that put your Mr. Coffee to shame. So go ahead and do it: Buy yourself a six-dollar coffee (after all, the reading material is free), pull a book off the shelf, and hunker down for the afternoon. It will take you a few trips to see how the latest vampire romance story ends, but the suspense makes the love story that much sweeter.

Rest for the Wicked You're borrowing, not buying—so be sure to leave the books in good condition. This means no dog-earing the pages or sneaking a novel into the bathroom with you.

Other Perks of a Bookstore-as-Library

- You can browse the magazines and newspapers too
- The arm chairs are comfy enough for a nap
- No membership card required
- There aren't any librarians to shush you

MAY 14

Watch the Game at Work

We are inclined that if we watch a football game or baseball game, we have taken part in it.

—John F. Kennedy

Many important sporting events take place during the day. The Chicago Cubs famously play day games most of the week. The first two rounds of the NCAA Tournament take place during the weekday. Many college football bowls are during the day as well. Watching these games is certainly better than working, so open a new Mozilla window and watch some sporty ball at work.

Depending on your workplace, this might be dangerous or it might be tolerated but frowned upon. Either way, you'll have to keep a low profile. Bring in a pair of earphones so as not to disturb those near you. Also, you should practice not cheering during a game a few times before trying it at work. But once it's safe, it's a great way to be able to enjoy the time you spend at work. Plus you'll have all the latest sports news to disseminate to your officemates. Your cool factor just increased by one.

Rest for the Wicked Many games available on ESPN.com and other network websites offer the "Boss Button." If you click this button, the screen immediately changes to a workflow chart or something else that looks like real work. Use it when your boss comes by.

Inappropriate At-Work Sports Game Behavior

- Tailgating
- Bodypaint
- Foam fingers
- Audible cheering
- Doing the Wave
- Drinking

MAY 15

Get Free Refills All Night

Let's all go to the lobby to get ourselves a treat!

—1953 ANIMATED MOVIE THEATRE SNACK BAR ADVERTISEMENT

Dinner and a movie is America's favorite date night. The only problem? A romantic meal and two tickets to the latest blockbuster can easily set you back fifty bucks.

It's tempting to lower the price tag by scrimping on dinner or trading the big screen for a made-for-TV movie, but where's the fun in that? Instead of cutting back, squeeze every penny you can out of the restaurant and the movie theatre concession stand: Exploit the free-refill policy.

Look for menu items described as "unlimited," "bottomless," or "endless." You might not think you can make a meal out of bottomless soft drinks and unlimited breadsticks, but you would be wrong. At the movies, splurge for the large popcorn and soda. Remember, you're spending money to save money. After five or six refills, those snacks will have paid for themselves.

Rest for the Wicked Eat a light breakfast and lunch. You don't want to miss out on any delicious breadsticks, soft drinks, or popcorn because you overdid it on your morning cereal.

Making the Most of the Refill

Sneak a Ziploc bag and an empty cup into the movie theater. As soon as you sit down, transfer your snacks to the empty containers and give them to your date. Refill the original packages. Repeat. And repeat again.

MAY 16

Have an Upside-Down Dinner

Life is uncertain. Eat dessert first.

—Ernestine Ulmer, American Writer

Dessert is obviously the best part of any meal, yet over and again we gorge ourselves on mediocre dinner fare until there's no room left for sweets. And each time we do that, our inner child dies a little inside. The solution is as elegant as it is simple: eat dessert first.

There are some things that just need to happen in order. Like thinking of an excuse before you call in sick to work. But the timeframe of eating dessert simply does not fall into that category. It's not like coating your stomach with steak will prevent the cheesecake from making you fat. So you might as well give in to your sweet tooth.

When your waiter gets to the table, kindly ask to see the dessert menu before you even look at the dinner options. Indulge yourself with ice cream, fruit tarts, French pastries, and anything else that catches your eye. Once you are filled to capacity, take a moment to see if you have room for dinner. You might not even need to bother.

Rest for the Wicked Finish all the pie that's on your plate, or else you won't get any chicken.

Other Upside-Down Adventures

- Work week (take Monday/Tuesday off)
- Road trip (start complaining, then get in the car)
- Fight (apologize first, then start punching)

MAY 17

Crash a Lunch Meeting

People who enjoy meetings should not be in charge of anything.

—Thomas Sowell, American writer

Lunch time rolls around and the egg salad sandwich you brought is about as appetizing as the bag in which you packed it. Suddenly, a ray of hope as the familiar scent of takeout wafts from the conference room.

You may not have been invited to the meeting directly, but you would be doing the company a disservice if you didn't attend. If you don't offer your expert opinion, countless minutes could be lost talking in circles.

Quietly sneak into the meeting room and grab a seat close to the lunch food. While you stuff your face, jot down a few notes and mumble in agreement so you look like you belong there. As long as you keep your head down, nobody will even notice you are there. It will be just like every other meeting you've ever been to.

Rest for the Wicked If anybody asks you a direct question—like what you're doing there—pretend to choke on some Szechuan chicken and head for the nearest exit.

Office Jargon Translated

- Synergy: Pawning off work on another department
- Action Item: Something we forgot to do
- Deadline: An utterly meaningless, arbitrary date

Buy a Puppy on a Whim

Whoever said you can't buy happiness forgot little puppies.

—GENE HILL, AMERICAN AUTHOR

You generally consult your significant other on all major life decisions. Buying a car, taking a new job, naming any existing or future children. Of course, this courtesy goes completely out the window the moment you set foot in a pet store.

Nobody knows what it is, but puppies have a mystical power that allows them to override the area of our brain dedicated to logic and reasoning. You never stood a chance. You might as well just accept your fate and take Fido home.

Don't feel bad about your reckless decision. Countless others—far stronger and wiser than yourself—have succumbed to their debilitating cuteness.

Prepare an elaborate story about how the puppy just jumped into your car while you were driving home. You might even be able to convince your partner that you won the little critter in a raffle. Just resist the urge to call ahead before you make your purchase. Remember, it's easier to ask for forgiveness than permission.

Rest for the Wicked Make sure you are holding the puppy when you tell your partner about the new pet. It'll make the news easier to take.

What Your Dog Says about You

- Golden Retriever – Dependable
- Chinese Crested – Alien
- Australian Shepherd – Hyperactive
- Chihuahua – Snobby
- Nintendog – Lonely

MAY 19

Go Uncamping

Some national parks have long waiting lists for camping reservations. When you have to wait a year to sleep next to a tree, something is wrong.

—George Carlin

Ah, camping—the sweet sting of mosquitoes, the fragrant aroma of canned beans, the intrinsic joy of burying your own waste.

Screw roughing it. Next time your loved ones ask you to join them in the wild, tell them you'll go uncamping instead. Bring a generator and a portable air conditioner. Pack your laptop, iPod, and a week's worth of DVDs. Cram a king-sized air mattress and a beanbag chair into your deluxe, three-room tent. Tuck champagne and tins of caviar in the cooler next to the hotdogs and beer. Or better yet, make arrangements to have a pizza delivered straight to the campsite.

After all, there's no reason to separate yourself from nature. Some of us just prefer to combine it with our other loves—like our PlayStation.

Rest for the Wicked To avoid any alfresco fistfights, be sure to set up your uncamping campsite out of earshot from anyone looking for peace and quiet.

Gourmet S'Mores

1 high-quality chocolate bar (such as Ghirardelli)
8 large oatmeal cookies
8 large marshmallows
skewers

1. Place pieces of chocolate on the flat sides of 4 oatmeal cookies.
2. Skewer the marshmallows and roast them until golden brown. Slide the warm marshmallows onto the chocolate and top with remaining cookies. Let the chocolate and marshmallows melt into a warm, gooey mess. Devour and enjoy.

Watch Movies All Day

I think cinema, movies, and magic have always been closely associated. The very earliest people who made film were magicians.

—Francis Ford Coppola

Ah, the weekend, the perfect time to catch up on all the errands and chores you've been neglecting all week. It can be so rewarding to check things off your to do list.

Of course, it can also be rewarding to sit on the couch and watch TV until your eyes bleed.

When was the last time you saw a good movie anyway? Let alone seven good movies back to back? Your list of to-dos has taken a back seat for weeks now. It can certainly wait another twenty-four hours while you catch up with your movie collection.

Dust off a few of your favorite flicks and plan the ultimate movie marathon. You can create a list of greatest hits, stick entirely to D-rate horror films, or watch an entire movie series in a single afternoon—you've got nothing but time.

Rest for the Wicked Stockpile popcorn, candy, pizza, and soda to avoid a break in the action.

Ultimate Movie Marathons

- *Lord of the Rings* trilogy (3 films) – 11 hours, 18 minutes
- *Star Wars* series (6 films) – 13 hours, 23 minutes
- *Harry Potter* series (8 films) – 19 hours, 31 minutes

Fart in a Crowded Elevator

I did not win the Nobel Fart Prize.

—Bart Simpson

Like real estate, farting is all about one thing: location, location, location. Whether you're in the privacy of your own home or in a public space among strangers matters greatly in how your fart will be received. Still, bystanders remain mostly powerless against olfactoral offenses. Which is why the next time you're stuck in a crowded elevator and have to let one rip, have at it.

The elevator is a perfect spot to fart because other people are trapped. They have nowhere to go and the air is creeping closer and closer to them. Lucky for you, your own fart smell is good, so it's not a problem. Some people may put their noses in their shirts or make a comment, but you just keep smiling away like you're skipping in the sun. As one final act of war against your elevator-mates, if people raise a fuss with you, silently point your thumb at the guy to your right.

Rest for the Wicked Don't do this after having a spicy bean burrito.

Other Rude Things to Do in a Crowded Elevator

- Talk on your cell phone
- Stretch
- Sneeze
- Jog in place
- Projectile-vomit
- Sweat profusely

Hire a Personal Back Scratcher

Happiness is having a scratch for every itch.

—OGDEN NASH, AUTHOR

Even when you don't have an itch, getting gently scratched is one of the most comforting feelings. Dogs become obedient and restful when you scratch them. Cats snuggle up to you. Other people moan approvingly from the feeling.

A stick with bristles on the end just doesn't do the trick. So invest in your comfort. Hire a personal back scratcher. It's an easy job, and some unemployed college graduate will happily take it up. Post an ad: Seeking a gentle, easy-going personal assistant who does not bite their nails. Before you know it you'll be living in luxury. Your personal back scratcher will be able to get all those hard-to-reach places: the upper back, under the shoulders. Plus having a personal back scratcher will free up your other two hands. Think of how much more you can get accomplished: with two extra hands, you can scratch four places at once!

Rest for the Wicked Nails should be sharp . . . but not too sharp.

Worst Things to Scratch

1. Chicken pox
2. Sunburn
3. Mosquito bites
4. Poison ivy rashes

MAY 23

Start a Fight Just for the Make-Up Sex

Sex alleviates tension. Love causes it.

—Woody Allen

Fights are an inevitability in any relationship. If you spend enough time with somebody, there's going to be the occasional disagreement. The good news is that the more bitter the dispute, the more heated and passionate the reconciliation.

Alas, you haven't had a fight in months, but don't despair. Just because you and your beau are getting along better than ever, doesn't mean you have to miss out on mind-blowing make-up sex. It's time to stir things up a little.

When you greet your significant other tonight, come prepared with a list of pet peeves and complaints and bombard your partner with everything you've got. Don't let up until your S.O. storms out in a fit of rage.

After you've both had a while to cool down, lay on the apologies. Once everything's smoothed over, it's time to attack one another with the reckless abandon only a truly epic fight can engender.

Sure it's a little manipulative, but your partner certainly won't be complaining when it's over.

Rest for the Wicked Don't take it too far, or you could be sleeping on the couch—or on the street—instead of in your lover's arms.

Best Places for Make-Up Sex

- Kitchen counter
- Bathroom floor
- Laundry room

Cash Out Your Savings Account

Too many of us look upon Americans as dollar chasers. This is a cruel libel, even if it is reiterated thoughtlessly by the Americans themselves.

—Albert Einstein

If you've ever seen a music video that takes place in a strip club (and really, who hasn't?), you know what $10,000 looks like. But do you know what it feels like? Not until you cash out your savings account and hold it in your hands.

Don't worry about the suspicious glances you get from the bank teller. This is your money, you've earned it, and you want to feel it between your fingers.

Common sense says to leave it in the bank where it will earn interest until you need it for something sensible, like a house or child's college education. But where's the fun in that? You want to have some time with your money before you have to spend it. And the first stop once you've felt its weight in your pocket? The strip club, of course. After all, it always looks like so much fun in music videos.

Rest for the Wicked Carrying a suitcase full of money is too cliché. Instead, wear cargo pants to the bank and stuff the dollar bills into the pockets.

Fun Things to Do with Money (Besides Spend It)

- Fill your bathtub with it and take a money bath
- Make a house of money (similar to a house of cards)
- Wallpaper your house with it
- Hide it in books so you don't discover it until later. Act surprised when you do

MAY 25

Hire a Hot Personal Trainer

The word aerobics came about when the gym instructors got together and said, "If we're going to charge $10 an hour, we can't call it jumping up and down."

—Rita Rudner

New Year's has come and gone, and with it so too has your New Year's resolution to get in shape. Nothing you seem to do can keep your motivation up. Even when you would reward yourself with a sip of beer after each situp. Those sips of beer became more frequent, and the situps less so. The fact is if you don't have a reason to go to the gym, you're not going to go. And therefore you have no choice but to hire a hot personal trainer.

It shouldn't be hard. Most personal trainers are young, in shape, and pretty hot. Are they qualified? If they can get themselves to look like that, then they must know something. But just to be sure, you should conduct an extensive interview process. Once you select the right candidate, you'll find yourself dreaming about going to the gym all day. Suddenly that motivation problem is solved.

Rest for the Wicked If you find your personal trainer is getting too hot during your workout, go-to thoughts can include grandma's cookies, baseball, and the comedy stylings of Garrison Keiller.

Buyer Beware

A 2002 investigation of the modern world of personal trainers found that 70 percent of those surveyed did not have a degree in any field related to exercise science.

Drink an Entire Bottle of Wine by Yourself

I cook with wine. Sometimes I even add it to the food.

—W. C. Fields, American comedian

It's been a long day, and your frustrations just seem to keep multiplying. After work, you walk in the door, throw down your keys, and immediately head for the wine rack. You pour a glass or two, willing away your workplace woes. You know it would be smart to put the bottle away, but tonight you really just don't want to.

So don't. Instead, kick off your shoes, order delivery, and treat yourself to not one or two glasses of wine, but the whole darn bottle. Everybody needs a little extra vino in their system now and then, and drinking a whole bottle in one night merely means you're a fun-loving soul—not that you're an alcoholic.

Whether you crack open a bottle of Two Buck Chuck or dig into a bottle of vintage cab that's been sitting in your wine rack for months, feel free to drink away. After all, studies have shown both red and white wines to be heart-healthy, and who doesn't want a working ticker?

Rest for the Wicked Drink several glasses of water before bed to reduce the risk of hangover.

Best Regional Wine Picks

- Chardonnay, Monterey, California
- Riesling, Finger Lakes region, New York
- Cabernet Sauvignon, Napa Valley, California
- Pinot Noir, Oregon

MAY 27

Fake a Headache So You Can Just Go to Sleep

And then Adam said, what's a headache?

—Author unknown

It happens to everyone—you climb into bed after a long day, feel your significant other's suggestive hand on your thigh and think, do we really have to do this tonight? Most evenings you would succumb to your S.O.'s advances to keep things on an even keel, but tonight you want to sleep, and dammit, you're going to sleep.

So instead of acquiescing, put on your best "I don't feel good" face, rub your temples a few times and gently tell your partner that since your head has been hurting all day, you need to sleep it off instead of engaging in any strenuous activity. If your partner puts up a fuss, kiss him or her a few times and promise a rollicking bedtime session tomorrow night.

Your partner may pout for a few minutes, but rest assured a night will come when he or she does the exact same thing to you. So for tonight, ditch the guilt and get to sleep.

Rest for the Wicked Keep a bottle of pain reliever by the bed so you can take some as part of your "I have a headache" scheme.

No More Excuses

Studies have shown that sex can actually help get rid of headaches. So on a night when you have a real headache, try to find some relief by getting busy between the sheets.

MAY 28

Memorial Day BBQ Hop

If you really want to make a friend, go to someone's house and eat with him . . . the people who give you their food give you their heart.

—Cesar Chavez

Follow the smell of smoke and burgers and hop from one backyard BBQ bash to the next. So what if you weren't invited? Everyone will assume you're a friend of someone else anyway.

Explore a variety of pasta salad preparations while seamlessly blending in with other Memorial Day revelers. As soon as the opportunity presents itself, challenge someone to a game of bag toss or bocce or some other backyard game. Make a friend. Establish your story. If you're looking chummy with just one person, everyone will think they're the one who invited you.

Keep a six-pack handy so it looks less suspicious when you wander in. Everyone likes beer, right? Don't forget to replenish the stash before you're on to the next stop.

Rest for the Wicked Don't let anyone know that you're crashing the party. Always have a back story handy so you don't get found out. Works best if you're operating alone.

Possible Back Story Ideas

- You went to college with the host's cousin
- You live upstairs/downstairs
- You live next door
- You're the landlord's husband/wife/daughter/son just saying "Hi"
- You're friends with Mike. No not that Mike. The other Mike. The one who couldn't make it.

MAY 29

Throw a BYOE (Bring Your Own Everything) Party

After all, what is your host's purpose in having a party? Surely not for you to enjoy yourself; if that were their sole purpose, they'd have simply sent champagne and women over to your place by taxi.

—P. J. O'Rourke

Take the idea of a potluck to the next level and outsource everything you need for a party to your guests. Don't just limit your guests to the typical six-pack and a bag of chips. You're providing the most important thing—the location—so it's only fair that your friends pull their own weight.

Keep a master list of everything you'll need. Things like cups and soda are expected, but what about those necessary items like toilet paper and dish detergent? Each time a guest asks if they can bring something, say "Yes" and assign them one of the items. Don't be afraid to include some things you've been needing around the house, too. If they seem confused when you ask them to bring cat food, just respond, "It's gonna be one hell of a party."

Rest for the Wicked Always establish a designated driver or make a plan for taking a cab home so no one is drinking and driving.

Party Must-Haves

- Alcohol
- Music
- Snacks
- Bottle opener
- Party game

MAY 30

Pass Off Takeout as Your Own Cooking

Please don't lie to me, unless you're absolutely sure I'll never find out the truth.

—Ashleigh Brilliant quotes English Author

Cooking for a crowd can be one of the most stressful activities imaginable. If you don't time everything just right, you're left with burnt food, hungry guests, and a kitchen full of shattered dreams. But even if you aren't a top-rate chef, you can still put together a stellar meal.

If you fake it, that is.

Ordering takeout and calling it homemade is certainly misleading, but on the grand scale of dishonesty it barely registers. Your guests get to eat a delicious meal, and you get to pretend you are Julia Child. Everybody wins.

Before your guests arrive, call up your favorite takeout restaurant, pick up a few of their most popular dishes, and stash them in your fridge. Keep everyone out of the kitchen for the entire night (no exceptions) and be sure to bang some pots around and chop up a few loose vegetables for effect. When it's time to serve, reheat the restaurant fare and transfer it into serving dishes. Your guests will never know the difference.

Rest for the Wicked Quickly dispose of any Styrofoam containers and any other incriminating evidence.

Crowd-Pleaser Meals

- Bacon-wrapped filet mignon
- Mushroom risotto
- Fettuccine alfredo
- Maple-glazed pork tenderloin

Consume an Entire Pizza by Yourself

You better cut the pizza in four pieces because I'm not hungry enough to eat six.

—Yogi Berra

With a telephone and a few extra dollars, anyone can enjoy the wonder that is the cheesy, gooey American pizza. But just because you don't have a party going on in your house doesn't mean you shouldn't go for the whole pie. After all, you're hungry—and you don't have to be.

Of course, a more practical person might order the deliverable minimum, eat a small portion, and save the rest for later. But leftover pizza simply isn't the same as a hot, oven-fresh pie. Besides, you can always hit the gym and make up for your evening of gluttony some other time.

Since this pizza is for you and you alone, feel free to go nuts. Get every topping on the menu, and even some that aren't. And don't even think about blotting it with a napkin first. The greasier the better.

Rest for the Wicked Avoid all food but nuts and berries for twelve hours prior to the pizza binge. You want your stomach to be empty, but not so empty that it shrinks.

Drinks That Go Well with Pizza

- $200 Cabernet Savignon
- Johnny Walker Blue
- Imported, oak-aged pilsner, retailing at $20/bottle

JUNE 1

Buy a Hobby

Beware the hobby that eats.

—Benjamin Franklin

Hobbies are great ways to add meaning to your life, but there's no denying they are immense time-sucks.

Some people spend years—lifetimes even—memorizing every species of spider or seeking out that one rare gum wrapper to complete their collection. While you could follow suit and start your own hobby from scratch, it's far easier to ride the coattails of someone else's blood, sweat, and tears and simply buy a hobby.

Pick a topic that interests you and poke around for a local trade show or convention devoted to the subject. Once there, track down a particularly impressive collection and buy it from the owner, lock stock, and barrel. Congratulations, you're now an official stamp collector, WWII enthusiast, or whatever else you'd like to be.

Whoever said money can't buy happiness clearly wasn't trying hard enough.

Rest for the Wicked Read up on your chosen hobby before trying to convince anyone that you're an expert.

Some Suggested Hobbies to Buy

- Stamps
- Glass figurines
- Buttons
- Baseball cards
- Action figures

Convert Your Living Room Into a Ball Pit

When my kids become wild and unruly, I use a nice, safe playpen. When they're finished, I climb out.

—Erma Bombeck, American humorist

There's little doubt that McDonald's success would be a fraction of what it is now were it not for the ball pit they employ at many of their locations. As a child, the sight of a pool of small multi-colored plastic balls was like a magnet. You just dropped everything and ran. Even as an adult there is some longing for those simpler times. So get back in touch with your younger self and convert your living room into a ball pit.

You'd be surprised how easy it is. Internet retailers like Amazon sell plastic balls (called "magic balls") used for ball pits. Order ten times as many as you think you'd need. Then when your delivery comes, just start unwrapping the bags and bags of balls until they're above your head. Then let your imagination run wild. Your own ball pit is a way to construct a fantasy world. It's also like having your own swimming pool, but one you can walk around in underwater without drowning. Invite your friends over and have a ball pit party. Play tag. Throw the balls at each other. You just became the envy of every child who lives on your block.

Rest for the Wicked Have a cell phone handy for when you get trapped and need to call for help.

The Dangers of Plastic Balls

There have been well-circulated urban legends that children have died after playing in a ball pit from poisonous snakes and hypodermic needle injections. Although there is no truth to these stories, workers at ball pits have reported finding dirty diapers, half-eaten food, and even syringes among the balls. So when you have your personal ball pit, remember to properly dispose of all needles and diapers.

Play in the Mud

There is an eagle in me that wants to soar, and there is a hippopotamus in me that wants to wallow in the mud.

—Carl Sandburg

As an upstanding adult, one expectation after another is piled on your shoulders. Make sure your hands are clean. Keep your clothes neat. Look respectable. Cinderelly, Cinderelly, Cinderelly!

But sometimes isn't it fun to do the opposite of what's expected? Now, we're not suggesting that you stop showering or start pulling on dirty clothes from the hamper. You're just taking a break from cleanliness. The best way—by which we mean, the most fun way—is to play in the mud.

If you ever played an outdoor sport, you know what we're talking about. The rain games are the best games. Well, you can achieve that same level of fun in your own backyard.

If you're feeling nostalgic, reconnect with your inner child over a stack of mud pies. If you're looking for a facial on the cheap, slather the stuff across your face and arms. Artistic types can etch their artwork into the mud canvas. Feeling rambunctious? Call up some friends and set up a mudball fight and a natural slip 'n slide. And once your friends are there and in on the fun, the possibilities are endless—but we can't print the most fun ones here.

Come on, you can send out your laundry tomorrow.

Rest for the Wicked If you're wary of hosing down your own backyard, wait for a summer rainstorm and head to the nearest park. Bring a soccer ball in case anyone asks how you managed to tear up a whole field.

Mud Races

If you're looking to turn a muddy afternoon into a team sport, you're not alone. Mud races are one of the fastest growing activities, attracting thousands of participants at each race.

Don't Tip for Mediocre Service

I don't tip because society says I have to. All right, I tip when somebody really deserves a tip. If they put forth an effort, I'll give them something extra. But I mean, this tipping automatically, that's for the birds.

—Mr. Pink, *Reservoir Dogs*

Your water glass has been empty since you finished your appetizer, someone else's crumbs are littering the table, and you had to grab a bottle of ketchup off a busboy's tray so you could eat your fries. Still, on any regular day, you'd cough up 15 percent when it came time to pay the bill.

But not today. Today it's good service or bust. Haven't seen your server in so long you forget if they're a man or a woman? No tip. Get an eye roll every time you ask for a refill on your coffee? No tip. Have to chase your server down to get $1 bills for all those $5 bills she gave you in change? You get the picture.

There's no need to fork over your hard-earned cash for a job not well done. Just remember to tip well and tip often when it is.

Rest for the Wicked If you're not leaving a tip, best to get out of there as soon as you've paid the bill. Otherwise, be prepared to provide an explanation.

Good Service Does Pay!

In 2007, an Indiana Pizza Hut waitress received a $10,000 tip from a regular customer so she could attend a local college.

JUNE 5

Pay for a Parking Ticket in Pennies

You know, somebody actually complimented me on my driving today. They left a little note on the windscreen, it said "Parking Fine."

—Tommy Cooper (British comedian)

There's no worse feeling than getting a parking ticket. Suddenly, that coffee you ran in for without paying the meter costs five times as much, and it feels like everyone in the whole world is against you. So give it right back to them: Instead of cutting a check like you're expected to do, take the opportunity to empty out your piggy bank—and pay the ticket in pennies.

It's legal tender—they have to take it. So have some fun with it and make it a game. The more coins you use to equal the amount of the ticket, the better. If you only have quarters or dimes, find a way to exchange them for pennies.

If they're going to take your money, you're going to take their time. Drop off the change and turn on your heel. There's no need to stay to make sure it's all there—they have your contact information if they need to get in touch.

Rest for the Wicked Do your research before pulling this stunt. Find out if there's a law against being a jerk or else prepare to be arrested.

Other Payment Options

- IOU (those are better than money)
- Pay in trade
- Marbles. Lots of marbles.

JUNE 6

Organize Your Life on Company Time

Yeah, I just stare at my desk; but it looks like I'm working. I do that for probably another hour after lunch, too. I'd say in a given week I probably only do about fifteen minutes of real, actual, work.

—PETER GIBBONS, *OFFICE SPACE*

When you have to be at work eight-plus hours a day, there's never enough time to take care of everything else on your To-Do List. Tasks pile up, only to be forgotten and remembered three weeks later. Lucky for you, there's an easy solution: Organize your life on company time.

It may require some finesse, but you can absolutely catch up on all those mundane little tasks you've been putting off. Pay the cable bill? Check. Reconcile your bank statement? Check. Make a much-needed dentist appointment? Check.

Let's be honest—people dick around at work all day, from Facebook stalking to Christmas-present shopping. If anything, your company should be glad to have an employee who does something valuable with his non-working-at-work time. And for you, thank God there will finally be enough hours in the day.

Rest for the Wicked Invest in a monitor mirror so you can see who's coming up behind you at work.

On Company Time

CUBICLE-DWELLERS CAN EASILY PULL OFF:

- Paying bills
- Writing birthday cards
- Catching up on the news

OFFICE-DWELLERS CAN EASILY PULL OFF:

- Knitting a sweater
- Reading all seven Harry Potter books
- Taking a nap

JUNE 7

Build a Couch Fort

The man who has no imagination has no wings.

—MUHAMMAD ALI

When you look at a couch, you probably see a nice comfortable place to hunker down and read a book. As every child knows, you are wildly underestimating its potential.

What you are actually sitting on are the building blocks for an impregnable fortress that doubles as a secret underground bunker. Provided you don't mind making a mess of your living room, of course.

Take all of the cushions, blankets, and throw pillows off of your couch and start your building process with a clean slate. Use the larger cushions to create a sturdy base, and pull materials from elsewhere in the house (comforters, end tables, chairs) to enhance your fort.

Once you have constructed a respectable stronghold, invite some friends over to relive their childhoods. You now have a secret place to discuss sensitive information (like which boy is cutest or whether Spider-Man could beat Wolverine in a fight).

You might think it a silly waste of time to build a couch fort, but there's something to be said for nurturing your imagination. If you don't give it some exercise, it's liable to wither away to nothing.

Rest for the Wicked Draw up blueprints for your fort before you start building. Making couch forts is serious business.

Items to Enhance Your Fort

- Blankets
- Christmas lights
- Finger paintings (for decoration)
- Guard dogs (for security)

JUNE 8

Stay Up All Night

There will be sleeping enough in the grave.

—Benjamin Franklin

For most people, nothing interesting happens between the hours of 10:00 P.M. and 6:00 A.M. But for the night owls, this is the absolute best time to be awake.

There must be something compelling people to forgo sleep, and tonight you are going to find out exactly what that might be. You've got your entire life ahead of you, does it really make sense to waste one third of it in bed with your eyes closed?

Put on a pot of coffee (or six) and hunker down for the long haul. You can occupy your time with aimless Internet browsing, mindless infomercial viewing, and an occasional late-night munchie session. Since you would otherwise be sleeping, you won't feel as guilty doing things that would otherwise be gross wastes of your time.

Rest for the Wicked When preparing warm munchies, stick to the microwave. The oven is off limits for sleep-deprived zombies.

Secrets to Staying Awake

- Combine coffee, soda, tea, ginseng, and caffeine pills in a single drink
- Jog in place or do jumping jacks
- Watch horror movie marathons

Go Skinny Dipping

Only when the tide goes out do you discover who's been swimming naked.

—Warren Buffett

After awhile, every day starts to feel depressingly similar to the one before. You wake up, go to work, come home, make dinner, watch TV, and go to bed. What you wouldn't give for a little spontaneity.

Luckily you don't have to sell all your worldy possessions and go backpacking around Europe to shake things up. Something as simple as taking a quick dip in your outdoor pool could be all you need. Naked, of course.

The average bathing suit is uncomfortable, restrictive, and leaves almost nothing to the imagination anyway.

Pick a spot for your risque swimming session—local pond, nearby beach, neighborhood pool—and head out. You don't need to bring much along, just a towel and a sense of adventure.

When you get to the water, there's nothing left to do but strip down and dive in. Swim a few laps in your birthday suit and enjoy the cool water against your skin before you hop out and towel off. Hopefully nobody saw you, but even if they did, that's half the fun.

Rest for the Wicked If you are self-conscious about your body, jump into the water first and then take off your clothes.

Rules for Skinny Dipping

1. Strip or go home. No free shows.
2. Underwear doesn't count.
3. No pointing, no laughing, no cameras.

JUNE 10

Waste Gas and Go for a Sunday Drive

A driver is a king on a vinyl bucket-seat throne, changing direction with the turn of a wheel, changing the climate with a flick of the button, changing the music with the switch of a dial.

—Andrew H. Malcolm

Gas prices are past the three-dollar mark and climbing, which has put a damper on travel plans that don't involve bicycle spokes or your own two legs.

But you know what? Sundays are for three things: sleeping in, brunch, and leisurely drives. So this Sunday, forget the prices at the pump and get behind that wheel. Wherever you live, chances are there's some beautiful scenery just an hour or two away—mountains or rivers, grassy plains or sandy beaches, covered bridges or horse-dotted pastures.

After all, there's nothing better than zooming down a country road on a summer afternoon with the windows down and the stereo up. So sleep in, eat that brunch, and get driving.

Rest for the Wicked If you spring for the bloody Mary at brunch, line up an alternate driver. The scenery's even better from the passenger seat.

Drive Your Cares Away

Automobile pioneer Henry Ford was an advocate of the Sunday drive. Though many Christians observe Sunday as a day of rest, he promoted it as a day of activity to generate more automobile sales.

Fake a Doctor's Appointment

Truth is beautiful, without doubt; but so are lies.

—Ralph Waldo Emerson

Everyone fakes being sick every now and then. But what about those times when you don't need the whole day off, just an hour or two?

It would be great if you could just tell your boss you need an hour to recharge, but most managers would laugh in your face if you tried that. Enter the fake doctor's appointment. For all the times you've come in early, stayed late, and skipped lunch, you deserve a little time off. It's just a shame you have to pretend to be at the dentist to get it.

Stroll into your boss's office and remind him or her that you need to duck out to see the doctor. Most will assume you already cleared it with them and they merely forgot. Keep any explanation to a minimum, as you don't want your boss asking too many questions.

Once you are free, get some distance from the office and sneak in some leisure time. Read a book, take a walk, stare at the clouds. Just remember that you only bought yourself an hour or two max. It doesn't take an entire afternoon to get your teeth cleaned.

Rest for the Wicked Come back sucking on a lollipop with a bandage on your arm to reinforce the lie.

Obscure Types of Doctors

- Nephrologist – kidney doctor
- Hepatologist – liver doctor
- Parasitologist – parasite doctor
- Pulmonologist – lung doctor
- Hematologist – blood doctor

Get the House to Yourself

I don't want to be alone. I want to be left alone.

—Audrey Hepburn

Family togetherness is a wonderful thing. Not half as wonderful, however, as having the entire house to yourself.

It's not that you don't love your family, it's just that sometimes everybody wants a little alone time. Which can be very difficult to obtain with a spouse, three kids, two dogs, and a fish.

Brainstorm a series of fool's errands that will keep your family occupied for a few hours. Draft an excessive shopping list or break a few essential household items and send them out for replacements. Anything to get them out of the house and out of your hair.

With the house to yourself, you are free to do whatever you want. Eat all the junk food you want, invite your friends over for an impromptu poker game, or just sprawl out on the couch with a book. Just make sure not to do any irreparable damage or you may never get the house to yourself again.

Rest for the Wicked Some people are more efficient than others. Give your family twice as many errands as you believe necessary, just to be safe.

Why Being Alone Is Better

- No fighting over the remote
- You have more money
- No diapers
- Your car doesn't double as a taxi

Grab a Pint of Ice Cream and Crawl Into Bed

Without ice cream, there would be darkness and chaos.

—DON KARDONG

One of life's greatest pleasures is crawling into a comfortable bed at the end of the day. This feeling of satisfaction is rivaled only by the joy of eating ice cream.

Unfortunately, we all know the rules for both of these experiences. You're not supposed to eat in bed. You're only supposed to have one serving of ice cream, and you're supposed to eat it out of a bowl.

Well, you're an adult now and there's no one to enforce those silly rules. Pop open a fresh pint of your favorite Ben & Jerry's (as long as it's not low-fat or frozen yogurt) and walk straight out of the kitchen, pausing only to grab a spoon. Tonight you're eating directly out of the pint, and not standing up at the kitchen sink either. You're going to see what happens when the luxury of whole milk, cane sugar, and Tahitian vanilla beans combines with the comfort of your very own bed. So bundle up in your fluffiest down comforter and lean back on a stack of pillows. You're taking dessert to a whole new level of decadence.

Rest for the Wicked Savor the experience. The only thing that can ruin the experience is rushing through your pint and giving yourself a Level One brainfreeze.

How to Make Dessert Even Sweeter

- Have someone else join you in bed—but tell him or her to bring a second pint
- Call in sick and eat your ice cream at 11 A.M. while watching *The Price Is Right*
- Spring for the fanciest pint at the grocery store
- Make ice cream sundaes

JUNE 14

Turn Your Cube Into an Office

I was sitting in my cubicle today and I realized ever since I started working, every single day of my life has been worse than the day before it.

—PETER GIBBONS, *OFFICE SPACE*

Waking up at the ass-crack of dawn and battling traffic on the way to work is bad enough. Do they really have to cram us into 4' × 4' boxes with when we get there?

Four walls. Enough space for a computer and a monitor. Perhaps even a door. That's not really asking too much. But since everybody else is so satisfied with the status quo, you need to take matters into your own hands.

Rummage around for some building materials and start working on your faux office space. Track down a large, unused bulletin board to serve as a makeshift door, while layered cardboard boxes can serve as a ceiling. To give yourself some extra storage space, duct tape a few shelves along the walls of your new "office."

Sure it will look like crap, but at least you will be able to work in private.

Rest for the Wicked Don't bother clearing your construction project with HR first. It's easier to ask for forgiveness than permission.

Benefits to Having an Office

- Nobody can look over your shoulder
- You don't have to wear headphones to listen to music
- People assume your job is important

JUNE 15

Stay at an All-You-Can-Eat Buffet All Day

The U.S. deficit is growing faster than someone who spent too much time at an all-you-can-eat buffet.

—Andrew Pyle, philosopher

There is nothing Americans love more than an all-you-can-eat buffet. These little treasures combine two of our favorite things—gluttony and food—into one irresistible package. Unfortunately, buffets have one big problem: you can't take any leftovers home.

So next time you hit up an all-you-can-eat venue, make the most of your money by staying the whole damn day. You shelled out $15, and dammit, you're going to eat at least three times that much food. For maximum consumption, you'll want to pace yourself. Start off with something light, like a salad, and then move into the heavier foods like meatloaf and turkey. Finish off with dessert, take a nap, then repeat the whole process.

To prevent the buffet owner from asking you to leave, you should probably keep a plate of food on your table at all times. But unless they can show you a clause on the buffet sign stating that it is only valid for one meal per day, you're all set for a day-long marathon of gluttony.

Rest for the Wicked Do not attempt at an Indian buffet unless you want to wreak havoc on your digestive system.

The Origins of Gluttony

The all-you-can-eat buffet concept has been attributed to Herb Macdonald, a Minneapolis-based hotel manager who introduced the idea in 1946.

JUNE 16

Make Out with a Stranger

Stolen kisses are always sweetest.

—LEIGH HUNT, ENGLISH AUTHOR

A deep, passionate kiss is an outward expression of an uncontrollable love shared between two people. Of course, it can also be an emotionless instance of public debauchery, under the right circumstances.

If you've never had a meaningless kiss with a stranger, then you really are missing out. Just think, no mushy feelings, no tearful goodbyes, just two sets of lips and a mutual desire to smoosh them together. Isn't about time you experienced the rush of excitement that can only come from locking lips with somebody whose name you don't even know?

While you could just approach a random passerby and steal a kiss, that's not only rude, it's probably illegal. Instead, choose a target and flirt with him or her with your eyes for a bit before approaching. Lean in to whisper your intentions into your mark's ear and wait for a reaction. If it's affirmative, plant a soft, passionate kiss right then and there before retreating as suddenly as you appeared.

Not only have you fulfilled your own sinful desire, but your partner in crime now has an unbelievable story to tell for quite some time.

Rest for the Wicked Keep your hands to yourself. You hardly know the person.

Tongue in Cheek

What many countries refer to as a "French kiss" is known as a "baiser amoureux" or "love kiss" in France.

JUNE 17

Get Your Groceries Delivered

Ever consider what pets must think of us? I mean, here we come back from a grocery store with the most amazing haul—chicken, pork, half a cow. They must think we're the greatest hunters on earth.

—ANNE TYLER, AUTHOR

However often you do it—once a week, once every two weeks, or once a month—going to the grocery store is the same experience every time. You know what you like to eat, you know where it is in the store, and you know the quickest and most efficient way to navigate your route. You also know you're going to have to wait about twenty minutes in line to check out.

In this modern world, however, there's another choice. You can have your groceries delivered. Go online and start filling up your virtual grocery basket. You already know everything you'll eat. Pay online and sit back and, for the hour you'd otherwise be grocery shopping, do something useful—like watch TV. Before you know it your food will be at your front door. If only the grocery store offered someone who could cook your food for you, too.

Rest for the Wicked Check your carton of eggs before the delivery person leaves to make sure they're still intact.

Survey Says

In 2010, 32 percent of consumers responding to a Food Marketing Institute survey said their primary grocery store offered online ordering, and 28 percent said they had done at least some online ordering at those grocers.

Buy an Expensive Cappuccino Maker

Behind every successful woman is a substantial amount of coffee.

—STEPHANIE PIRO

With the cost of a cup of coffee exceeding that of your basic breakfast sandwich these days, it's economically wise to bid adieu to the barista and make your own at home. But you shouldn't settle for mediocre coffee just because you're making it yourself.

If you buy your own fancy cappuccino maker, you'll have the best of both worlds—premium cups of Joe that you don't have to pay a premium to enjoy.

Forget the miniscule espresso machines masquerading as decent coffee makers. You're in the market for something big and expensive. Preferably industrial quality. However much you spend, you'll just make up the difference by using it a lot. Every time you make your own cappucino at home, that's an extra few dollars in your pocket. A few thousand cups later, and your new indulgence has already paid for itself!

Rest for the Wicked Don't tell anybody that you've got the espresso hookup, or you're friends will start lining up outside your door.

Demystifying Coffee Vocabulary

- Espresso – a highly concentrated drink made by forcing pressurized hot water through finely ground coffee.
- French Press – a cylindrical machine used to steep and coffee grounds in water and then strain out unwanted particles.
- Kopi Luwak – a variety of coffee made from beans eaten and defecated by the palm civet, a small cat-like creature.

JUNE 19

Dine-and-Ditch on Your Friends

Desperate times call for desperate measures.

—Proverb

Dining out with your buds can be quite the bonding experience, but the impending bill may take away your appetite. Sometimes, you need to resort to bold measures to save face in tough economic times.

The next time you're eating out, pull a fast one. The trick is to pick the perfect moment to up-and-leave your pals with the check. After ordering several alcoholic drinks and downing half your meal, start fidgeting in your seat. Look nervously at random people in the restaurant and mumble that you "just gotta go" before launching out of the booth. Your friends will be too confused to notice you never dropped money on the table.

Remember, they're your friends! They are allowed to cover your bill for the night. You'd help them out, too, if you weren't so goddamn broke.

Rest for the Wicked Exit the restaurant discreetly to avoid a nasty look from your waiter.

Reasons You Shouldn't Have to Pay

- You listen to Mike's stupid stories without complaining
- Lauren has owed you $20 for five years
- You never liked them anyway

JUNE 20

Claim an Empty Office

It is better to take what does not belong to you than to let it lie around neglected.

—Mark Twain

Layoffs have been hard on everyone lately. It's also left a couple of empty offices around your workplace. Every day you peer in and wonder if they're gonna use that space for anything. It's been two months. Your cubiclemates are constantly sniffling, coughing, and playing their radio without headphones. You deserve to claim that empty office as your own.

Move your stuff in early, before work starts. Get your computer set up, put up some family photos, move your chair in, and lean back. It's best to move in, then tell your superior that the CEO told you you could take any open office space until it was needed. It gives you an alibi, and if they need the space you look inconvenienced more than anything else. Once you establish yourself there over time, the office will slowly become your property. Then, you can slowly expand your empire by annexing adjacent offices and desks. But it's best to exercise patience. Don't look too far ahead.

Rest for the Wicked Leave some papers and folders on your old desk so it doesn't look completely abandoned. It may throw people off for some time while you establish your presence in your new office.

Things to Do in Your Own Office

- Decorate it as you please
- Look out upon the peons
- Listen to your music with the door closed
- Sleep under your desk
- Fart to your heart's content

JUNE 21

Take an Hour-Long Shower

Cleanliness is next to godliness.

—PROVERB

Most days when you're getting ready, time is of the essence. Taking a shower is just that thing you have to do before getting dressed, so you're usually in and out of the bathroom in under ten minutes. Rarely do you take your time in there and really savor the experience.

Next time you take a shower, give yourself a full hour to stay under the water. Patiently scrub each toe and wash behind your ears. Use one of those pumice stones on your feet, sloughing away dead skin and thoroughly exfoliate every inch of skin. When is the last time you let your fingers get good and pruned, anyway? Completely lather up before shaving every inch of your body and then just stand there, doing nothing, for a solid twenty minutes.

When it's time to shampoo your hair: lather, rinse, and then actually repeat. And then again. Bring a radio into the bathroom and sing along at the top of your lungs while massaging conditioner into your scalp for the third or fourth time.

Rest for the Wicked Make sure none of your family members or roommates will need the bathroom while you're in there—nothing ruins bath time like someone knocking on the door saying they need to pee.

Songs to Sing in the Shower

- "The Longest Time," Billy Joel
- "Fly Me To The Moon," Frank Sinatra
- "Daydream Believer," The Monkees
- "Bohemian Rhapsody," Queen
- "Paparazzi," Lady Gaga

JUNE 22

Steal Your Neighbor's Flowers

Flowers are the sweetest things God ever made, and forgot to put a soul into.

—Henry Ward Beecher

You can't be bothered with such trivial things as planting flowers or tending to a garden. That takes a level of effort that you're just not willing to give. Your neighbor, however, is a regular Martha Stewart. She's out there every morning on her knees, weeding the beds and spreading mulch. At night, she dutifully soaks the ground with a garden hose. The result of all her effort is a garden teeming with life in a variety of colors and shapes.

Be honest: it actually looks nice. You're a little jealous of those flowers, aren't you? Kind of wish you'd planted some of your own, after all?

When your neighbor is out, sneak over into her yard and snip off a few blossoms to enjoy in your own home. Arrange them artfully in a vase and admire all the hard work that went into growing them. Then pat yourself on the back since you weren't the one who had to do it.

Rest for the Wicked Don't cut so many flowers that she'll notice they're gone. Instead, go for a more random, mixed bouquet approach—one flower here, another flower there—and she won't suspect a thing.

What Different Colored Roses Mean

- Red: Love and romance
- Pink: Admiration and appreciation
- Yellow: Friendship
- White: Remembrance
- Lavender: Love at first sight

JUNE 23

Rev Your Engine at a Stoplight

It's not how you stand by your car, it's how you race your car.

—EDWIN, FROM *THE FAST AND THE FURIOUS*

When you roll up to a stoplight, there's very little to do but stare straight ahead and think of all the mundane errands you are about to run on yet another boring, average day. If you look over at the car next to yours, it's almost certain the driver will sport the same glazed-over look that you have.

You are both in desperate need of something unexpected to shake up your days. Just this once, engage the driver to your side by shifting your car into neutral and giving a gentle press on the accelerator. Let your engine roar. On the road, this is an official declaration of war. You're telling your roadmate that you're ready to race your 2001 Toyota Camry for road supremacy. They can either accept your challenge by revving their own engine, or choose to ignore you. Either way, it's all in good fun. The mere act of revving your engine will bring you back to the good old days when going for a drive was actually fun, instead of a chore.

Rest for the Wicked Do not rev your engine if you happen to pull up next to Vin Diesel.

Racing for Slips

Most U.S. drag races are a quarter mile, and racers compete for cash or sometimes for ownership of the losing car.

JUNE 24

Rent a Clean Apartment

What after all Is a halo? It's only one more thing to keep clean.

—Christopher Fry, English writer

Because it happens so gradually, you often don't realize your once-clean apartment has transformed into an uninhabitable toxic waste dump. When you finally do notice, it's far too late.

Let's face it, no amount of spot cleaning is going to fix this problem. It would take an effort ten times more intense than the last time your parents came to visit. And you certainly don't have time for that. No, the only real solution is to take the easy way out and just find a new place to live.

Check your local online listings for furnished apartments and find a temporary sublet in your area. You're not looking for anything permanent, just a place to hang your hat until you summon up the nerve to tidy up your current dwelling.

You may have to spend a few months living with roommates, but it's worth it if you can avoid cleaning whatever substance that is living in your kitchen sink.

Rest for the Wicked See if you can have your current apartment condemned to break your lease and avoid paying double rent.

Temporary Cleaning Methods

- Sweep everything under a rug
- Throw away unsalvageable dirty dishes
- Pour baking soda over the source of any offensive odors

JUNE 25

Take a Bookstore Book with You Into the Bookstore Bathroom

A bookstore is one of the only pieces of evidence we have that people are still thinking.

—JERRY SEINFELD

It's a fact of nature that human beings like to read when they go to the bathroom. It's a great way to multitask and take advantage of what would otherwise be wasted time. And no place tempts you more with this than a bookstore. When you're perusing the latest new releases and suddenly you have to make your latest new release, you'll find yourself surrounded by thousands of books to choose from. Maybe you find one and maybe you start to head to the bathroom, and all of a sudden you see the sign: "Do not bring unpurchased books into the bathroom with you."

It stops you for a second, and the choice is before you. Either turn back or keep walking. Just think, they're practically tempting you with the selection. Just take a quick glance around and make sure no one's watching, then march into the bathroom with determination and read to your heart's content.

Rest for the Wicked Reserve one hand for the book, and the other hand for all other bathroom-related things.

It's a National Holiday

The Bathroom Reading Institute has declared June National Bathroom Reading month.

JUNE 26

Make Your Significant Other Sleep on the Couch

When I'm alone, I can sleep crossways in bed without an argument.
—Zsa Zsa Gabor

Sharing the bed with someone has many upsides—rampant cuddling, spontaneous morning sex, consistent spooning. But everything has its downsides, and speaking of downsides, why won't your boyfriend/girlfriend move over and quit hogging the goddamn covers all the time?

Yes, there are some things even a king-sized bed can't fix. It's OK to want to stretch out once in a while. So tonight, tell your loved one, "Sorry, honey, you're sleeping on the couch." After all, it's only one night. Think of the possibilities! You could sleep right in the center of the bed. You could sleep diagonally with your head in one corner and your feet in the opposite. You could stretch out horizontally. You could wrap yourself up in the comforter like a human hot dog.

And how sweet it is. Once you've had your fill of sleeping solo, you'll be happy to invite a warm body back into the bed. But if you're going to brag about it, be prepared to be exiled occasionally yourself.

Rest for the Wicked Couches are optional—if you have a guest bed, that'll do too.

A Not-So-Good Night's Sleep

Not all couples make good bedfellows. According to a 2005 National Sleep Foundation survey, 23 percent of partnered adults frequently sleep solo because of their partners' snoring, kicking, or other sleep problems.

Hire a Butler

It is said, that no one is a hero to their butler. The reason is, that it requires a hero to recognize a hero. The butler, however, will probably know well how to estimate his equals.

—Johann Wolfgang Von Goethe, German author

On their own, life's daily chores are not too troublesome. But when you have to pick up the dry cleaning, drive the kids to soccer practice, pay your bills, get the car fixed, and cook everyone dinner in a single day, it can be a little overwhelming. If only you could dump your responsibility on somebody else.

Your friends and family could pick up the slack, but chances are they'd gripe and groan the whole time. A butler on the other hand, would sort your dirty laundry with nary a complaint. And he'll never judge you for not being able to handle it all yourself.

Once you've tracked down a reputable butler, it's time to brainstorm all of your least favorite daily duties and pawn them off on Jeeves. Make a long list of to-dos for your butler so you get your money's worth. Don't hold back on even the most gross and unpleasant tasks. Your butler is getting paid to do them.

Rest for the Wicked Ask for references before giving your butler the keys to your life.

Notable Pop Culture Butlers

- Alfred Pennyworth (Batman series)
- Ask Jeeves (search engine mascot)
- Bentley (P-Diddy's "umbrella guy")
- Wadsworth (*Clue* movie)
- Igor (*Dracula*)

JUNE 28

Go Off Your Diet

I don't mind that I'm fat. You still get the same money.

—Marlon Brando

Starting a new diet is easy; it's following through with it that's the challenging bit. Whether it's smearing your morning bagel with butter instead of margarine or sneaking a midday candy bar, eventually you are going to backslide. So you might as well go for broke.

Sure you want to get in shape and lose a few pounds, but that's a problem for another day. Think of the ensuing binge as one last hurrah before you replace your daily breakfast burrito with a granola bar.

Instead of counting calories and doing sit-ups, today your focus will be seeing how many M&Ms you can fit in your mouth and inventing a meal between breakfast and brunch. Just be sure not to attack your non-diet with the same carefree attitude you used for your real one. If you must eat a salad, make sure it's doused with plenty of creamy dressing and topped with no fewer than four strips of bacon.

Rest for the Wicked Lock all your granola bars and rice cakes in a drawer and give the key to a close friend.

Recipe for Fool's Gold Sandwich

1 pound of cooked bacon
1 loaf of French bread, sliced down the middle and toasted
1 jar of peanut butter
1 jar of grape jelly

1. Spoon peanut butter and jelly onto toasted bread and add bacon.

JUNE 29

Play on a Playground

The world is a playground, and life is pushing my swing.

—Natalie Kocsis, American cartoonist

When you were a kid there were few things more magical than exploring the local playground. You could spend an entire day hanging on the monkey bars or launching yourself from the swings.

Sadly, you aren't a kid anymore. Now the closest you get to spinning on the merry-go-round is the two seconds it takes to walk through the revolving door as you enter the office each morning.

But what's stopping you from recapturing your childhood? It's not like there's a forcefield surrounding all playgrounds that locks out anyone above the age of fourteen. Playgrounds are designed to be played upon. So what are you waiting for?

Run, don't walk, to the nearest playground and head straight for the biggest slide you can find. Climb up and down the cargo net, run the wrong way up the slide, and even play with the stupid giant tic-tac-toe game. Pay no attention to the confused stares of your fellow "adults." They're just jealous.

Rest for the Wicked Bring a child along so you seem less creepy.

Best Playground Games

- Capture the Flag
- The Ground Is Lava
- King of the Hill
- Throw Wood Chips at Each Other and Call It a Game

Sample Every Ice Cream Flavor

Ice cream is happiness condensed.

—Jessi Lane Adams

Unless you live next door to a Baskin Robbins, you're probably stuck satisfying your evening sweet tooth with a leftover, half-eaten carton of ice cream. And let's be honest, freezer-burn isn't all that satisfying.

The next time your sweet tooth strikes, don't settle for anything less than all thirty-one flavors—and do it without paying for a single scoop.

Instead of politely nibbling one flavor and then ordering a scoop, ask for another sample. After all, you can't be expected to choose if you don't know all of your options. Just feign uncertainty and work your way through the freezer case. You'll know you're finished when you have a fistful of tiny plastic spoons and a sugar rush to rival any six-year-old in town. Throw a buck in the tip jar and head back home to sleep the sweetest of dreams.

Rest for the Wicked It's tempting to order willy-nilly and shout out flavors as they come to mind, but it pays to be methodical. Working left-to-right ensures that you hit all the flavors, but a zig-zag approach prevents the staff from catching on right away.

America's Favorite Flavors

1. Vanilla
2. Chocolate
3. Butter Pecan
4. Strawberry
5. Mint Chocolate Chip

JULY 1

Open a Speakeasy

I drink only to make my friends seem interesting.

—Don Marquis, American humorist

Back in the Prohibition days, thirsty Americans flocked to underground dens of sin known as "speakeasies" to drown their sorrows with illicit hooch. Back then, all you needed was a secret password and some discretion and you were in the club.

Alcohol is legal again, yet somehow it's harder to get a drink today than it ever was in the 1920s. If you aren't wearing the right clothes or driving the right car, you'll be lucky to even get within a mile of some clubs. But that's only because there aren't other options.

Tonight, instead of traipsing all the way to the new hip club, you're going to open the trendiest bar in town—right in your basement.

Head to the liquor store and stock up on the cheapest booze you can find, and be sure to cover every variety. Just remember, you're going for quantity, not quality. Spread the word among your hipster friends that there's a cool underground scene that just opened and wait for the lines to start forming.

Rest for the Wicked Install a small peep hole into your door so you can get a good look at guests without letting them see inside.

Prohibition Slang

- Hooch – Bootleg liquor
- Rum runners/bootleggers – Traffickers of illegal alcohol
- Wet blankets – Killjoys
- Flappers – Risque, bawdy women fond of late-night dancing and short hair.
- Spifflicated – Drunk

JULY 2

Incorporate Lobster Into Every Meal

If you work on a lobster boat, sneaking up behind someone and pinching him is probably a joke that gets old real fast.

—Author Unknown

Everyone knows the best days of your life are those when you wake up in the morning feeling like a king—as if nothing in the world can stop you. You deserve to eat like a king on those kind of days, and there is only one food that will fit the bill: lobster.

You probably don't consume lobster with the frequency of, say, chicken, so you might as well go all out and incorporate this delicacy into every single meal. At first, lobster might seem like a limiting food, but the options are truly endless—lobster omelet, lobster salad, lobster ravioli, lobster with butter—the list goes on!

The bad news is that your wallet is bound to take a hit from your lobster binge. But as long as you make it a rare extravagance rather than a recurring habit, you have nothing to apologize for. Eat up!

Rest for the Wicked When eating fresh lobster, don a bib to avoid getting food all over yourself.

Try These Famous Lobster Eateries

- Five Islands Lobster Co., Georgetown, Maine
- Bob Lobster, Newbury, Massachusetts
- Red's Eats, Wiscasset, Maine

JULY 3

Perfect Your Cannonball

One never dives into the water to save a drowning man more eagerly than when there are others present who dare not take the risk.

—Friedrich Nietzsche

There's a reason pooldecks are made of waterproof surfaces: They're going to get wet. So, if you're on a pooldeck, you run the risk of getting wet, too. Why not drive that point home by practicing your cannonball in a pool lined with sunbathers?

You did it when you were younger. It was always a hit at pool parties when you were a pre-teen. It's time to relive your glory days by participating in and winning a cannonball competition—where the only competitor is yourself.

Tanning doesn't require water; swimming does. So if you happen to attempt the biggest splash-producing jump in the history of pool entries, it's because you didn't have a choice. If the tanners are afraid to get wet, they should go tan somewhere where the splash can't reach them. Like, in a tanning bed.

Rest for the Wicked Before taking the plunge, find out how long you can hold your breath. Then, stay underwater for as long as possible after cannonballing into the pool so that people's anger has a few more seconds to dissipate.

Other Pool Activities to Get People Wet

- Jackknife-jump into the pool
- Water guns
- Duck, duck, goose (with water)
- Water balloons

Buy Illegal Fireworks

The 4th of July combines the two things Americans love most in one day: alcohol and explosives.

—David Letterman

It's the anniversary of our great nation, and what better way to celebrate than by blowing up a small portion of it.

Sure, fireworks may be illegal in many states, but so is speeding and jaywalking and downloading pirated music. Police have bigger things to worry about than a few cherry bombs. Besides, you'd be disgracing our Founding Fathers if you didn't honor their memory with a proper pyrotechnics display.

Head to your local fireworks emporium and check out the section reserved for the more "patriotic" customers (usually located in a back room). Forget lame sparklers and noisemakers, you're looking for bottle rockets, Roman candles, and M80s. Once you've gathered enough artillery to level a small village, you should be able to put on a first-rate fireworks show. Or at least blow up a few garbage cans.

Rest for the Wicked Enlist local miscreants to instruct you on proper demolition protocol.

Homemade Tennis Ball Bomb

Cut a hole in a tennis ball and stuff with the heads removed from strike-anywhere matches. Cover the hole with tape and throw ball against a hard surface. Run.

Eat Only the Best Parts of Food

I am the President of the United States, and I'm not going to eat any more broccoli.
—George H. W. Bush

No two servings of food are created equal. And if you've ever been to a potluck or a Tuesday night dinner at home, you've probably thrown an elbow or two while duking it out for the tastiest bites at the table.

Today, there will be no fighting. Instead of tripping siblings and strong-arming cousins, you're going to treat yourself to the best parts of the food and throw away the rest.

We all know the best of the best. Crispy-crackly and sugary muffin tops are infinitely better than their soggy bottoms halves. For breakfast, just crack those suckers in two and send the paper-wrapped bottom sailing into the trash. And while you're at it, order up a cinnamon roll and eat just the gooey, cinnamon-streaked center. On your lunch break, tear off the bread crusts and eat a sandwich any five-year-old would envy. When dinnertime rolls around, order your favorite pizza—but ditch the bland and doughy crust to focus on the melty cheese. Finally, satisfy your sweet tooth with only the choicest selections of homemade brownies. Whether it's crispy edges you crave or the fudgy centers that drive you wild, eat your fill and leave the rejected pieces in the pan. After all, don't you deserve the best?

Rest for the Wicked Feeling guilty about throwing out food? Drop off your unwanted food in the office kitchenette. It will be gone before you're back at your desk.

The Least Desirable Pieces of Food

- End pieces of a loaf of bread
- The first watery squeeze out of a mustard bottle
- Burnt edges on Mom's meatloaf
- Bruises on fruit

JULY 6

Steal Cable

Television! Teacher, mother, secret lover.

—Homer Simpson

It's 3 A.M. and you're flipping through the channels. There's a home shopping show on, some infomercial for a workout product, and an interview with the local school board president. You look out the window and see your neighbor watching the Comedy Central roast of Rob Reiner. Looks funny. Sure wish you could watch too, huh?

Well, don't be so hard on yourself. Just pay a cable professional $50 and have them split the cable between your neighbor and yourself. There's enough information sailing through those thin black cables for the both of you. It's not like their entertainment value diminishes at all. And what the cable company doesn't know won't hurt them.

Now your viewing options include the ballgame, movies, and drama cop shows. Plus, with cable, there's a whole bunch of home shopping networks that you could only dream of before.

Rest for the Wicked Only use a cable guy personally referred to you to avoid getting caught.

Shows You Suddenly Discover You Like After Getting Cable

- *SpongeBob SquarePants*
- *Top Chef*
- The History Channel's World War II coverage
- *Jersey Shore*

JULY 7

Steal Someone's Reservation

I never eat in a restaurant that's over a hundred feet off the ground and won't stand still.

—CALVIN TRILLIN

You arrive at Le Petit Chateau at 7 P.M. on a Saturday night expecting to have a romantic French dinner with your significant other. Sadly, hundreds of other diners had the same idea and have beat you there. You now have three options: sit your sorry butt down and wait for a few hours, pay off the maitre d', or steal someone else's reservation.

With a party of less than four, it's easy to steal a reservation. If the wait is long—like longer than 45 minutes—some people will inevitably bail. Just follow the maitre d' like a hawk. After he announces a certain name three times with no response, jump in. "Yes, we are the 'Smith' party." If the number is higher than your party, just say your friend had to leave. Before you know it you'll be enjoying the finest wine and cheese the restaurant offers. Bon appetit, Mr. and Mrs. Smith.

Rest for the Wicked Have someone other than the person who initially put their name in with the maitre d' execute the ruse, in case the maitre d's memory is better than average.

Avoid the Wait

The iPhone app WaitList, launched in 2010 by The A.V. Club and Invoke Media, is an app that relies on user-generated information to predict wait times at local restaurants. Although its accuracy is still questionable, as more people use the service the more effective it will be.

Join a Protest

Nothing is as frustrating as arguing with someone who knows what he's talking about.

—Sam Ewing, former Major League Baseball player

Remember when you used to care about stuff? When the mere mention of "health care reform" made your blood boil, and you couldn't watch the evening news without shouting at the TV? Nowadays you only get worked up when the barista screws up your coffee order.

You may have lost some of your political passion, but it's never too late to break out the old poster board for an impromptu protest.

It doesn't matter if your cause of choice is legalizing gay marriage or getting *Arrested Development* back on the air, just pick something you are passionate about and get to work on some angry signs.

When you are ready to protest, choose a location that gets plenty of foot traffic and parade your opinions for all the world to see. Depending on your opinion and location, you may experience some backlash. Don't be discouraged. Protesting is more about being heard than being right.

Rest for the Wicked If you can't think of a cause to champion, protest taxes. Everybody hates taxes.

Protesting Essentials

- Comfortable shoes
- Nice weather
- Unwavering belief in the superiority of your opinion
- Eco-friendly snacks

JULY 9

Adjust Your Scale

The best measure of a man's honesty isn't his income tax return. It's the zero adjust on his bathroom scale.

—Arthur C. Clarke, British science-fiction author

Maintaining a respectable weight is a lot like flossing. It's not really that hard to keep up with, but you'll be damned if you're going to bother to do it. But as the pounds pile on, the extra weight can start to get to even the most thick-skinned of gluttons. If only you could un-eat all of sweets and hot dogs that got you into this mess.

While a little exercise and a strict diet might help you shed the extra poundage, you really need to attack the problem at its source: the bathroom scale. You have better things to do with your time than run on a treadmill.

Turn the dial on the side of your scale so the arrow is a little to the left of zero. Step on, and you've magically dropped a few pounds. Just like that, instant lipo. You can probably get away with up to ten pounds before anyone starts thinking the scale is broken.

See, and you thought losing weight was hard.

Rest for the Wicked Be very wary which way you turn the dial. You want to instantly lose poundage, not gain it.

Methods for Looking Slimmer

- Wear shirts with vertical stripes
- Never tuck in your shirt
- Dress in all black
- Surround yourself with fatter friends

JULY 10

Cool Off in a Public Fountain

The cistern contains: the fountain overflows.

—William Blake

It's the middle of the day, it's oppressively hot and humid, and there's no relief in sight. Unless of course you want to dive headfirst into a public fountain.

Come to think of it, that's exactly what you want to do. You're hot, and there's a nice cool supply of water right there. It's a no-brainer really.

When it comes to swimming in what is essentially a sculpture, approach doesn't really matter. Feel free to slowly wade in or kick off your sandals and do a cannonball right into the center. Regardless of how you go about it, you're sure to attract some dirty looks. Don't pay them any attention though. You're cool as a cucumber now, and that's all that matters.

Rest for the Wicked Bring a change of clothes to work unless you're comfortable sitting around in your underwear.

World's Tallest Fountain

Standing over 85 feet high and 65 feet wide, the Trevi Fountain is the largest fountain in Rome, and is perhaps the world's most famous fountain.

JULY 11

Score a Ride on a Stranger's Boat

You have to be careful on the deck because of the "hatches," which are holes placed around a sailboat at random to increase the insurance rates.

—Dave Barry

You've been cooped up indoors for what seems like an eternity and are finally anxious to make the most of the summer season. Unfortunately, you still don't know anyone who owns a boat. This time around though, you're not going to let that stop you.

Grab a friend (safety first!) and take a stroll down to the local pier, taking note of good sailing prospects. Like that friendly-looking portly gentleman who keeps eyeing you from his sailboat, or the Cougar who won't stop giving you a "come hither" look. After playing coy for a few minutes, walk over and flirt it up—chances are you'll be on board in no time.

That's not to say you won't be able to find a boat buddy closer to your own age group, but boats equal money, so don't be surprised if you find yourself flirting with the newest president of AARP. Don't feel bad about it either—you get an afternoon on a boat, and they get an ego boost. Everybody wins!

Rest for the Wicked Allowing your sailing companion to rub sunscreen on you will result in both brownie points and UV protection.

Famous Boaters

- Noah
- The Kennedys
- Christopher Columbus

Organize a Cool-Kids Table in the Lunch Room

Now, if you break any of these rules, you can't sit with us at lunch. I mean, not just you. Like, any of us. Okay, like if I was wearing jeans today, I would be sitting over there with the art freaks. Oh, and we always vote before we ask someone to eat lunch with us because you have to be considerate of the rest of the group.

—GRETCHEN WIENERS, *MEAN GIRLS*

A quick scan of the lunch room yields your typical mix of groups—the geeks, the goodie-goodies, the antisocial people, and the weirdos. You seriously don't fit in with any of those people, so there's only one thing left to do: start a cool-kids table. Clearly, they're just as necessary in real life as they were in high school.

First, identify your cool coworkers—typically they will be around your age and would certainly not be wearing something weird like elasticized pants or a beret. Next, figure out what time you should eat. Avoid the 12 to 1 P.M. crunch, because the lunch room will be filled and you'll get hangers-on to your group. Finally, tell your preselected colleagues and make it happen.

With a cool-kids table in place, you'll look forward to lunch hour even more than you already do. And THAT is something to celebrate.

Rest for the Wicked Continue going out to lunch one or two times a week to maintain your cool kids aura of mystery.

Tips for Starting Your Cool-Kids Table

- Never invite more than four people to sit with you—you have to remain selective
- Never eat before noon—you're not old enough for the early bird special yet
- Take it outside whenever it's nice—who wants to be cooped up inside all day?

Sit in a La-Z-Boy at Work

People who work sitting down get paid more than people who work standing up.

—OGDEN NASH, POET

You've spent a lot of time with your work chair. You've had it a long time now, and your butt groove is starting to sink the cushion. You can feel the wooden frame under the padding. It is not comfortable, safe, or practical. The time has come to upgrade to a real office chair.

In this time of decisive action, be bold. Order a La-Z-Boy. It might actually make you look forward to going to work. You'll be the envy of your office and the point of conversation for weeks. And anytime someone new comes in, you have something light and funny to talk about right off. Most importantly, you can recline in it.

During your lunch break or those nights that you have to work late, you can lean back and doze off. The La-Z-Boy will have everything you need for work: a cup holder, a cooler in the side (where you can store drinks and deli-style sandwiches), and a pouch for pens and pencils. When you're comfortable, you're happy. Sit on a throne and work in style.

Rest for the Wicked Make sure you can adjust the height of your desk should the recliner's arms not fit under your desk.

Other Chair Options

- The wooden IKEA chair
- The padded stacking chair
- The rolling mid-back posture chair
- The armless chair
- The leather executive chair

JULY 14

Screw Cancer—Go Out and Bake in the Sun

The University of Miami is not a campus with visible school spirit—just visible tan lines.

—LISA BIRNBACH, AUTHOR

Sun exposure's linkage to skin cancer is perhaps the saddest health care revelation of the last few decades. Gone are the days when women would lather themselves with baby oil during marathon outdoor tanning sessions, and men would rather endure weeks of sunburn than put on, God forbid, sunscreen.

But even though tanning may be past its prime, don't let the Surgeon General prevent you from enjoying the sun. This summer, grab your sunscreen (even if it's SPF 4) and scamper outside with your beach towel to soak up as many beautiful golden rays as possible.

Everyone knows people look hotter with tans, and you obviously don't want to be the only pale-faced kid on the block. Plus, sun is a great source of Vitamin D—so take THAT, doctor.

Rest for the Wicked Wear sunglasses to protect your peepers while tanning.

Tannest People in the United States

- The entire cast of *Jersey Shore*
- Angelo Mozilo, former CEO of Countrywide Financial
- Lindsay Lohan, when she's not under house arrest

JULY 15

Ignore Household Chores

My favorite way of getting out of doing chores is by acting like I'm asleep. But it never works.

—Devon Werkheiser, American actor

It's a beautiful day out, and you've got a sink full of dishes and an overflowing laundry basket waiting for you. Thus begins the mental battle of trying to convince yourself that it's better to stay in and clean than going outside to frolic.

News flash: it's not. Cleaning sucks and you should be out enjoying the fresh air instead of inside inhaling chemical fumes. So today, do whatever the hell you want as long as it doesn't involve cleaning, tidying, vacuuming, polishing, or scrubbing of any kind.

And don't waste your time feeling guilty about not cleaning. You don't live in a *Good Housekeeping* photo shoot, and last time we checked, your name wasn't Monica Geller either. So just get over it and clean tomorrow.

Rest for the Wicked Leave the house to forget about the mess.

Do's and Don'ts . . .

- Don't put anything away
- Don't clean the bathtub
- Don't dust the living room
- Do have as many beers as you want

JULY 16

Steal Candy from a Baby

A lot of people like lollipops. I don't like lollipops. To me, a lollipop is hard candy plus garbage. I don't need a handle. Just give me the candy.

—DEMETRI MARTIN

It's late in the afternoon and an insatiable sugar craving hits. Alas, your coworkers depleted your secret candy drawer months ago. Lucky for you, it's Bring Your Child to Work Day.

Despite what you may have heard, taking candy from babies is not easy. What they lack in physical strength and intelligence they make up for in blood-curdling screaming ability. Also, their inherent cuteness deters all but the most hardened candy thieves. But you're hungry, dammit.

Employ a clever distraction to eliminate mom and isolate the infant. Phone in a bomb threat, have her car towed, whatever it takes. Now, with lightning fast speed and agility, approach the target and liberate the candy. Before the baby realizes what hit it, quietly return to your desk and consume the evidence.

There will be crying, but you must not give in to your inevitable feelings of guilt. Besides, if you chose your target wisely, it will be months before it develops the cognitive skills necessary to implicate you in the crime.

Rest for the Wicked Check the office for baby monitors and nanny cams. Perfect balloon-animal-making skills to distract the target.

Easier Ways to Get Candy

- Get a haircut
- Be a good boy or girl at the doctor
- Visit your grandmother

JULY 17

Communicate Solely in Expletives

Life is a four-letter word.

—Lenny Bruce, comedian

When we're in a rage, nothing feels better than to unleash a barrage of four-letter words on the offender. It's therapeutic, nonviolent, and generally quite fun. It's a shame we reserve such eloquent prose solely for our most frustrating moments.

The thing is, those swears and vulgarities are so fun to say. It'd really make more sense to talk that way all the time in order to get your fill.

Today, start your day off with an %$#@ing coffee, hop on the @#&% %$!#ing train and attend your morning meeting with that ^#& %@!&ing son of a !@^#. Maybe later you and friends will #@!$ like $#&ing &%^#!@s, just like in the good old days.

Don't be bashful; use your expletives loud and proud, and if anyone has a problem with it, then they can !$#% off.

Rest for the Wicked The caveat to using profane language is in the presence of children. Parents get really @%&#ing mad about that.

Best G-Rated Curses

- "Dangnabbit!"
- "Oh, fruitcake!"
- "Blast and tarnation!"
- "Sweet swirling onion rings!"

JULY 18

Sneak Into Your Neighbor's Pool

I've just been handed an urgent and horrifying news story. And I need all of you to stop what you're doing and listen. Cannonball!!!

—Ron Burgundy, *Anchorman*

In summertime, nothing beats a day at the pool. You stretch out as a warm breeze filters across your sun-kissed skin, allowing your body to find true relaxation. Then, right on cue, hordes of screaming children run toward the waterslide and the afternoon rush of gabbing soccer moms arrive to ruin your peaceful day.

You are in desperate need of something a little more private. Lucky for you, you have a neighbor. Your neighbor has a pool. So by the transient nature of property, you also have a pool.

Today you're going to pull on your swimsuit and take control of that pool as though you're the one paying the pool boy to clean it. You can even bring along some snacks and a pitcher of margaritas for the party. After all, what your neighbors don't know won't hurt them.

To avoid arousing suspicion, you should probably wait until nightfall—or at least until midday when you're neighbors have all gone to work—to stake your claim. It's less likely that you'll be seen that way. Even better, wait until your neighbors have gone on vacation.

Rest for the Wicked To avoid a potential 911 call, limit your pool party to four people or fewer.

How to Perform a Proper Cannonball

- Give yourself a running distance of five feet or more
- Leap into the air upon reaching the side of the pool
- After taking off, crouch into a ball and wrap your arms around your legs
- Shout "Cannonball" as loudly as possible

Supersize Everything

Is she fat? Her favorite food is seconds.

—Joan Rivers

In the good old days, the hallmark of a good restaurant was how much food they could cram onto a single plate. Unfortunately, the health-conscious brats of the world have ruined it for everyone.

Despite what some might think, you were not designed to function on a single lettuce leaf and a thimbleful of Vitamin Water. So stop pretending like you can. When you place your lunch order today, keep in mind the following motto: bigger is better.

Upgrade your tiny side of mixed greens to a gargantuan superhero salad complete with hard-boiled eggs, bacon, and heaps of dressing. Forget the tiny chicken sandwich and order a Philly cheesesteak or a footlong meatball sub instead. As for dessert, nothing short of a triple-scoop sundae with hot fudge, chopped nuts, and a mountain of whipped cream will suffice.

You'll know you've had enough when your pants button pops off or the restaurant asks you to leave—whichever comes first.

Rest for the Wicked Never attempt this act of extreme gluttony on a first, second, or even twenty-seventh date. In fact, you probably should go this one solo.

"Do You Want to Dinosize That?"

McDonalds originally released its "Supersized" fries and sodas in 1993 as "Dinosized" to capitalize on the popular movie Jurassic Park. They changed the name after the promotion.

Sneak Onto a Golf Course

Although golf was originally restricted to wealthy, overweight Protestants, today it's open to anybody who owns hideous clothing.

—Dave Barry

If you want to play on the best courses in the world, a single round of golf can set you back hundreds of dollars. Unless, of course, you are willing to be a little sneaky.

Take a look around a golf course and notice what isn't there. Fences, security guards, attack dogs, alarm systems. There is literally nothing to prevent you from hopping on for free, aside from a few pimple-faced caddies and your own conscience.

What are you waiting for?

Throw on your ugliest pair of plaid shorts, grab your clubs, and head to the links. If you act confident and tee off straight away, nobody is going to question your legitimacy as a paying customer. If it's a fancier course, they may even treat you to some free drinks or a nice cigar while you swindle them out of a free round of golf.

Rest for the Wicked The first hole is usually right next to the clubhouse, so skip over to the second or third to avoid detection.

America's Swankiest Courses

- Shadow Creek – Las Vegas, Nevada: $500 per round
- Pebble Beach – Pebble Beach, California: $495 per round
- Trump National Golf Course – Los Angeles, California $375 per round

JULY 21

Feed Your Pets Filet Mignon

We can judge the heart of a man by his treatment of animals.

—IMMANUEL KANT, PHILOSOPHER

Pets are the the perfect companion. They never judge when your dignity's gone out the window and they're always up for a good snuggle. The only thing they ask for in return is food. Whether your cat smells a tuna fish sandwich or your dog spots a fallen crumb, they go nuts over anything edible.

Yet perversely, their one joy is met with nothing more than dry, pet food pebbles. Shouldn't you give them something to really purr over?

In people terms, the crème de la crème of dining is filet mignon. Bring the French cuisine to the pet bowl and let them enjoy meat the way it should be. Shut off any thoughts about price or dietary concerns and simply witness the pure delight as your furry companion chows down. You can even turn it into a dinner for two and pull up a chair and your own filet. After this meal, there will be no doubt that your pet will love you for life.

Rest for the Wicked A whole filet is a choking hazard, not to mention a mess. Be sure to cut the filet mignon into bite-size pieces.

Lap of Luxury

- Couch time on the "forbidden" loveseat
- One-hour petting session
- Visit to the aquarium (cat)
- Visit to the tennis court (dog)

JULY 22

Skip Out on Dinner with the In-Laws

Just got back from a pleasure trip: I took my mother-in-law to the airport.

—Henny Youngman

As if one overbearing set of parents wasn't enough, tradition saw fit to slap us with a fresh new pair the moment we get married. Best of all, unlike your adoring parents, this new set doesn't even like you. In all likelihood, they downright hate you.

Yet, despite their unbridled disdain for you, they invite you over for dinner every Sunday. You've bit the bullet and put up with their incessant nagging and general disappointment for years. Enough is enough.

Tonight, you are going to do what you've always dreamed, but never dared to do: just say no. Forget the excuses, don't bother faking sick, just don't go. Sure, your spouse will want to murder you, but at least you won't have to sit through another slide show of your in-laws' Alaska cruise.

Since you have the evening to yourself, make a relaxing dinner for one, pour yourself an expensive glass of wine, and toast to the first night of an in-law-free existance.

Rest for the Wicked Get a blanket and pillow and set them up on the couch. Because that's where you'll be sleeping tonight.

Ace Ventura, In-Law Detective

Actor Jim Carrey was originally cast to star as Gaylord "Greg" Focker in the hit film *Meet the Parents*. Greg's unfortunate last name was his idea.

Stay at a Five-Star Hotel

The great advantage of a hotel is that it's a great refuge from home life.
—George Bernard Shaw

By and large, there's no place like home. The thermostat is set just the way you like it, the grooves in the couch perfectly match your derriere, and you know where everything is in the kitchen. But when the dishes start to pile up and the chores become overwhelming, perhaps its best to jump ship for the evening.

Hotels offer a temporary escape, but you're too good for just any one-star hovel. Tonight you deserve to live it up in a five-star palace.

Pack an overnight bag and kiss your responsibilities goodbye for the evening. It's only for one night anyway. Your family, pets, and chores can all wait until the morning. Once you've checked in, it's time to start living like a rock star (minus the destructive tendencies). Order up an expensive bottle of wine and sprawl out on the king-sized bed to unwind. A nice soothing bubble bath in the jacuzzi tub should put all your cares and worries out of your mind.

Rest for the Wicked Leave a debit card instead of a credit card at the front desk. You don't want to spend more on room service than you have in the bank.

Most Expensive Hotel Rooms

- Royal Penthouse Suite at President Wilson Hotel, Geneva, Switzerland – $65,000 per night
- Royal Villa at Grand Resort Lagonissi, Athens, Greece – $50,000 per night
- Shahi Mahal Presidential Suite at Raj Palace, Jaipur, India – $40,000 per night
- Hugh Hefner Sky Villa at Palms Casino & Resort, Las Vegas – $40,000 per night

Pretend It's Your Birthday

All the world is birthday cake, so take a piece, but not too much.

—George Harrison

Ah your birthday, that one special day where everything goes your way. Piles of gifts, your very own birthday cake, dinner out at your favorite restaurant. Pity it only comes once a year.

Why is someone as forward-thinking as yourself adhering to a tradition as outdated as the annual birthday? An event as monumental as your birth surely deserves at least a bimonthly celebration. Sure you weren't born on this particular day, but that's a secret you can keep to yourself today.

Fill your house with birthday balloons and streamers to set the mood and invite your friends and family to celebrate your special day. Most will be so embarrassed they forgot that they will shower you with presents and bend over backwards to make your "birthday" memorable.

Milk it for everything it's worth, because when your real birthday comes around you'll be hard-pressed to convince anyone to take you out again.

Rest for the Wicked Conveniently "forget" your ID at home.

Best Birthday Freebies

- Hollywood Video – free rental
- Brunswick Bowling – two free games
- Houlihan's – free entree
- Medieval Times – free admission
- Friendly's – free ice cream cone

Park in the Executive Space

One way to make sure everyone gets to work on time would be to have 95 parking spaces for every 100 employees.

—Michael Lapoce, American comedy writer

No matter how hard you try, for some reason you can never make it to your office by 9:00 A.M. Maybe it's the thirteen times you hit the snooze button, or the twenty minutes you spend trying to find your keys each morning. The fact that you have to park two miles away from the front door certainly isn't helping either.

There's no sense in sacrificing sleep for the sake of punctuality, and your keys aren't about to start finding themselves. It seems the only logical way to get to work on time is to snag a better parking space.

Cruise right past all the suckers walking from their cars and head straight for the space marked "Reserved – CEO." It will almost certainly be vacant—most CEOs are too busy golfing and cruising on yachts to come into the office.

Once you're parked, pause to enjoy a brief feeling of superiority before strolling the last twenty feet to the door—on time for once.

Rest for the Wicked Tip the parking garage attendant a few extra bucks to look the other way.

Breakdown of Average Commute

- 8:15 – Leave for work
- 8:16 to 8:50 – Sit in traffic wishing you'd walked
- 8:51 to 8:57 – Scan for parking spots, checking the clock every ten seconds
- 8:58 to 9:04 – Sprint to the office like you are being chased by killer bees
- 9:05 –Tiptoe into your cube, praying your boss doesn't notice you are late

Wear Sexy Lingerie Under Jeans and a T-Shirt

I wear women's leggings under my clothes, but no lingerie.

—Dennis Rodman

When you pull on a pair of jeans in the morning, the obvious next step is to throw on the nearest t-shirt and slide into a pair of sneakers. It's comfortable and all, but unless you're Brooke Shields circa 1980, it doesn't exactly signal sex appeal. Besides, most of us prefer to have something between ourselves and our Calvins.

Well, there's a quick way to keep the outfit, but add a little punch.

Every woman has them: fancy undies bought as a special set for a special night, but that don't get much regular use. And let's face it: half a square yard of fabric can cost a pretty penny. You paid good money and you might as well get something out of it. The next time you pull on a casual outfit, skip the faded cotton underwear and reach for your raciest, laciest lingerie. Sure, you probably bought those skivvies because you wanted them to be seen, but walking around with a little hidden secret makes the sexiest lingerie even sexier.

Rest for the Wicked Be unexpected but practical: Don't swap out your underwear on a day you're playing dodgeball or raking the yard. After all, you want that lingerie looking fresh for the next time it's worn after hours.

Top Five Nicknames for Underwear

1. Undies
2. Tighty-Whities
3. Chonies
4. Skivvies
5. Unmentionables

Deliver Yourself Home

Human nature is above all things lazy.

—Harriet Beecher Stowe

When you're coming home from a night out, the otherwise short walk home might as well be a journey of 100 miles. What's worse, your evening of drinking and dancing has left you starving.

Rather than hoof it home and munch on leftovers, you might as well call up the local pizza parlor and kill two birds with one stone.

Whip out your cell phone and order up a fresh pie to be delivered to your house. Head over to the pizza shop and intercept the delivery boy before he heads out. A bright smile and the promise of a generous tip should be enough to convince him to bring you along for the ride.

Besides, if he doesn't bring you along, who's going to pay for the pies?

Rest for the Wicked Make sure you have enough cash to cover the food. Otherwise who knows where you'll get dropped off.

Alternate Transportation Options

- Hitchhike
- Call an ambulance
- Steal a bike
- Pay someone to carry you

Party in an Abandoned Building

When you invite the whole world to your party, inevitably someone pees in the beer.

—Xeni Jardin, American columnist

Hordes of sweaty people gyrating to pop music, rivers of alcohol spilling from overflowing glasses, who doesn't love a good party? Well, the person who has to clean up afterwards, for one.

When you select a venue for your next shindig, perhaps it might be wise to choose a location that doesn't have wall-to-wall carpeting and a collection of antique vases. Like an abandoned warehouse.

For starters, there's far more room in an abandoned building than there is in your tiny duplex. Also, an abandoned building comes pre-trashed, so nobody is going to notice if you leave behind a few scattered beer bottles and some stale pretzels. Bonus.

Call a few hundred of your closest friends and head to the industrial section of town. If you throw up some streamers, install a fog machine, and hang a disco ball from the ceiling beforehand, nobody will be able to tell they are dancing next to a rusty packing machine.

Rest for the Wicked Scout out all the exits ahead of time, in case the cops show up.

Alternate Party Venues

- Local dive motel
- Large open field
- Police station (it's the last place they'd expect)

Max Out Your Per Diem

It's not your salary that makes you rich, it's your spending habits.

—Charles A. Jaffe

You don't need to have been in Latin Club to translate the phrases Semper *ubi sub ubi* (always wear underwear) and *carpe diem* (seize the day). So why is another common Latin phrase so often misused?

If you encounter a lot of travel or living expenses for work, you're allotted a per diem from the company. Chances are, you pinch pennies to stay well within the upper limits of your dollar amounts. But why are you limiting yourself? Just this once, you should max out your per diem.

Think about it. Some HR administrator in a corner office has already determined that your per diem is a reasonable amount for you to spend. They expect you to spend that amount. Maybe they don't want you to spend it all, but it's certainly not stealing. The per diem is like an extension of your salary. And when you think of it that way, not using it is almost like the company is stealing from you! So go ahead: order the filet mignon at dinner and fill up your car with premium gasoline. Squeeze every penny out your company account. After all, you'll be damned if you're not going to carpe diem.

Rest for the Wicked Check the rates before you move from the Motel 6 single to the penthouse suite at the Plaza. You don't want to get stuck paying for terrycloth robes and fruit baskets out of your paycheck.

Latin Phrases in American English

- Et cetera (and the rest)
- Veni vidi vici (I came, I saw, I conquered)
- Pro bono (for the public good)
- Per apera ad atra (through hardships to the stars)
- E pluribus unum (Out of all things one, one out of all things)

Pee in the Pool

Sometimes you just have to pee in the sink.

—Charles Bukowksi, American novelist

Though beach parties and all-day tanning definitely make the summertime worthwhile, nothing can feel better than a dip in a pool on a humid day. Nothing, except, not exiting that pool when you feel the urge to urinate.

Peeing in the pool will keep you cool and save you energy. Sitting in the sun all day tires you out, and there's no point wasting calories walking in and out of the house to wee. Just make sure you're alone when you "peel the pool," as other swimmers may notice a temperature change in the water.

Before you exit the pool, swim around a bit to "clean" the pee from your swimsuit. Don't worry too much about germs; the chlorine is sure to kill some of them.

Rest for the Wicked Make sure that urine doesn't change the water's color, as it could lead to an awkward confrontation with the pool owner.

Best Public Peeing Places

- The wave pool
- A hot tub
- The ocean

JULY 31

Have Sex in a Library

I have always imagined that Paradise will be a kind of library.

—Jorge Luis Borges, Argentinean poet

Libraries are truly underappreciated resources. Most have air conditioning to escape the summer heat, free WiFi to browse the Internet, and all the books you could hope to read in a lifetime of lazy Sundays. Best of all, since almost nobody uses them, you can pretty much do anything you want between the bookshelves. That's right, *Anything.*

Doing the nasty in public is a popular fantasy, but the risk of getting caught is too much for most people. The library solves this problem quite nicely, as you are just as likely to get caught bumping uglies in the travel/leisure section of the library as you are in your own bedroom.

The next time you have to return some overdue books, grab your partner and head to the least trafficked area of any library—the history section. Take a look around to make sure nobody's watching, and get down to business as discreetly as possible. Just be sure to keep any moans of ecstasy to a whisper. You're in a library, after all.

Rest for the Wicked Before you get your groove on, send the librarian on a fool's errand to search for a book that doesn't exist. It'll buy you some much-needed sexy time.

Other Discreet Public Options

- Hiking trails
- Empty subway car
- Beach at night
- Golf course after hours

AUGUST 1

Buy a Garden

Gardening requires lots of water—most of it in the form of perspiration.

—Lou Erickson

We'd all love to be "that person." You know, that person who buys all their plants in the form of seed packets, who lovingly nestles them in soil-filled egg cartons, who owns a top-of-the-line, high-intensity plant light for this singular purpose.

But who has the time? This year, let someone else do the work. Hit up your local garden center for some seedlings already sprouted. Pick your favorite flowers—if your thumb is less than green, annuals like zinnias, marigolds, and geraniums are some of the easiest to keep alive. In the vegetable department, tomatoes, lettuces, and zucchini may be your best bet. And don't forget the herbs! You can plant them right around the perimeter of your larger plants.

When summer guests compliment you on your flourishing garden, go ahead—pretend to be "that person." Just make sure you've tossed the evidence first.

Rest for the Wicked Don't forget to throw out the plant markers that come from the store—they're a dead giveaway.

Fruit or Vegetable?

In 1893, the U.S. Supreme Court ruled that the tomato should be legally classified as a vegetable. Why? Fruits could be imported tax-free, while vegetables couldn't. Because tomatoes are eaten with main dishes, the court ruled them to be a vegetable.

Only Eat Fast Food for a Day

My idea of fast food is a mallard.

—Ted Nugent

Expensive meals like lobster Newberg or duck confit are jaw-droppingly decadent, but sometimes you just need a good old-fashioned fast food burger. Not only is fast food delicious, you just can't beat the convenience of a meal that goes from the grill to your mouth in less than five minutes.

Unfortunately, fast food is about as healthy as the oil in which it's deep-fried, so it should really only be an occasional indulgence. On the other hand, you could always just blow through a year's worth of indulgences in a single day. If you can eat ten burgers a year without any ill effects, it stands to reason that you could eat the same amount in twenty-four hours. As long as you don't make it a habit, one over-the-top day won't kill you. Probably.

Start yourself off slow with a doughnut and coffee and work your way up to burgers and fries by lunchtime. Hit up all your favorite fast food joints throughout the day, but make sure you stick solely to fast food. If it doesn't have a dollar menu, you don't want to be eating there.

Rest for the Wicked Only hit up each fast food venue once to avoid judgmental fry cooks.

Calorie Count

- Breakfast – McDonalds: Egg McMuffin (300), hash brown (130), black coffee (0) – 430 calories
- Lunch – Wendy's: Crispy Chicken Deluxe (460), medium fries (420), medium Frosty (340) – 1,220 calories
- Dinner – Burger King: Whopper (670), medium fries (440), medium soda (290) – 1,400 calories
- Fourth Meal – Taco Bell: 2 beef Chalupas (820), caramel apple empanada (310), small soda (200) – 1,530 calories
- Grand Total – 4,580 calories

AUGUST 3

Stomp on Sandcastles

And so castles made of sand fall in the sea, eventually.

—Jimi Hendrix

There's nothing so pleasant and enjoyable as crafting the perfect sandcastle. Aside from stomping around and crushing one to oblivion, of course.

Stomping on sandcastles gives you all the pleasure of city-wide destruction and mayhem without any of the guilt associated with destroying actual buildings. Who wouldn't want to try it?

Wait until all of the families have taken their kids off the beach for the day and have a free-for-all with the abandoned sandcastles. Pretend you are an invading monster and stomp your way from one delicate structure to the next.

As you survey the devastation, take comfort in the fact that the sandcastles were doomed from the beginning. The sea is far more destructive than you could ever be.

Rest for the Wicked Watch out for hidden moats and holes while you rampage. Even monsters aren't immune to broken ankles.

World's Sandiest Sandcastle

In 2007, a group of artists constructed the world's largest sandcastle in Myrtle Beach, California. It stood almost fifty feet high and took ten days to construct.

AUGUST 4

Crank Up the A/C

No pleasure, no rapture, no exquisite sin greater . . . than central air.

—Azrael, *Dogma*

Environmental advocates are everywhere these days, and they have the blue and green bins to prove it. Not only are they forcing us all to reduce, reuse, and recycle, but now they're on a rampage to curb global warming and our beloved air conditioners are on the chopping block.

This aggression will not stand. It's time to take up arms against your eco-friendly foes by wantonly wasting energy today.

Crank every air conditioner in your house until it's a frosty 50 degrees and you have to throw on a sweater to keep the goosebumps at bay. If your A/C units are struggling to keep up, crack open your freezer for some extra cool air.

Peel back the blinds and watch as hordes of sweaty tree huggers swelter in the boiling sun. Just be thankful it isn't you and pour yourself another mug of hot cocoa in the comfort of your chilly sanctuary.

Rest for the Wicked Just remember, this is a one-day indulgence. You can't afford to live in a temperature-controlled bio dome forever.

Cheaper Ways to Cool Down

- Place a block of ice next to your fan
- Keep the blinds closed
- Order delivery instead of turning on the oven
- Leave all the lights off

AUGUST 5

Spend the Day Staring at Clouds

Too low they build who build below the skies.

—Edward Young

What with all the time people spend on computers these days, it's easy to forget that it's possible to have fun outside without the aid of a screen. Today, you're going to give yourself a reminder in the form of some good old-fashioned cloud gazing.

First, cancel any obligations or plans you may have for the day. You don't want anything getting in the way of your goal of unabashed idleness. Next, hoof it to the nearest park, throw down a blanket, and lie down in a field of flowers to stare straight up at the sky. Observe each cloud as it moves from one side of the sky to the other, and create a story in your head to correspond with the ever-changing aerial landscape.

Most importantly, resist the urge to check your cell phone or interact with anything electronic. This day's all about you, the sky, and your imagination.

Rest for the Wicked Don a pair of sunglasses if the bright sun inhibits your serenity.

Best Cloud Observatories

- Open fields
- Large tree branches
- Sunny beaches
- Outside car windows

AUGUST 6

Blame Your Coworker

Blame someone else and get on with your life.

—Alan Woods

You're sitting at your desk counting the minutes down until the end of the day when the scariest e-mail possible pops up on your computer. It's from your boss. "Please see me in my office in five minutes." It's the moment of truth. Have you done anything wrong? Have you missed any deadlines? What can this possibly be for?

No matter what it is, it's important to blame the office jerk for whatever you're about to be confronted about. Nobody likes the office jerk. He talks so loudly on the phone it disturbs everyone else and he makes bad jokes about people's appearance. He even accidentally hit "reply all" to your company-wide party invitation and said he'd rather eat glass than go. So when you're confronted with low sales numbers or a bad presentation, the office jerk is really the problem, because he told you to do it that way even though you wanted to do it the right way. God, he's such a jerk.

Rest for the Wicked Make sure the office jerk is not the boss who confronts you.

Most Likely Reasons You're Actually Getting Called Into Your Boss's Office

- "Can you work late tonight?"
- "This tie or that tie?"
- "What do you think of this speech?"
- "What's an eight-letter word for 'portable canopy?'"

Lead on a Telemarketer

I don't answer the phone. I get the feeling whenever I do that there will be someone on the other end.

—FRED COUPLES, AMERICAN GOLFER

If your phone rings between the hours of 6:00 P.M. and 7:30 P.M., chances are you will be speaking to the lowest form of human existence if you pick it up: a telemarketer. While you could certainly ignore the incessant ringing, it would be infinitely more fun to mess with them.

When the telemarketer breaks into his spiel, act as if you have never been more interested in anything in your life. "Holy crap, I can get ten Spanish to Finnish dictionaries for the price of nine?! Where do I sign?"

Once he has answered every question about his product you can possibly think of, tell him you need to get your wallet and put the phone down for at least ten minutes. When you return, confess that you already have whatever he's selling and promptly hang up.

Yes telemarketers are only doing their jobs, and yes it's cruel to give them false hope, but they really waive their right to human decency by interrupting your dinner. Besides, think of all the people you saved by keeping Joe AT&T on the line.

Rest for the Wicked Try to stifle any laughter. It's a dead giveaway you aren't serious.

Phrases to Get Rid of Telemarketers

- "If you're calling about Deborah, she was already dead when I got home."
- "You sound like you have a pretty mouth. Am I right?"
- "Can I come over? I'd prefer to talk face to face."

AUGUST 8

Have Sex in an Elevator

The only unnatural sex act is that which you cannot perform.

—Alfred C. Kinsey

High-rise buildings may not be the most romantic settings imaginable, but they do offer one oft-overlooked piece of equipment to aid in a casual rendezvous. The humble elevator.

It's private, roomy enough for two, and there's the tantalizing risk that you might get caught. The question isn't "Why should you have sex in an elevator?" It's "Why wouldn't you?"

Grab your significant other (or a willing stranger) and head straight to the nearest office building, the taller the better.

Hit the button for the top floor, and when the car starts moving, strip down and go to town. Just be sure to finish up before you reach your destination, otherwise you're in for an awkward exchange if anybody's waiting to use the lift.

Rest for the Wicked Don't attempt this task if you are prone to claustrophobia.

Alternative Office Nookie Locales

- Empty stairwell
- Remote supply closet
- Copy room
- CEO's corner office (Don't worry, CEOs are never at work.)

AUGUST 9

Splurge on Useless Gadgets

A new gadget that lasts only five minutes is worth more than an immortal work that bores everyone.

—Francis Picabia, French Painter

There was a time when your bulky laptop and flimsy flip phone were innovative pieces of technology. Now they're about as state-of-the-art as a fountain pen.

Your outdated electronics still technically work, but think of all the faster, sleeker gadgets out there that you could be enjoying. Splurging on flashy new technology might not be the most economical decision you make all day, but it will be the coolest.

Run, don't walk, to your local gadget emporium and stock up on top-of-the-line computers, mp3 players, smart phones, and home theater equipment. Heck, even pick up a few luxury items you don't even need like an automatic wine opener or an electric towel warmer.

Take your new gadgets and bask in the glory of owning all state-of-the-art equipment. You've got a solid six months before they are completely obsolete.

Rest for the Wicked Research your gadgets online to ensure you are buying the most state-of-the-art models.

Best Gadget Stores

- The Sharper Image
- Brookstone
- Best Buy

AUGUST 10

Throw Out Your Leftovers and Go Out to Dinner

The most remarkable thing about my mother is that for thirty years she served the family nothing but leftovers. The original meal has never been found.

—Calvin Trillin, author

Oh, the dreaded leftovers: they sit forgotten in the back of your fridge for days, remembered only if there's no other food in the house. Tonight, you know you should eat them, but pasta from the Italian joint down the street just sounds so good . . .

Do yourself a favor—throw out your leftovers and just go out. They will never be half as good as the original thing, so why even try? Whether you want a Mediterranean feast or a humongous pizza, your stomach will thank you for giving it something exciting, new, and delicious.

And don't bother wasting your dinner out feeling guilty. If your leftovers were worthy of your stomach, you would have eaten them the first time around.

Rest for the Wicked Always throw out leftovers that have been in your refrigerator longer than four days.

World's Worst Leftovers

- Meatloaf
- Macaroni and cheese
- Wedding cake
- Pancakes

AUGUST 11

Read the Cliff's Notes for Book Club

My friend invented Cliff's Notes. When I asked him how he got such a great idea, he said, "Well, first I . . . I just . . . well, to make a long story short . . ."

—Stephen Wright, American actor

Every month it's the same. You've had thirty days to read the latest novel for your book club, yet it's the night before and you haven't even cracked open the cover.

Normally you'd stroll into the meetup with a host of excuses and your tail tucked between your legs, but this time is going to be different. Because this time you're going to do something you haven't done since high school. You're going to cheat.

But truthfully, is it really so wrong to take a peek through the Cliff's Notes? It's certainly better than reading nothing at all. And now you'll actually have a clue what the story is about for once.

Hit up your local bookstore and head straight for the telltale black and yellow covers. If you have time, flip through the synopsis to get a general feel for the story. Otherwise simply tuck the Cliff's Notes version into the original book and smuggle it into book club. Your friends will think you're merely checking a passage, when in reality you are consulting your own personal cheat sheet.

Rest for the Wicked Rip the cover off the Cliff's Notes, as it's very recognizable.

Alternatives to Cliff's Notes

- Wikipedia
- Sparks Notes
- Watching the movie
- Books on tape

AUGUST 12

Take Cabs Everywhere

The civilized man has built a coach, but has lost the use of his feet.

—Ralph Waldo Emerson

For an entire day, ignore the bus and avoid the subway. Instead, every time you leave your apartment, hail a cab to take you where you need to go. Sure you could walk to the corner store for that gallon of milk, but who says you have to?

Conduct all personal business from the backseat of a taxicab, turning it into an office-on-wheels of sorts. Answer e-mails, call your grandmother, and pay your bills while watching the city fly by outside the window.

On the subway, there are all sorts of things that are frowned upon, like speaking loudly on a cell phone or applying makeup. Well, from the backseat of a cab, you don't have to worry about that. This is your personal livery service for the day and you'll file your nails if you want to. And if the driver has a problem with it, just raise the partition.

Rest for the Wicked Always wear your seat belt when riding in the back of a cab and keep enough cash on you to include a tip that's between 15–18 percent of the final fare.

Suggested Movie List

- *Taxi Driver,* 1976
- *The Fifth Element,* 1997
- *Alfie,* 1966
- *Taxi,* 1978
- *D.C. Cab,* 1983

Become a Meatatarian

Vegetables are interesting, but lack a sense of purpose when unaccompanied by a good cut of meat.

—Fran Lebowitz, American Writer

These days, it seems everyone has some sort of dietary restriction. Some only eat fish, others can't stomach dairy, and a few won't touch anything that has even been in the same room as a carb.

Well, if you can't beat 'em, join 'em. Today your diet will consist entirely of good old-fashioned animal flesh. Like nature intended. While it may not be the healthiest diet ever conceived, it's by far the most delicious.

Start yourself off with a few strips of bacon and some breakfast sausage. For lunch, try a hamburger or a sandwich without the pesky bun. Finally, finish your day off with a thick, bloody steak wrapped in prosciutto with a side of barbecued jumbo shrimp. Resist the urge to supplement your meals with useless vegetables. They're just filler anyway.

Rest for the Wicked Check labels carefully to ensure no hidden vegetables have contaminated your food.

World's Meatiest Dish

Dubbed "The Feast," the world's largest meal consists of cooked eggs stuffed into a fish, stuffed into chickens, stuffed into a sheep, stuffed into a camel. The result takes twenty-four hours to cook.

AUGUST 14

Jet-Set for the Afternoon

If some people didn't tell you, you'd never know they'd been away on a vacation.

—Kin Hubbard, American humorist

One of the best ways to pass the time during a slow work afternoon is to think of all the exotic places you'd rather be. If only you were a rich socialite instead of an underpaid desk jockey.

Then again, while you may not have mountains of cash to travel the world, you can certainly scrape together enough for a short twenty-four-hour jaunt. You may have to dip into your rainy day fund, but isn't that precisely what it's there for?

Forget itineraries or travel agents, just throw a few essentials into a bag and head straight for the airport. Pick a destination at random (Paris, Tahiti, Buenos Aires, London) and hop on the first available flight. Don't worry about minor details like where you'll stay or what you'll do once you arrive; you have the whole flight to figure that out.

Rest for the Wicked Stick with just a carry-on bag. If you need to check a bag, you don't understand the concept of jet-setting.

Jet-Setting Essentials

- Oversized sunglasses
- Small dog(s)
- Limo driver
- American Express Black Card

AUGUST 15

Hire a Hot Pool Cleaner for Your Tub

I've been dating younger men since my twenties, When I was twenty-nine, I dated someone twenty-one . . . younger men are just more fun. I like their energy.

—DANA DELANY, AMERICAN ACTRESS

If television has taught us nothing, it's that there is nothing better than lounging on a patio chair while a scantily clad twenty-something cleans your pool. If only you had a pool of your own—and disposable income—you could see for yourself.

Well, let's think about exactly what makes a pool a pool. If you define it as simply a large container filled with water, well then, by golly, you've got everything you need to live out your fantasy sitting in your bathroom. You just happen to call it a bathtub.

Track down your local pool-cleaning service and let them know you have a special job for the right candidate. Since your "pool" is really dirty and requires lots of cleaning, explain that you need someone who is in shape and up to the task. When your temporary servant arrives, don't bother trying to pass your tub off as a pool. Just pull up a chair, pour yourself a margarita, and tell your cleaner to get to work . . . but not to rush through it.

Rest for the Wicked Pre-dirty the tub so you have longer to admire the view.

Optional Tasks for Your Pool Cleaner

- Change dead light bulbs (while you hold the ladder)
- Feed you grapes
- Apply sunscreen to your back (every five minutes)

AUGUST 16

Buy Only Junk Food at the Supermarket

My body is a temple where junk food goes to worship.

—Unknown

Your grocery list is starting to look like the ingredient list for your dog's all-natural organic kibble. Free-range, locally raised chicken breasts. Kale and chard. Brown rice and lentils. No, you wouldn't dream of buying a bag of potato chips! Not that they're not good, but . . . come to think of it, potato chips are really frickin' good.

So just this once, hit the local supermarket—not Whole Foods, not Trader Joe's, but the regular supermarket. Skip the perimeter (that's where they keep all the healthful stuff), and go straight for the aisles. Then fill your basket with the worst of it: greasy potato chips, neon cheese balls, chemically created baked goods, ice cream in a tub, cheese in a can, cookies in a tube. Does it get any more wicked than this?

When you get home, go at it. Eat the cookie dough straight from the tube. Get cheese dust all over your fingers and syrupy chocolate sauce under your fingernails. Eat until you feel like you might vomit. Tomorrow morning you can hit the reset—and kale may have never tasted so good.

Rest for the Wicked Be sure to throw out those potato chip bags and Twinkie wrappers once you're done binging. People might judge.

"Twinkie Defense"

The term "Twinkie Defense" was coined in 1979, when Daniel White claimed that eating too much junk food was his reason for killing Harvey Milk and San Francisco Mayor George Moscone.

AUGUST 17

Take a Nap at Work

No day is so bad it can't be fixed with a nap.

—CARRIE SNOW, AMERICAN COMEDIAN

Perhaps it's the low, incessant hum of your aging computer, but something about being in an office can make you feel like you haven't slept in days. You should be finishing up a report, but all you can think of is the down comforter and memory foam mattress waiting for you at home.

Rather than fight against your droopy eyes, you might as well embrace the inevitable: you need a nap. Once you've had your beauty rest, you'll be ten times more productive than you were before. If anything, you're doing the company a favor by catching a few winks.

Turn off your computer, grab a roll of paper towels (makeshift pillow), and find a quiet place to curl up for awhile. Nothing crazy, just a twenty-minute cat nap in the abandoned office on the second floor. Chances are nobody will even notice you were gone, which should say something about the true importance of your job.

Rest for the Wicked Set an alarm on your phone so you don't sleep through the entire day.

Best Places to Sleep

- Under your desk
- Empty conference room
- Janitor's closet
- Parked car

AUGUST 18

Participate in Obnoxious PDA

A kiss is a lovely trick designed by nature to stop speech when words become superfluous.

—INGRID BERGMAN, SWEDISH ACTRESS

When it comes to public displays of affection, there are a few general rules. Be as discreet as possible, keep your hands where we can see them, and please—for the love of god—no tongue. Good thing you care as much about decorum as you do about the mating habits of African fruit flies.

Nobody has the right to tell you when, or how far, you can shove your tongue down your partner's throat. If they don't like it, they can find another bench to sit on.

Throw caution to the wind and hug, kiss, grope, and nuzzle your significant other to your heart's content. Not enough seats at the restaurant? Just sit on your partner's lap. No space on the subway? Just hug each other as close as possible. If you are obnoxious enough, the rest of the world may just give you some privacy for a change.

Rest for the Wicked Keep it PG-13. You want to be annoying, not wind up in prison.

Most Offensive Forms of PDA

- Hands in each other's back pockets
- Playing footsie
- Incessant baby talk

AUGUST 19

Go to a Nude Beach with Clothes On

Clothes make the man. Naked people have little or no influence on society.

—Mark Twain

The first time you hear about nude beaches is probably sometime in early adolesence, and if you're like most people, you have overactive hormones that make it clear this is a place you should visit. Not to break free from the shackles of society's norms, but just to get a glimpse of the full, naked body in all its beautiful glory.

Now that you're old and out of shape, the thought of being on a nude beach might frighten you more than entice you. There's a fear that fellow nudists would pass judgment on your hairy, flabby, nutritionless torso. So rather than subject yourself to the type of shallow judgments that you would certainly have if you saw your naked self, get the best of both worlds. Throw on your swim trunks, dab some sunscreen on your nose, and have at it. Nude beaches allow patrons to be nude. They don't require it.

Rest for the Wicked Wear dark or reflective sunglasses. Wandering eyes will warrant at best a chuckle and at worst a slap in the face.

Questions Not to Ask at a Nude Beach

- How's it hanging?
- Can you hold these for a second?
- How much longer will it be?

AUGUST 20

Steal Veggies from the Community Garden

I have a rock garden. Last week three of them died.

—RICHARD DIRAN, AMERICAN WRITER

As you watch your neighbors toil and putter in the soil, you can't help but wonder why they spend so much time in the community garden. That is until they let you taste one of their fresh summer tomatoes and every corner of your mouth explodes with glee.

It's too late to start growing your own produce, but it's never to late to grub off of theirs.

Most community gardens are practically overflowing with veggies. Far too many for the participating gardeners to consume. If you don't grab some now, they'll sit on the vine and rot. And you can't let that happen.

Better start harvesting.

Wait for the dead of night and hop over the rickety fence surrounding the garden. Take your pick of the plumpest carrots, the juiciest tomatoes, and the spiciest hot peppers. Once you've gathered all your arms can carry, flee to a secluded area to eat the evidence.

Rest for the Wicked Bring a neighborhood cat along to use as a patsy.

Easiest Food to Steal Unnoticed

- Berries
- Tomatoes
- Peppers

AUGUST 21

Jump the Subway Turnstile

A smart person knows all the rules so he can break them wisely.

—Lubna Azmi

You may think turnstile jumping is just for unruly teenagers and drunken homeless people. But can you imagine the exhilaration? The running start, the over-the-turnstile leap, the wind from the subway in your hair as you run full-speed toward the closing doors of the train. Pure adrenaline. It's worth a try.

There are several ways you can go about this. You can plan to do it late at night on a weekday when there are few riders and no attendants on duty. You could also make it a crime of opportunity, doing the deed spontaneously at a time when you wander into an out-of-the-way stop with virtually no one around. But perhaps the best method is to plan your jump at a station with a short distance between the turnstile and the platform. Wait until your train pulls into the station, make your leap, and run like the wind. Chances are anyone who sees you won't have time to catch up before the doors close and the train barrels away.

Sure, you might get a big fine or even get arrested. But if you're that worried, pay the fare first, then go back and jump it just for fun.

Rest for the Wicked Beware of undercover public transit police officers—not everyone who can arrest you will be wearing a uniform.

Lounge At Your Own Risk

Possibly the least serious "crime" you can be cited for on the New York City subway: taking up more than one seat.

AUGUST 22

Rent an Expensive Car and Claim You Own It

To attract men, I wear a perfume called "New Car Interior."

—Rita Rudner

As long as your car gets you where you're going, it doesn't have to be flashy or fast. But on some days, you'd give anything to trade in your clunker for a deluxe model.

You can imagine it all: leather soft as a baby's bottom, studio-quality sound system, and the ability to hit sixty in 3.5 seconds. Heads will turn when you roll down the street, and it won't be because of the rattle in your engine or the smoke billowing out of your exhaust.

If you can't shake the urge for automobile extravagance, give into it. But before you sign on that dotted line, remember that you're not James Bond and you can't swing $800 monthly payments. You can, however, get an expensive rental car for a day (or a week) and claim it's yours. Whether you want a super-sleek frame and glittering rims or impeccable handling and ventilated seats, you'll be able to find it at the nearest Hertz for a tiny fraction of the down payment. And as long as those keys are in your hand, you can convince anyone you own it—even yourself.

Rest for the Wicked Remember the old saying: You break it, you buy it. Get all your jollies out while the car is in your possession, but try to bring it back in one piece. The last thing you want to do is pay for a deluxe model you never even owned.

The Best Cars of American Film

1. The DeLorean DMC12—*Back to the Future*
2. 007's Aston-Martin—any (and every) James Bond movie
3. 1961 Ferrari GT—*Ferris Bueller's Day Off*
4. The Batmobile—the *Batman* series
5. The Black Trans Am—*Smokey and the Bandit*

Make Your Own Hollywood Star

You're not famous until my mother has heard of you.

—Jay Leno

Unless you are reading this book on the set of a major motion picture, chances are you will never have your own star on the Hollywood Walk of Fame. But that doesn't mean you can't make your own.

It might not be Hollywood, but somewhere in your immediate vicinity lies a wet slab of cement, just waiting for somebody to stick his or her hands into it. And that somebody is you.

Whatever they are building, there's no way a few innocent handprints will impair its structural integrity. If anything, you're helping the construction workers by testing whether the concrete is dry yet.

Call your local municipal office and check for the nearest construction site. Wait until lunchtime and make your move quickly before anyone realizes what's going on. You should have just enough time to dip your hands and sign your masterpiece before it's time to skedaddle.

The signature may be a dead giveaway, but it's a small price to pay for eternal fame.

Rest for the Wicked Bring a damp cloth to remove the evidence from your hands.

The Birth of a Star(s)

There was no single first person to receive a star on the Hollywood Walk of Fame. All of the original inductees were installed at the same time.

Blow Your Rainy Day Fund

I'm living so far beyond my income that we may almost be said to be living apart.
—E.E Cummings

We all have a rainy day fund—some small stash of money that we hide away for a later date. You know you're supposed to save it, but will it really matter if that account balance drops down to zero?

Don't stop to think about the rent check. This isn't your savings account. You're not dipping into the college fund of your future children. Bills will still get paid.

Who cares if the sun is shining and you don't need anything new? You earned this money and with it, the right to spend it however you'd like. So go out with a clean conscience and drop a few hundred bucks. You weren't using the money before, so why would you miss it now? Besides, what were you going to buy on a rainy day, anyway? Umbrellas?

Rest for the Wicked Double-check your account numbers before you withdraw your rainy day fund. Nothing will take the sunshine out of the next morning like finding out that your rent check bounced.

Ways to Blow a Few Hundred Bucks

- A weekend in a luxury hotel room
- Designer clothing
- A five-course dinner
- A spa day
- A flat screen

AUGUST 25

Eat the Last Cookie

Think what a better world it would be if we all, the whole world, had cookies and milk about three o'clock every afternoon and then lay down on our blankets for a nap.

—Barbara Jordan

There it sits, an island oasis in a sea of buttery crumbs: the last cookie. You want it, desperately. But so does your friend across the table, the friend sitting next to you, and probably his girlfriend too. Yet you all just sit there, chatting politely and sipping your coffee, trying not to let your eyes dart to that last morsel of sugary goodness taunting you like Eve's apple.

What to do? Take it. Don't ask—just take it. Keep talking, keep drinking your coffee, but reach out and grasp that cookie and take a bite. Savor it. Tomorrow, it's back to manners, back to politeness, back to "No, no, you have it, I insist." But just this once, that cookie is yours.

After all, someone has to eat the last cookie. Might as well be you.

Rest for the Wicked If there's any social fallout, feign ignorance: "Wow, guys, I thought there were more cookies in the kitchen. Next batch is on me."

A Monster by Any Other Name

Cookie Monster revealed in a 2004 song that prior to discovering his love of cookies, his name was Sid.

Buy Every Seat for a Movie

No, I'm sorry, these are taken. They're in the lobby buying popcorn . . . what are you doing? These are taken, these are taken!

—Elaine, *Seinfeld*

You've got the perfect Sunday planned—a trip to the movies to see the latest action flick, complete with popcorn, soda, and candy. Unfortunately, your perfect day turns into a perfect nightmare when loud, obnoxious movie patrons talk during the film and rip the plastic off of candy boxes every five seconds. Enough already!

Next time you hit the movies, spare yourself the annoyance of other humans and buy up every seat in the theater. You might get a few odd looks at the ticket counter, but at least this way you can enjoy a movie in peace without wanting to throw something at the kid kicking the back of your seat for two hours.

Given the cost of movie tickets these days, you might have to take out a loan to buy more than ten seats. It'll be worth it, though—after all, silence is golden.

Rest for the Wicked Try out different seats before the movie starts to find the best vantage point for your private viewing.

Worldwide Highest-Grossing Films of All Time (as of 2010)

1. *Avatar,* 2009
2. *Titanic,* 1997
3. *The Lord of the Rings: The Return of the King,* 2003
4. *Pirates of the Caribbean: Dead Man's Chest,* 2006
5. *Toy Story 3,* 2010

AUGUST 27

Pee in Public

I gotta pee.

—Forrest Gump

Inevitably, in life, we will all find ourselves in the following predicament. We're out in public, there is no available bathroom, and we really, really have to pee. This can happen through no fault of our own. Our options are to either 1) pee our pants; or 2) find somewhere discreet to pee.

Clearly the latter is the proper response.

Some find it gross or unsavory, but it's not the worst thing a person can do. It's not only convenient, it's also the environmentally friendly way to pee. When you pee in nature, there's no wasted toilet water. Plus, if you find the right spot, you might even help hydrate a plant. So next time someone asks you what your carbon footprint is, tell them that while you may have three refrigerators and run the A/C with the door open, you just peed in the park, so maybe they should rethink their lifestyle.

Rest for the Wicked Look out to make sure nobody is around when you pee. In some states, the law defines public urination as a sex offense. No bathroom emergency is worth that.

Most Popular Things to Draw with Your Pee in the Snow

1. Snow angels
2. Middle finger
3. Signing your name
4. Any Jackson Pollock painting

AUGUST 28

Reclaim Your Yard

I always thought a yard was three feet; then I started mowing the lawn.
—C. E. Cowman

There's something charming about those overgrown shrubs and flowers creeping over your fence and deck railings, isn't there? Kind of like a wild garden from a Dickens novel. And you always were a bit charmed by Miss Havisham.

But wait, wasn't Miss Havisham a decrepit old woman whose garden was overrun and unkempt? And come to think of it, those aren't flowers in your backyard—those are weeds. Right. Time to wrangle some friends, pop open a twelve-pack, pull out the ol' garden tools, and get to work. Or hire someone else to take care of it! Sure, digging up weeds and trimming back hedges is no one's idea of self-indulgence, but watching someone else take care of it sure is. And think about how much better you'll feel when it's done!

Rest for the Wicked Consider renting a mulcher, which will turn the organic pruning waste into compost you can use for landscaping or gardening.

Hollywood Magic

In the 1990 film *Edward Scissorhands,* set designers made the giant hedge sculptures by wrapping metal skeletons in chicken wire, then weaving in thousands of small plastic plant sprigs.

AUGUST 29

Waste Food

People shop for a bathing suit with more care than they do a husband or wife. The rules are the same. Look for something you'll feel comfortable wearing. Allow for room to grow.

—Erma Bombeck, American humorist

Your mother always told you to clear your plate or else you wouldn't get any dessert. Lucky for you, your mother isn't here right now.

Nobody is immune to the occasional miscalculation when it comes to food. But just because your eyes were bigger than your stomach does not mean you should force feed yourself. If you're not hungry anymore, simply throw the rest away.

Don't bother breaking out the Tupperware, simply open up the trash and dump your extra food in. Let's face it, you would just watch it rot in your refrigerator anyway.

Yes, there are millions of starving children out there, but it's not like you can wrap up your leftover lasagna and mail it across the ocean. Stop agonizing over your wasted meal and donate some money to a charity or volunteer at a soup kitchen if you want to make a difference.

Rest for the Wicked Wait a few minutes to make sure you are actually full. Once it's passed the rim of the garbage can, it officially makes the transition from food to trash.

Only Foods Worth Saving

- Pizza
- Chili
- Birthday cake
- Apple pie

AUGUST 30

Be a Litter Bug

I know a man who doesn't pay to have his trash taken out. How does he get rid of his trash? He gift-wraps it, and puts in into an unlocked car.

—Henny Youngman

Properly disposing of garbage is easy when you are within a stone's throw of a trash can. When you are stuck holding a candy wrapper full of melted chocolate with nowhere to toss it, that's a different story.

If everybody gave up on trash cans, it would only take a few days before we were drowning in filth. But you're only one person. Surely nobody would notice if just you dumped your trash wherever you pleased.

Gather up all of your stray receipts, coffee cups, empty bottles, and other assorted trash and hurl them out the nearest window. For good measure, empty out your pockets and toss anything that isn't money right onto the ground.

As for your random papers, loose rubber bands, and assorted office crap, just sweep them right onto the floor. Congratulations, you finally cleaned up your work station, and you didn't even have to stand up.

Rest for the Wicked Keep an eye out for cops and hippies. Neither group takes kindly to littering.

Trash Decomposition Timeframes

- Apple core—1 to 2 months
- Cigarette butt—1 to 5 years
- Aluminum can—80 to 200 years

AUGUST 31

Buy a Whole New Wardrobe

Our minds want clothes as much as our bodies.

—Samuel Butler

Unless you fancy yourself something of a fashionista, you probably fall prey to the same wardrobe cycle as the rest of us. You buy a new T-shirt or sweater and it promptly becomes your go-to item of clothing, making an appearance at least four times a week. This, of course, begs the question of what you used to wear. Before you've solved that mystery, you tire of your new shirt and buy something even newer. The cycle begins again.

Today, you break the pattern.

Instead of limiting your shopping trip to one pair of jeans or a single jacket, spring for a whole new wardrobe. Ask any MIT doctoral student. They'll tell you that this is a mathematically sound decision. Let's take T-shirts, for example. If you pull on the same tee every four days, you'll wear it out in about three months. But if you rotate through thirty-seven shirts, they'll be worn so infrequently that each one will last approximately four years. And by then, those clothes will have paid for themselves. In fact, it's practically like someone paid you to shop. You can't argue with that logic.

Rest for the Wicked Feeling guilty about emptying a full closet to make room for you new wardrobe? Don't fret. Donate the old threads to Goodwill or The Salvation Army.

Clothes That Won't Improve Your Wardrobe

- Overalls
- Members Only jackets
- Jorts
- Parachute pants
- Pleated khakis

SEPTEMBER 1

Don't Pay Your Bills

A man who pays his bills on time is soon forgotten.

—Oscar Wilde

It's the first of the month, and time to cash your big fat paycheck. Unfortunately, it's also time to pay off the stack of bigger, fatter bills accumulating on your counter.

Then again, what's your rush? Those bills have been piling up for weeks. It certainly couldn't hurt to ignore them for a little while longer. It's not like the cable company is going to go under because you didn't pay your $39.95 subscription fee.

Take your overflowing pile of bills and file them under "S" for "some other time." You're still going to pay them—just not today. For now, you have more important things to spend your hard-earned money on, like a night on the town or an electric wine chiller. All the things you've always wanted but never had the readily available funds to afford. Don't worry, your bills will still be waiting for you when you get back from your shopping spree.

Rest for the Wicked Many companies will waive a recent bill if you threaten to cancel the service. It's worth a shot.

Methods for Avoiding Creditors

- Change your name
- Answer the phone in Spanish
- Declare bankruptcy
- Good, old-fashioned running

SEPTEMBER 2

Get a Tattoo

My body is my journal, and my tattoos are my story.

—JOHNNY DEPP

Some people change their appearance by the hour, but most of us pretty much look the same whether it's Monday, Saturday, March, or November. There's a lot to be said for consistency, but sometimes you've got to shake things up a little.

And what better to break you out of your cookie-cutter monotony than a spontaneous tattoo? Sure you are glad that you never got that butterfly on your ankle when you were a teenager, but you're all grown up now and better qualified to handle such a permanent life decision.

The wonder of tattoos is that there is no right or wrong. If you've always wanted Yosemite Sam blazed across your chest, by all means, get it done. Think a golden triforce on your hand is too nerdy? Think again. You are only limited by your imagination—and your boldness.

Rest for the Wicked Draw the tattoo in marker first before you make it a permanent part of your body.

What Your Tattoo Says about You

- Bicep – Hyper aggressive
- Lower Back – Skanky
- Hand – Over confident
- Face – Psychopathic
- Top of the Foot – Insecure

SEPTEMBER 3

Have a Five-Course Meal on Your Lunch Break

There is no sincerer love than the love of food.

—George Bernard Shaw

Few things are worse than the sound of an alarm clock pulling you out of a sweet dream and into the cold reality of another workday. When you've hit snooze one too many times, there's barely enough time to get dressed and comb your hair, let alone pack a lunch.

Make the best of a bad situation by taking yourself out to lunch—and not just any lunch. Treat yourself to a five-course meal.

You could grab some fast food, but that will never duplicate the complex flavors and nutritional balance of the brown bag lunch you surely would have packed yourself. Only a five-course meal—complete with appetizer, soup, salad, entrée, and dessert—can provide the culinary quality and quantity your body craves. And that's not all. The sophisticated calm of the restaurant offers the perfect atmosphere to rest your mind. At the end of the meal, you'll have gotten all you need for a super-productive afternoon at the office. So what if there are only ninety minutes left in the day? You deserved that three-hour lunch break.

Rest for the Wicked Don't indulge in a five-course meal if you have a big client meeting or if the boss's boss is in town. You can always pass off your five-course meal as a trial run for an upcoming business dinner, but it will be better if no one notices.

Worst Bagged Lunch Options

- Leftover tuna casserole
- Egg salad sandwich
- Hummus and carrot sticks

SEPTEMBER 4

Forget Recycling; Throw It All Away

Recycling and speed limits are bullshit, they're like someone who quits smoking on his deathbed.

—Chuck Palahniuk, American novelist

Throwing away garbage used to be simple. Whether it was a half-eaten hamburger or a misguided chemistry experiment, the process was the same: Open lid, dump in trash, move on with life. Now it's gotten so complicated you could have ten pieces of junk and eleven different bins to put them in.

As you sit there, empty cereal box in hand, debating whether the plastic bag counts as a separate entity or as part of the box, think about how much time you'd save if you just threw everything in the trash—and then do it. No more scrubbing sticky peanut butter from the bottom of jars, no more cutting up plastic six-pack rings. Just you, a trash can, and your garbage.

While your small act of rebellion might hurt the environment, mother earth has bigger concerns than your minor negligence—and honestly, how much of the stuff in your recycling bin is actually recycled anyway? Not 100 percent of it, that's for sure! Besides, there are plenty of things you can do to offset your negative impact—like using the time you've saved to go shopping for eco-friendly clothes.

Rest for the Wicked Remove your address number from your overflowing garbage bins to prevent retaliation from the trash collectors.

New Recycling System

- Old sandwich = trash
- Beer bottle = trash
- Newspapers = BBQ kindling (always save)
- Styrofoam container = trash
- Broken garbage can = ?

Embellish Your Resume

Desperate times call for desperate measures.

—PROVERB

With America's economy still on the fritz, finding a job has become more difficult than ever. Some jobs receive thousands of applicants, all more qualified than the next. How are you supposed to compete with resume points like Harvard, MBA and Special Olympics volunteer?

Easy: embellish your resume. In case your prospective employer does a background check, it's probably not smart to lie about your GPA or current job title. But it's safe and easy to exaggerate your current and past job responsibilities. "Assisted with networking reception logistics" becomes "Coordinated and managed networking reception logistics," and so on. Just be careful not to fib too much—otherwise it could bite you in the ass if your new employer demands your "expertise" on something you know nothing about.

If at first you feel nervous embellishing your resume, don't be. How do you think everyone else out there is getting jobs?

Rest for the Wicked Don't lie about things that can be easily verified, such as your criminal history or your college major.

Risky Resumes

A 2008 Career Builder survey found that of almost 9,000 respondents, 8 percent reported that they fudged some aspect of their resume.

SEPTEMBER 6

Fill Your Coffee Mug with Booze

To alcohol! The cause of, and solution to, all of life's problems.

—Homer Simpson

Just as you were starting to enjoy your weekend, Monday hits you like a sack of bricks and the dreary work week begins anew. All your office provides to help you cope is a pot of instant coffee and the occasional danish. What you really need is something a little stronger.

You don't want to get plastered on the job, but there's certainly no harm in doctoring up your morning coffee with a dash or two of whiskey. It'll perk you up a lot better than coffee alone, and help ease you into the day.

If you don't keep a bottle of spirits at the office for just such occasions, throw a few shots in a water bottle and smuggle it in. Mix in some orange juice and you have yourself a morning screwdriver. If your coworkers get wise, just offer them a little of your bootleg hooch and swear them to secrecy.

Rest for the Wicked Carry a pack of gum or mints to mask the smell of booze.

Monday Funday Recipe

1 part gin
1 part triple sec
1 part vodka
6 parts orange juice
splash of grenadine

1. Combine ingredients in a small shaker with ice. Shake for several seconds, pour into an opaque water bottle with straw (to contain alcohol smell).

SEPTEMBER 7

Hire a Styling Team

Looking good and dressing well is a necessity. Having a purpose in life is not.
—Oscar Wilde

It's no coincidence that movie stars look fantastic whether they are walking the red carpet or grabbing the morning paper. They have a team of people styling their hair, hiding their wrinkles, and coordinating their outfits.

You may not be a movie star (yet), but that doesn't mean you can't be treated like one. If only for a day.

Comb through the classifieds and piece together a crack team of hair stylists, makeup artists, and wardrobe connoisseurs to follow you around for the day. Their job is to make you look your best, and you should settle for nothing short of perfection.

Once your entourage has crafted the ultimate diva look, it's time to show yourself off around town. Whether you head to the local coffee shop or just strut around the park, try to put on your best imitation of a spoiled movie star. You may just attract a paparazzo or two.

Rest for the Wicked Treat your temporary employees like garbage, to complete the illusion of stardom.

The Hollywood Look

- Oversized sunglasses
- Effortless hair (that actually took three hours to style)
- Torn, shabby looking clothes (that actually cost a fortune)
- Ten pounds of makeup
- Liposuction/tummy tuck (optional)

SEPTEMBER 8

Bring Along an Ugly Friend

It is better to be beautiful than to be good, but it is better to be good than to be ugly.
—OSCAR WILDE

When it comes to love—or, at the very least, getting laid—you don't need undue competition to thwart your progress dead in its tracks.

Make a list and check it twice. Include at least ten of your most grotesque friends, and then rank them in order from most to least attractive. Eliminate everyone but the ugliest, and then invite the unwitting soul over for a popcorn-and-pajamas movie night.

In the meantime, primp. Wear your most flattering outfit. Then, when your friend arrives in sweats, reveal that there's been a change of plans and head to the local watering hole.

Your friend will look horrible—and potentially deranged—while you'll look dapper and comparatively sane. Sit back, relax, and enjoy the attention as all potential suitors bypass your unappealing friend in favor of you.

Rest for the Wicked To save the friendship, agree to ugly yourself up and return the favor next time.

Rules for Wingmen (Wingwomen)

1. If there is a grenade, you must jump on it. No questions asked.
2. Don't speak unless spoken to, and never say anything funny.
3. Find your own ride home

SEPTEMBER 9

Crash a Wedding

Bachelors know more about women than married men; if they didn't, they'd be married too.

—H. L. Mencken, American journalist

As long as you aren't involved in the planning portion of a wedding, hanging out at the actual party is a blast. Pity all of your friends are either already married or forever alone. In order to party it up wedding style, you're going to have to take matters into your own hands.

On the one hand, crashing a wedding is dishonest, illegal, and potentially dangerous. On the other, it guarantees you unlimited booze, permission to dance like an idiot, and desperate single people as far as the eye can see. Clearly, it's worth the risk.

Check newspaper archives for local wedding announcements and start preparing your back story. When you arrive, head straight for the dance floor and hide among the other drunken partiers. If other guests starts asking too many questions, hightail it to the nearest bathroom to throw them off the trail.

Once you've scored a couple of drinks and enjoyed a decent free meal, quietly exit the party—preferably with a bridesmaid or groomsman in tow.

Rest for the Wicked Use a fake name in case you encounter a stage-five clinger.

Wedding Crasher Rules

Rule #1: Never leave a fellow Crasher behind.
Rule #7: Blend in by standing out.
Rule #13: Bridesmaids are desperate—console them.
Rule #55: If pressed, tell people you're related to Uncle John. Everyone has an Uncle John.

Start a Pillow Fight in Public

We just want to inspire girls to have pillow fights and then drive to the beach and break up with their boyfriends!

—Ben Romans

Let's face it, pillow fights are awesome. Everyone gets to unleash their repressed aggression, and nobody gets hurt. So why must they be relegated to children's sleepovers and sorority houses?

Today you can bring the pillow fight to the mainstream by staging an epic battle in public.

Head to your nearest department store and buy out every pillow they've got. Now, take your arsenal to the streets, wait for unsuspecting commuters to start heading to work, and start smacking. Be direct, aim true, and strike hard. Be as aggressive as possible without causing any real physical harm.

It shouldn't take long for everyone to figure out what's going on and grab some pillows from your pile to join in. Sure they may be a few minutes late to work, but they'll have the most fun morning commute ever.

Rest for the Wicked Don't attack anyone holding coffee or wearing glasses. It's just mean.

Pillows for Everyone!

The largest pillow fight flash mob took place during the International Pillow Fight Day on March 22, 2008.

Show Up Late to Work

If you're gonna be late, then be late and not just two minutes—make it an hour and enjoy your breakfast.

—David Brent, *The Office*

Unless you are an ice cream taster at Ben & Jerry's, you probably aren't too excited to get to work in the morning. Yet every morning you rush out the door so you can be a model employee and arrive before 9:00.

Well, today's going to be different. This morning you're actually going to enjoy your breakfast and ease yourself into work mode. Your boss may think otherwise, but rest assured the office will still be standing if you show up an hour late.

When the alarm goes off, hit the snooze button once, twice, or even twenty-seven times. Treat yourself to a nice long shower and take the time to iron and starch your shirt. Forget the cold bowl of cereal or the granola bar on the go, today you are treating yourself to bacon, eggs, and a thick slice of French toast.

Now that you are good and relaxed, you might actually get some work done for a change when you finally do make it into the office.

Rest for the Wicked Use the side entrance when entering the building. Your boss might not even notice.

Day in the Life of a Slacker

- 10:30 – Arrive at work
- 10:31 – Coffee break
- 11:31 – Lunch hour
- 12:31 – Second lunch hour
- 2:00 – Doctor's appointment
- 3:00 – Leave early to pick up kids

SEPTEMBER 12

Only Eat Dessert

Just think of all those women on the Titanic who said, "No, thank you," to dessert that night. And for what!

—Erma Bombeck, American humorist

As any child will tell you, any meal—no matter how delicious—is just a necessary evil on the long windy road to dessert. Yet for some reason, most adults insist on eating their meal first. What's worse, some get so full from the meal that they don't even bother with dessert at all.

Well, that certainly isn't going to happen to you today.

To ensure you don't miss out on any sweet, gooey goodness, every item of food that passes your lips today will either be sugary, chocolatey, fruity, or some combination of the three.

Start your day with a big stack of chocolate chip pancakes and a glass of chocolate milk. For lunch, you can stuff your face with everything from cannolis and cupcakes to apple pie and French pastries. Without the burden of filling foods like bread and pasta, you'll be surprised how many different desserts you can fit into a single meal.

For the grand finale, bake yourself a nice, tall, birthday cake, scarf down the entire thing by yourself, and slip into a peaceful sugar coma.

Rest for the Wicked Keep a few candy bars in your pockets in case you get hungry between meals.

Recipe for Toast Cream Sundae

1 slice cinnamon raisin bread
1 scoop vanilla ice cream
2 tablespoons whipped cream
2 tablespoons hot fudge
chocolate sprinkles

1. Toast bread and set inside of a small bowl.
2. Pile on ice cream, whipped cream, and fudge. Top with sprinkles and serve.

Throw Out Your Significant Other's Junk

Don't spend two dollars to dry clean a shirt. Donate it to the Salvation Army instead. They'll clean it and put it on a hanger. Next morning buy it back for seventy-five cents.

—Unknown

You're cohabitating with your significant other, and your new place looks totally awesome (if you do say so yourself). There's just one problem: that hideous ceramic cookie jar in the shape of Yogi Bear prominently displayed on the kitchen counter. Not to mention the neon, light-up Budweiser sign your beau wants to hang on the bedroom wall. Oh, and those two huge boxes of worthless comic books and faded high school basketball uniforms that have nowhere to go.

What to do? Toss 'em. Now, this may seem harsh, and by no means should you trash anything with real sentimental value. But it's possible your significant other needs help. Maybe he or she really wants to get rid of that stuff but simply doesn't have the heart to do it. Have you seen *Hoarders*? This could be your future.

Best to nip it in the bud while it's still manageable. And if your sweetie complains, simply nod sympathetically and say, "You're welcome."

Rest for the Wicked If you suspect tossing the junk might be break-up material, consider boxing up everything and going through it together before making the trip to Goodwill.

Top Five Valuable Pieces of "Junk"

- Ansel Adams negatives: Bought for $45, estimated at $200 million
- Copy of Declaration of Independence: Bought for $4, sold for $2.4 million
- Jackson Pollock painting: Bought for $5, sold for $50 million
- Eighties-era video game from Stadium Events: bought for less than $50, sold for $41,300
- Martin Johnson Heade painting: bought for $29, sold for $882,500

SEPTEMBER 14

Drive Through Traffic on the Shoulder

Life is too short for traffic.

—Dan Bellack, American author

Some people think there are two certainties in life, but there are actually three. Death, taxes, and traffic. Because if you are in a rush, you can bet your life you'll be running into some congestion on your trip.

Aside from sprouting wings, the only surefire way to avoid traffic is to take matters into your own hands and sneak into the breakdown lane. It's a risky move, but you're an important person with important things to do. You can't waste your time waiting for a horde of rubberneckers to get their ass in gear.

Check your mirrors and wait until the coast is clear. Before anybody realizes what's going on, ease into the shoulder and cruise past your fellow motorists. Ignore the angry honking and obscene hand gesturing. They're just jealous you saved twenty minutes they'll never get back.

Rest for the Wicked Pull back your side mirrors to avoid colliding with a fellow motorist.

World's Longest Traffic Jam

In August of 2010, congestion became so severe on the China National Highway that cars were backed up for sixty miles. The traffic jam lasted more than ten days, with some drivers traveling as little as .5 miles per day.

SEPTEMBER 15

Bet It All on Black

You cannot beat a roulette table unless you steal money from it.

—ALBERT EINSTEIN

To be a successful gambler, you could study probabilities and spend countless hours grinding out wins and losses to come out ahead. Or you could always bypass all that and just go for broke.

Betting your hard-earned cash on a spinning wheel may seem stupid, but how is it any different from playing the stock market? Besides, it's your money, and you are well within your rights to fritter it away however you choose.

Head to the casino and walk straight to the roulette wheel. Whether you want to bet $10 or $10,000 your next move is the same: convert it to chips and smack it down right on black. If you win, cash out your earnings and spend it on anything from an expensive meal to a new car. Just don't stick around the casino to find out how quickly you can lose it back.

Rest for the Wicked Leave your credit cards and extra cash at home to remove temptation should you lose.

Roulette Odds

- Any single number – 37:1
- Row 00 (00, or 0) – 19: 1
- First Column – 2.167: 1
- Black/Red – 1.111: 1

SEPTEMBER 16

Attend a Religious Service for Snacks

Jesus died for somebody's sins but not mine.

—Patti Smith

Regardless of your religious beliefs—or lack thereof—you can agree on one thing: free snacks are a good thing.

At first, attending a religious service simply to obtain free food may seem horribly dishonest. At second glance, it's still pretty awful. But hey, if there's one thing all religions preach, it's forgiveness.

Choose your service wisely. Not all religious houses offer free grub, and it would be a shame to sit through an entire sermon with nothing to show for it but a greater appreciation for your fellow man.

Once you've found your spot, pay attention to the other worshippers and mimic their behavior. If everybody sits down, don't be the only idiot who kneels. You'll stand out like a freeloading sore thumb. You only need to make it through about an hour of preaching before it's chow time.

Rest for the Wicked The more time you spend stuffing your face, the less you'll have to spend discussing dogma.

The Seven Deadly Sins

- Wrath
- Greed
- Sloth
- Pride
- Lust
- Envy
- Gluttony

SEPTEMBER 17

Fake an Injury to Cut the Amusement Park Lines

Success has always been a great liar.

—FRIEDRICH NIETZSCHE, PHILOSOPHER

The thing about amusement parks is that it's quite unamusing to wait forty minutes in line for a ride. If you want your thrills to be timely, you're stuck with the kiddie ride that creeps along at two miles an hour. By the time you get to the front of the seven-loop roller coaster line, the park is about to close.

Aside from buying those expensive member passes, it is possible to skip the lines by milking sympathy and feigning a hobble. Or a broken wrist. Or a sprained toe. When you're injured, you get to jump to the front with everyone's blessing.

Warm up those acting skills for your next park visit and get that spot in line you've always wanted. A prop is key, so make sure you've got a pair of crutches or a sling. (Who knew that old bike injury would come in handy?) Better yet, grab a wheelchair from the welcome center. With a few pitiful looks, you should be ushered to the front and having the ride of your life.

Rest for the Wicked Pick an injury that's not too serious. You want to be allowed to ride, after all.

Theme Park Thrills

The International Association of Amusement Parks and Attractions (IAAPA) found that rides are the number one reason Americans visit amusement parks. Roller coasters earned the favorite spot at 46 percent.

Claim a Store-Bought Dish Is Homemade

I was thirty-two when I started cooking; up until then, I just ate.

—Julia Child

People love organizing potlucks. Sure, some may view them as an opportunity for their guests to show off their favorite new dish or impress everyone with their best family recipe. But let's call them what they really are: an excuse for the organizer to shirk some of the party-planning responsibility. In other words, it's a copout. So next time you're invited to a potluck, bring a dish that you made at home—if your home is a grocery store.

The key to pulling this off is getting rid of the evidence before you arrive at the party. Remove the wrapping and trade in the black plastic tray for something from your cabinet.

When you arrive at the party, expect compliments on your picture-perfect dessert. There will undoubtedly be one guest who tries to call your bluff, but thinly veils it in a compliment by saying it tastes just like his favorite childhood store-bought baked good. Just tell him it must have been all the time and energy you put into it—then scoff at his lowbrow taste in snacks.

Rest for the Wicked People will ask for the recipe, so either memorize one you've found in a cookbook or food magazine, or just say, "Oh, it's an old family recipe. My mom would kill me if I told anyone!"

Best Store-Bought Dishes to Claim as Your Own

- Coffee cake
- Guacamole
- Salsa
- Cupcakes (just mess up the frosting a bit)
- Pound cake

SEPTEMBER 19

Go to a Strip Club

I think onstage nudity is disgusting, shameful, and damaging to all things American. But if I were twenty-two with a great body, it would be artistic, tasteful, patriotic, and a progressive religious experience.

—Shelley Winters

Maybe you don't want to be "that guy." Maybe you're a woman and worry you'd look out of place. Or maybe you're a die-hard feminist (male or female) and feel they're terribly degrading. Whatever the reason, it's time for you to go out and experience the bizarre joy of the strip club—if only just this once.

Now, we're not saying all strip clubs are created equal. Some are frightening places that attract the basest levels of humanity. Skip those. But plenty of clubs are surprisingly nice, even what you might call "classy joints," making them ideal places to spend a leisurely evening surrounded by well-proportioned women who just happen to take their clothes off. And contrary to popular belief, women are always welcome. In fact, some dancers claim they're the best tippers. So man or woman, gather some friends and some one-dollar bills and go make an evening of it.

Whether or not you stay true to your original opinion of these sordid contributors to American entertainment, it's worth going to see what they're all about. And if you find yourself enjoying the experience, even better.

Rest for the Wicked Bring only as much cash as you're willing to spend. Men and women alike have been known to get carried away with the tipping.

King and Queen of the Pole

The International Pole Championship is a pole-dancing competition held annually for women and men. The 2010 competition was held in Tokyo.

SEPTEMBER 20

Buy Stuff to Smash

To build may have to be the slow and laborious task of years. To destroy can be the thoughtless act of a single day.

—WINSTON CHURCHILL

In the movies, it's ordinary for characters to hurl dishes and pottery in a fit of fury. But in real life most of us won't even go so far as to punch a pillow. Instead we count to ten and bottle up all rage to discuss with our shrink later.

Even on a calm day, it's easy to imagine the thrill of wreaking havoc on your living room. A sideswipe to a lamp and a violent toss of a framed picture offer a far greater rush than your weekly kickboxing class.

Instead of dealing with the aftermath of broken valuables, take a cue from the movies and purchase your own props. Next time you see a yard sale sign or pass a Salvation Army, stop to gather some knickknacks and outdated electronics. At home, clear some space and lay down a tarp (you'll have to clean up, after all). Then let the refuse fly.

All those old relics would have wound up in the trash anyway; you'll at least have had some fun with them.

Rest for the Wicked With all the shards you'll create, you need protection. Ski goggles and a pair of work gloves is the uniform of choice.

Handy WMDs

- Bat
- Boxing gloves
- Crampons
- Hammer
- Slingshot

SEPTEMBER 21

Bike Without a Helmet

Believe me! The secret of reaping the greatest fruitfulness and the greatest enjoyment from life is to live dangerously!

—Friedrich Nietzsche

There are many great things about biking. It's environmentally friendly, efficient, fun, and inexpensive. Too bad you have to wear an oversized salad bowl on your head in order to ride one.

Sure a helmet can save your life, but it's also uncomfortable, hot, and ridiculously stupid-looking. They're fine for uncoordinated children and the elderly, but not for someone as graceful and athletic as yourself.

It's only protecting your brain, and how much were you really using that anyway?

Today, instead of delicately balancing pounds of plastic on your cranium, leave your helmet in the garage where it belongs. Feel the wind whipping through your hair as you fly down hills and zip in and out of traffic.

Since you don't have a helmet to block your view, take in the gorgeous scenery as you ride. But not for too long. You don't want to fall and hit your head—it's surprisingly fragile without protective gear.

Rest for the Wicked Keep it under 10 mph, or learn to fall on your feet.

Helmet Alternatives

- Turban
- Saucepan
- Plastic bucket
- Sponges and belt

Get Custom-Made Clothes

I base most of my fashion taste on what doesn't itch.

—Gilda Radner

A finely tailored suit can make an ordinary man look like a king. When the pants fit right, comfortably around your butt and breaking right at the shoe, you can stand on a sidewalk with your jacket flung over your shoulder like a Brooks Brothers model. And people will notice.

Wouldn't you like to look that good every day? Get your clothes all custom made. Take your ten favorite outfits to a tailor and tell them to go to work. The rest of your things you can give away. Then buy the rest of your clothes and have them all tailored to your specifications. Get your signature stitched into the back pocket of your jeans. Have your shirts cut in such a way that they're hugging your rockin' abs. Finally create those ironic and sarcastic T-shirts that you've kept stored away in your head all these years.

It's time to unveil the new you. It's the same as the old you, just shinier.

Rest for the Wicked Chafing can be an issue with printed shirts, so keep some spare cotton shirts in the closet.

Proper Fit Defined

According to British suitmaker Seiden Bach, a properly fitted suit should have the following characteristics:

- It should not be too loose, like you borrowed it from your older brother
- It should not be too tight, so that if you tighten your shoulders it will tear
- The buttons should rest slightly on your body
- The lapels should be flat when your arms are hanging loosely at the sides
- The pants should start at the navel, and the cuffs should be brushing the top edge of the shoe, resulting in a slight break in front
- The seat should not be too baggy, but also not tight enough to see the outline of your butt
- The undershirt should protrude ¼" to ½" from the jacket sleeves
- The collar should cover ½" to 1" of your neck above the jacket

Return a Broken Item

What we have to do, what at any rate it is our duty to do, is to revive the old art of lying.

—OSCAR WILDE

It happens to the best of us. Mere moments after opening a new expensive gadget we unceremoniously drop it on the floor and break it to a thousand worthless bits. The honest thing to do would be to head back to the store and pony up the cash for a new one.

But honesty is so overrated.

Sure you're the one who dropped it, but whose fault is it really? You wouldn't be in this mess if the thing wasn't so slippery in the first place. And how do they know it didn't just disintegrate when you opened the package?

Gather up any stray fragments of your priceless piece of technology and head back to the store. With the best poker face you can muster, calmly request a replacement. Respond to any questions about how it broke with a blank stare and a shrug of your shoulders. You may lose a few karma points for your deception, but at least you get to keep your hard-earned cash.

Rest for the Wicked Practice your "poker face" in the mirror so you can confidently deliver the line, "It looked like that when I opened the box."

Unreturnable "Broken" Items

- Diapers
- Tissues
- Chewing gum
- Prophylactics

SEPTEMBER 24

Lie about Your Age

Age is something that doesn't matter, unless you are a cheese.

—Billie Burke

You know what's fun? Being young. You get to do stupid things, make mistakes freely, and have a great body and wrinkle-free face, to boot. And while aging has its upsides—hello, acquired wisdom and legally available alcohol!—the grass will always seem greener on the younger side.

Fortunately, it's no one's business how old you are. So lie about it. If you're on the far side of thirty, hop back over that fence and be twenty-four again. Hit the bars in your favorite mid-twenties ensemble (tube tops for the ladies and button-down shirts for the men are still popular choices). Dance the night away in the club with some sweaty dude wearing Axe body spray. Find a local frat party and do a few keg stands. Flirt blatantly with the twenty-three-year-old barista at your local Starbucks. If anyone asks (but why would they?), claim to be sticking within your age range.

After all, you're only as old as you feel. And if you're feeling twenty-two tonight, by all means, go shotgun some beers.

Rest for the Wicked Make sure to keep your driver's license hidden at all times.

The Eyes Have It

You can't judge a person's age by their eyeballs. Why? A human's eyes will stay roughly the same size from infancy to old age.

Commandeer Control of the TV Remote

Men definitely hit the remote more than women. Men don't care what's on TV, men only care what else is on TV. Women want to see what the show is before they change the channel, because men hunt and women nest.

—Jerry Seinfeld

There's a lot of crap on TV. And, frankly, your family's tastes aren't cutting it. Flipping between *Millionaire Matchmaker, NYPD Blue,* and CNN isn't providing the kind of consistency of entertainment that you're hoping to zone out to right now. Plus they're watching too many commercials and missing too much of the key action sequences on each of the three shows you're trying to watch simultaneously. They've shown they're not capable of handling the responsibility of holding the TV remote.

The time has come to take control of the operation. Snag the remote and start captaining the ship. Your choice in entertainment is better than anyone else's who's in the room and your ability to accurately estimate commercial break times is unparalleled. Plus, you want to watch what you want to watch. It's that simple. The time for politely deferring to your family is over. Stage a coup, and take over the TV remote throne.

Rest for the Wicked Try to have spare batteries nearby in case an ensuing fight results in the batteries being ejected from the remote.

Death of the Channel Dial

The first remote intended to control a TV was called "Lazy Bones." It was developed by Zenith in 1950 and connected to the TV by a wire.

SEPTEMBER 26

Buy Out the Toy Store

As men get older, the toys get more expensive.

—Marvin Davis, American businessman

There's an unfortunate Catch-22 when it comes to the world of tin soldiers and china dolls. When you are kid and it is socially acceptable to play them, you don't have any money to buy them. When you are an adult with more money than you know what to do with, it's suddenly weird to play with toys.

Life sure can be cruel. Good thing you're too self-assured to care what anybody thinks about you.

Head over to your local toystore and start stocking your cart with all of the coolest toys that your parents refused to get you when you were a kid: remote-controlled robots, elaborate pretend tea sets, high-tech video games, low-tech board games, and every Barbie doll and accessory on the shelf.

If you feel a little creepy skipping past the cash register with an entire aisle's worth of toys, just remember, whether you're seventeen or seventy, you're never too old to enjoy a good toy.

Rest for the Wicked Be sure to read the instruction manuals before you start playing. A lot has changed in the decades since you were a kid.

All-Time Coolest Toys

- The Red Ryder BB Gun
- Radio Flyer Wagon
- Silly Putty
- Super Soaker
- Etch-A-Sketch

SEPTEMBER 27

Use the TV as a Babysitter

When I got my first television set, I stopped caring so much about having close relationships.

—ANDY WARHOL

You know that mom at playgroup who insists her children have never watched a second of television? She's a pain in the ass and not to be trusted.

Every time your kids start to drive you crazy, you fantasize about sitting them in front of the TV and escaping for a little "me time"—even if that just means drawing a bubble bath for yourself. Well, who says you can't?

These days, television shows like *Sesame Street* and *Dora the Explorer* are both entertaining and educational for young minds. Besides, a couple hours of TV never hurt anyone. You turned out just fine, right?

Block out the inappropriate channels so your kids don't accidentally stumble across something scary or graphic. Better yet, pop in a Disney movie or two or three and keep them entertained for hours.

Rest for the Wicked Resurrect the baby monitor so you can still keep a watchful eye on them if they start to fight or get into something they shouldn't.

How Do You Get to Sesame Street?

The quintessential children's television program *Sesame Street,* which first debuted in 1969, can be seen in more than 140 countries.

SEPTEMBER 28

Turn Your Living Room Into a Theater

You know what your problem is, it's that you haven't seen enough movies—all of life's riddles are answered in the movies.

—Steve Martin

Charging $15 for a ticket and another $15 for stale popcorn and flat soda should have sparked mass revolts by now. Instead, hordes of moviegoers fork over their hard-earned cash without complaint.

It's about time somebody took a stand. Today, you're going to boycott the overpriced theaters and create your own cinema experience at home.

The first thing you'll need is a proper big-screen. Don't waste your time with puny 55-inch TVs; think pull-down projector screens that cover the entire wall. Massive surround-sound speakers are a must, as are reclining theater chairs outfitted with cup holders. An old-fashioned popcorn popper and soda machine will complete the experience.

Now kick back and enjoy the show. It may have cost a small fortune, but your home theater will eventually pay for itself. You just need to watch a few thousand movies at home.

Better get started.

Rest for the Wicked Don't charge your friends admission. It's obnoxious and almost certainly illegal.

Films Worth Seeing in a Theater

- *Gone with the Wind*
- *Avatar*
- *Lord of the Rings Trilogy*
- *Apocalypse Now*
- *The Matrix Trilogy*

SEPTEMBER 29

Invoke the Five-Second Rule

If I drop food on the floor, I pick it up and eat it! Even if I'm at sidewalk cafe! In Calcutta!

—George Carlin

When it comes to cooking, there are few tragedies worse than watching all your hard work slowly cascade to the floor. You know you should just throw it away and start from scratch, but is it really worth all the extra effort?

Nobody saw you drop it. As long as it didn't land in a pile of pet hair, there's nothing a little a quick rinse in the sink can't fix.

Don't stop to think about the last time you mopped the floor. Simply grab the remnants of your meal and rearrange it back on the plate. Just remember, you may have to sacrifice the portion that actually made contact with the ground if your floor is especially dirty. Or at least make sure nobody is looking before you eat it.

Rest for the Wicked Blow on your food prior to ingestion. This will kill approximately 0.0 percent of germs.

Unsalvageable Foods

- Soup
- Pasta
- Cereal (if you've already added milk)
- Ice cream
- Pudding

SEPTEMBER 30

Create an Online Dating Persona of Your Ultimate Self

I've been on so many blind dates, I should get a free dog.

—Wendy Liebman

Any online dating veteran knows that "just being yourself" is the fastest route to standing Friday night plans with a container of Kung Pao chicken and back-to-back reruns of *Frasier.* There's a lot of competition out there, and the pressure to appear charming, successful, and devastatingly attractive in a 500-character profile can be nearly unbearable.

So why not fake it? Next time you edit your profile, don't make it for you—make it for the ideal you. Maybe that person is an architect or a stage actress or a commercial airline pilot. Maybe he's competed in the Tour de France and finishes four triathlons a year. Maybe she's done extensive postgraduate work on the plains of Namibia and has a vacation home in the Maldives. Maybe she's a spy.

Whatever it is, put it out there and see what you catch. Exchange some messages as your ideal self. Share your ultimate life experiences as fact. Have fun with it. After all, it's just a version of you that hasn't come to be—not yet, anyway.

Rest for the Wicked Your ultimate self should probably restrict his or her communications to the electronic variety. Keep your regular dating profile active in case you'd like to meet any matches in person.

Make Me a Match

Matchmakers in Manhattan can charge upwards of $20,000 for their services, with a bonus expected upon marriage. Who knew online dating was such a bargain?

OCTOBER 1

Purposely Fart at Important Life Moments

My philosophy of dating is to just fart right away.

—Jenny McCarthy

Let's face it. You're on stage doing something serious and everyone is looking at you. Maybe it's your bar mitzvah. Or your graduation. Or you're getting married. Who really cares? Does it really matter? Are you going to take this moment that seriously?

Hell no, you're not. Because you're in a tuxedo. And nobody is expecting it. And you're a comedy genius, which means you realize that there is nothing funnier than a well-timed, unexpected, loud and unignorable fart to shake things up. That's why you ate a can of beans an hour earlier, to prepare for this moment. And when it comes, dear lord, will it be glorious. Hire a videographer and instruct him or her to get reaction shots of your family. It will be the best investment of your life. This video may be the launching pad for your Internet fame, and you'll want to be able to show your kids the tape one day.

Rest for the Wicked Warn your elderly family members of what is to come. You don't want anyone to faint from shock.

Ways to Make It Up to Those Whom You Offended

- Apology cards
- Flowers
- Free whoopie cushions
- Coupon book for one free punch in the face

Jump Into Leaf Piles

Autumn is a second spring where every leaf is a flower.

—Albert Camus, French novelist

One of the things they don't tell you in homeowner school is that you will spend most of your fall weekends removing dead foliage from your lawn and organizing it into neat little piles. They also didn't tell you that it is impossible to shake the childhood urge to dive headfirst into said piles.

If only there were a way to indulge that desire without negating all that hard work.

Well, you're not the only one with trees in the area. Surely your neighbors have equally inviting leaf piles in which you can play. It seems their piles aren't nearly as orderly as your own. If anything you'll be doing them a favor by scattering the leaves again. Clearly they could use the practice.

Check around for witnesses before performing a cannonball right into your neighbor's pile. Take some time to revel in the leafy goodness: construct a leaf hat, build a leaf fort, fall backward and make leaf angels. Once you've had your fill, hightail it out of there before anyone catches on and hands you a rake.

Rest for the Wicked Wash your clothes immediately to remove incriminating leaf residue.

Dangers to Watch Out For

- Animal "leavings"
- Jagged rake tines
- Broken bottles

OCTOBER 3

Get Drunk Before Noon

An intelligent man is sometimes forced to be drunk to spend time with his fools.

—Ernest Hemingway

There's a universally shared belief that it is morally reprehensible to start drinking before 12:00 P.M. Most of us oblige without asking questions, but it's quite possible we're missing out on something magical as a result.

For starters, you are more in need of a drink first thing in the morning than any other time of day. A shot of tequila is at least ten times more effective at waking you up than even the strongest cup of coffee. What's more, imagine how much more enjoyable your day will be if you are already sloshed before it's even really begun.

Start your morning off right with a good, old-fashioned shot of whiskey, and wash it down with your favorite microbrew. If you prefer wine, by all means crack a bottle of your favorite vintage and sip away until noon. This isn't about getting trashed off whatever's cheap and available, it's about indulging in your drink of choice whenever you damn well please—not when society deems it's acceptable.

Rest for the Wicked Enlist a drinking buddy to help you with this activity. Drinking before noon may be okay, but drinking alone before noon is the epitome of sad.

Irish Coffee Recipe

6 ounces warm coffee
1.5 ounces Irish Whiskey
.5 ounces Bailey's Irish Cream

1. Brew a cup of our favorite coffee, add whiskey and Bailey's, and serve.

OCTOBER 4

Build the Ultimate Sundae

I doubt whether the world holds for any one a more soul-stirring surprise than the first adventure with ice cream.

—Heywood C. Broun, American Writer

For some things, it's important to set limits. Like how many cats to keep in a one-bedroom apartment. Luckily, the same does not hold true for ice cream.

The hard week you've had to endure calls for more than just a few scoops of vanilla. What you need are mounds of almonds, hot fudge, and a tower of whipped cream that reaches to the ceiling. In essence, the world's greatest sundae.

Since nobody's around to naysay your absurd indulgence, the sky's the limit. Start with a base of at least ten different flavors of ice cream. Don't waste your time with minuscule toppings like sprinkles and chocolate chips. Stick to big ticket items like bananas, entire bags of candy, and whole cookies. For the finishing touch, whip up a batch of homemade whipped cream and top your creation with a jar of maraschino cherries.

People often forget that fat is a necessary food group, and you've certainly got that covered here.

Rest for the Wicked If you lack a bowl big enough for your sugary creation, simply construct it on your kitchen counter and eat fast.

Vessels to Contain Your Sundae

- One or more punch bowls
- Garbage can (purchased new)
- Kitchen counter (eat fast)

Charge a Personal Item to the Company

I haven't reported my missing credit card to the police because whoever stole it is spending less than my wife.

—ILIE NASTASE, PROFESSIONAL TENNIS PLAYER

In the age of corporate credit cards, it can be incredibly tempting to charge something for yourself to the company. After all, most companies are highly profitable, and yet they continue paying you barely enough to live on. So next time the urge to buy strikes, go for it.

It wouldn't be prudent to charge an obvious, large-ticket item like a new bike or the *Friends* on DVD collection to your company. Instead, charge something small from an inconspicuous vendor—like a new planner from FedEx Office, or a book from Barnes & Noble. If you lump your goodie in with other items that you actually need for work, the chances of anyone noticing your rogue purchase are minimal.

And if you're really nervous about this undertaking, buy something super cheap, like a candy bar or a soda. You'll still have the opportunity to feel like a badass.

Rest for the Wicked Don't make a habit of charging personal items to the company, unless you want to land in jail.

For a Hamburger Today . . .

The modern credit card was first used in the 1920s to sell fuel to automobile owners.

OCTOBER 6

Sneak Into a Concert

For those of you in the cheap seats, I'd like you to clap your hands to this one; the rest of you can just rattle your jewelry!

—JOHN LENNON

So your favorite band is coming to town. In your lifespan, you've probably spent $500 on CDs, LPs, branded hoodies and T-shirts, posters, bumper stickers, not to mention that ill-advised fan-club membership back when you were 13. And now they want $80 for a spot in the nosebleeds, a place where your only hope of seeing the sweat drip from the lead singer's brow is on a giant screen?

No, thanks. This time, be a rebel and sneak in. How? Try scanning the perimeter of the venue for the weak link in security—the guy picking at his nails, eating a hot dog, playing solitaire on his smartphone. Then simply find a lively crowd of people entering the venue and work your way in among them. Look confident and casual, make eye contact, smile, and whatever you do, keep moving.

If anyone questions you, just say you must have wandered out looking for the bathroom. And if all else fails—run. Run like the wind.

Rest for the Wicked Wear dark or neutral-colored clothing so you'll blend in with the crowd easier if you're fleeing from security.

Other Ways to Sneak into a Concert

- Hop a fence
- Have a friend press their fresh hand stamp against your hand until it rubs off
- Pick up a small child and ask someone to open the back entrance door for you
- Rally the crowd and bum-rush the entrance

OCTOBER 7

Skip Work and Go to the Beach

Life moves pretty fast. If you don't stop and look around once in a while, you could miss it.

—FERRIS BUELLER

You wake up to a beautiful day. You are within driving distance of a beautiful body of water, beside which lie beautiful bodies basking in the sun. You long to be one of them.

But you are due at work in an hour. Accounting is expecting you.

The choice is yours: Finance—or fun?

Follow your gut—and call in sick to work. You know the drill: You have the flu; you ate bad Chinese last night; you've developed a sudden allergy to shellfish.

The only accounting you're going to do today involves beach chairs, bikinis, and booze. Type the location of the nearest ocean, river, lake, or country club pool into your GPS. Load up your transport with all of the sinner's accoutrements: towels, umbrella, ghetto blaster, sexy novels, KFC bucket, and a cooler full of Beach-Proof Margaritas.

Slip into the skimpiest bathing suit you own. Don a sunhat or baseball cap. And don't forget a killer pair of sunglasses.

You look good. You know you do. Now go play hooky.

Rest for the Wicked Use plenty of sunscreen. You can explain away a little color, but a bright red sunburn will arouse unwelcome suspicion.

Beach-Proof Margaritas

3 ounces tequila
1 ounces triple sec
½ ounce lime juice
6 ounces sour mix

1. Keep all the ingredients in separate, sealed plastic bags. Once you are ready to mix, pour the ingredients into an empty plastic soda bottle. Seal the bottle, shake, and enjoy straight from the bottle.

OCTOBER 8

Throw a Raging House Party and Hire a Cleaning Service to Clean Up the Mess

Nature abhors a vacuum. And so do I.

—Anne Gibbons

The plus sides of partying at your own place are plentiful. You get to show off your awesome digs. You always know exactly where the bathroom is. You can pass out in your own bed without calling a cab. You get to be in charge. But you know what sucks? Cleanup. Cleanup sucks so bad that chances are you'd rather pass out on a stranger's lawn than hose someone's vomit off your patio while nursing a Sunday hangover.

Luckily, this is why we have cleaning services. And while you may balk at the cost, just think of the time and effort and headaches you'll avoid. Plan a brunch with friends the day after your party and go nurse a mimosa while someone else sweeps up cigarette butts, scrubs sticky kitchen floors, and banishes whatever unthinkable things have appeared in your toilet.

Because house parties are fun, cleaning is not. Take the latter out of it, and you've got a recipe for some damn good memories—and an entire day to sleep them off.

Rest for the Wicked Cleaning services don't appreciate surprises, so make sure you tell them ahead of time what sort of mess they'll be dealing with.

Things to Remove from Party Areas

- Portable electronic devices (laptops, MP3 players, digital cameras)
- Anything breakable (vases, lamps, wall art, family photos)
- Rugs or pillows that stain easily
- Finicky plants that don't like being watered with beer

Create a Super Secret Candy Stash

Research tells us fourteen out of any ten individuals likes chocolate.

—Sandra Boynton, American humorist

There are two certainties when stocking an office candy drawer. 1) You will gain five pounds the first month; and 2) your coworkers will flock to the sound of rustling wrappers like moths to a flame.

Enter the double secret candy stash; Sharing is for suckers.

Just because you want an afternoon snack does not mean you should have to feed your entire office. If your coworkers like candy so much, they can very well buy their own. Besides, the last thing your hyperactive cubemate needs is more sugar.

First and foremost, create a decoy candy drawer with mints and licorice to draw attention away from your real stash. Now you need to find a hiding place for your real stash.

Storing your sweets in an unlocked drawer is simply out of the question. That's the first place they'd look. Instead, try more creative hiding places like a hollowed-out dictionary or your monthly expense reports binder.

Rest for the Wicked Dispose of stray wrappers immediately after consumption so you don't arouse suspicion.

Best Candy Hiding Places

- Underneath a loose floorboard
- Bucket labeled "Not Candy"
- Inside a box of granola bars

OCTOBER 10

Steal Your Friend's Stories to Make Yourself Sound Cool

A lie is just the truth waiting to be itself.

—TERRI GUILLEMETS

You know that story about your friend's wild night in New Orleans by heart because you've heard him tell it so many times. That big, crazy tale is a crowd-pleaser for sure—so why not make it your own? How about the time you caught the shark during that deep-sea fishing trip in college? That didn't happen to you either? Well, no one needs to know that.

The truth is, your life is pretty boring these days. You're at work on time every day and your bills are always paid—there's not much happening in the way of adventure. Adopting a few of your friend's stories as your own will give you the excitement you're lacking, Besides, without them, you might never get laid.

Rest for the Wicked To ensure you don't get found out, only use the stories when meeting someone new for the first time. That way, if they hear the story from someone else, they'll assume the second person was the one stealing stories from you.

Anatomy of a Good Story

- Look your audience in the eye
- Keep it short and simple
- Gesture with your hands
- Build up to the big climax
- Pause for effect

OCTOBER 11

Go Bungee Jumping

Jump, and you will find out how to unfold your wings as you fall.

—Ray Bradbury

There are few feelings more exhilirating than freefall. Whether it comes from a jump off the high dive or a drop on a roller coaster, once you're freefalling, you have no control over the situation any more. It's time for you to let go. Experience the ultimate freefall and go bungee jumping.

Bungee jumping has been in style ever since Alicia Silverstone did it at the end of the Aerosmith video "Cryin'". But unlike jumping from an airplane or the fall from a roller coaster, bungee jumping's thrill comes as much from the fall as it does from the rebound. It might be scary, but facing your fears is a big part of life. And it's safe . . . mostly. Plus doing some daredevil bungee jumping will give you some much needed street cred, which you lost ever since that time you jumped behind a bush when a distant firecracker went off.

Rest for the Wicked Wear a helmet.

World's Highest Jump

As of 2011, the world's highest commercial bungee jump, according to the *Guinness Book of World Records,* is at the Macau Tower in China. It stands 764 feet high, more than the length of two football fields.

Sneak a Horror Film Into Movie Night

The length of a film should be directly related to the endurance of the human bladder.

—Alfred Hitchcock

After a long week, it's finally Friday. Time for a nice relaxing movie night with a few friends. Best of all, it's your turn to choose the flick.

Unfortunately, it is physically impossible to select a film everyone can agree upon. You can, however, use the opportunity to mess with your friends. Particularly the one who refuses to watch anything but rom-coms.

To set up your clever prank, choose a horror movie with a rather ambiguous title like *The Red Shoes, Senseless,* or *Love Object,* and bill it as a heartwarming love story. Assure your friends that the dark, suspenseful opening scenes and creepy music are just metaphors foreshadowing a classic "opposites attract" love story later in the film. Then sit back and enjoy your friends' screams of horror as the first slasher murder scene ensues.

While the experience may be traumatic for everyone involved, at least you'll have the house to yourself when the next movie night rolls around.

Rest for the Wicked Make sure your friends don't see the movie box before the movie starts!

Least Romantic Horror Movies

- *The Human Centipede*
- *The Fly*
- *The Silence of the Lambs*
- *Alien*

Stage a Subway Dance Party

There is a bit of insanity in dancing that does everybody a great deal of good.

—Edwin Denby, American poet

Anyone who has ever ridden the subway knows there is one golden rule of commuting: You do not, under any circumstances, attempt to engage your fellow commuters. No eye contact, no smiling, and absolutely no talking.

Today, armed with a boombox and a total disregard for public humiliation, you are going to give your fellow subway drones a break from the constant monotony. They may not realize it, but deep down they are dying for a good old-fashioned dance party. If nothing else, it will give them something to talk about when they reach their destination.

While a boombox or a cell phone with a speaker are ideal, you can simply belt out your favorite tune and bust out your least embarrassing dance moves to start your impromptu episode of *Soul Train*. If the other passengers don't join in right away, don't be discouraged—your contagious enthusiasm will soon win them over.

Rest for the Wicked Plan your dance party around busy commuting times. There isn't enough room to turn around during rush hour, let alone dance.

Best Dance Party Songs

- "YMCA," The Village People
- "Billie Jean," Michael Jackson
- "Bootylicious," Destiny's Child
- "Dancing Queen," ABBA
- "Milkshake," Kelis

OCTOBER 14

Don't Bother Washing Your Hands

You know when I wash my hands? When I shit on them! And you know how often that happens? Tops, tops, three times a week.

—George Carlin

Our modern society is obsessed with cleanliness. We shower twice a day, we carry little sanitizer bottles with us at all times, and we'd rather die than eat something that fell on the floor. Whatever happened to the five-second rule?

Today, in the name of slovenliness, you are going to forgo the most sacred of cleaning rituals: washing your hands.

The first word that comes to mind, quite naturally, is "gross." But think about all the harm caused by constant hand washing. Without exposure to germs, your body is completely unprepared should one sneak through. By skipping the suds, you can fortify yourself against an attack.

Go about your normal day, but avoid soap at all costs. Not before you eat, not after you sneeze, not even after you use the bathroom. If you can't resist the urge to wash up, run your hands under some hot water for a few seconds. Just steer clear of anything with the word "sanitizer" on the label. You really don't want a substance that kills 99.9 percent of anything that close to your skin.

Rest for the Wicked Revert to the "fist bump" as your greeting of choice.

Foods to Avoid

- Chicken wings
- Hamburgers
- Lobster
- Tacos
- Cheese fries

OCTOBER 15

Invent the Ultimate Beau

When a man says that he is perfect already, there is only one of two places for him, and that is heaven or the lunatic asylum.

—Henry Ward Beecher, U.S. Congregational Minister

For single folks, nothing stings more than reminders of a significant other you most certainly do not have. Just once you'd like to give an answer to the question, "So, are you seeing anybody?" other than, "No, but my cat did something really cute today."

Instead of waiting around for Mr. or Mrs. Right, who's to stop you from making up your own? The perfect relationship already exists in your head anyway, all it needs is a name—and a made-up background.

Since your beau is imaginary anyway, dream big. Perhaps your new fling has a Ph.D. from Harvard and reads to the blind at the local children's hospital every Saturday. Did you mention he's the Duke of Norfolk? When your family asks where your dreamboat is, emphasize that he or she wanted to be there but had to fly to Europe to advise the King of France.

Don't think of it as a lie, just a few minor embellishments stacked together in succession.

Rest for the Wicked Give your new sweetheart a generic last name. This way, a potential Facebook search will yield some results (and boost credibility to your story).

More "Unique" Hobbies for Your Beau

- Plays in an acid jazz band
- Studies ethnomusicology
- Paints miniatures
- Does voice-overs for cartoons

OCTOBER 16

Cancel All Your Meetings

A meeting moves at the speed of the slowest mind in the room.

—Dale Dauten, American author and professional speaker

Just when you thought you were actually going to get some work done, your diligent computer calendar sends you a foreboding alert. Drop everything, it's meeting time.

Of all the copious distractions and time sucks in an office, nothing destroys productivity better than a group of people talking in circles for an hour. So why do you bother going?

Think about all of the times something useful has come out of meeting you attended. Can you count them on one hand? One finger?

Open up your calendar and wipe your day clean of every brainstorming session, progress report, team check-in, and anything that even resembles a meeting. Pretend to fall ill, invent an off-site project, whatever it takes. Just don't go within 100 feet of a conference room.

Instead of just sitting around talking about doing things, today you are actually going to get things done. It should be a novel experience.

Rest for the Wicked Take your computer away from your desk to work so nobody can track you down and drag you to a meeting.

Things Worse Than Meetings

- Performance reviews
- Company socials
- Organized company softball

Take Up Smoking

A cigarette is the perfect type of a perfect pleasure. It is exquisite, and it leaves one unsatisfied. What more can one want?

—Oscar Wilde

Smoking used to be the epitome of cool. Now most people would sooner admit they club baby seals for a living than reveal they indulge in the occasional cigarette.

For the most part, the stigma makes sense. Cigarettes smell bad, they turn your teeth yellow, and they cause all sorts of health problems. Which will make it all the more easy to give up when you take up smoking just for one day.

Grab your coat and follow the clouds of smoke to find the resident chimneys in your building. Most will be happy to bum you a smoke if you don't want to buy your own pack. Puff away and relax for a bit; you now have an excuse to sneak out of the office for five minutes every hour for the day. Which can be far more addictive than the cigarettes themselves.

Rest for the Wicked Soak yourself in Febreze to hide your temporary habit.

Cigarettes 2.0

In 2003, Chinese pharmacist Hon Lik invented the e-cigarette, a device that heats up a nicotine-laced liquid and produces harmless water vapor instead of carcinogenic smoke.

OCTOBER 18

Get a Full-Body Massage

To me luxury is to be at home with my daughter, and the occasional massage doesn't hurt.

—Olivia Newton-John

You pretty much have two opportunities in life to get massages. The first is when a new massage place is opening up in a mall, and they offer customers a free five-minute massage to give them an idea of what to expect. The other is when your significant other decides to be generous and offer you a massage. Usually it comes with strings attached.

But rarely can you really unwind and enjoy a full-body massage that completely relaxes you. It's time to treat yourself to such a thing. Find a professional massage therapist and get the full treatment. It's been so long, and your muscles are tighter than you think. Plus it helps with your circulation and relieves joint pressure. Lie down and get ready for an hour of professional relaxation. Once you're finished, you'll feel so refreshed, your muscles will feel loosey-goosey. You'll feel like you can do anything. It's the best investment you'll ever make.

Rest for the Wicked Do the masseuse a favor and shower up beforehand. Nobody wants to massage a sweaty, oily back.

Tips for Giving a Massage

1. Find a warm, comfortable location
2. Offer the massagee towels and pillows
3. Use massage oil
4. Use slow movements for a soothing feeling
5. When applying pressure with the thumb, provide support with the other fingers

Organize a Beer Olympics

The Olympics remain the most compelling search for excellence that exists in sport, and maybe in life itself.

—DAWN FRASER

Like blue jeans, alcohol goes well with everything. Whether you're on a first date or watching the president's State of the Union address, drinking has a special place in our most enjoyable activities.

One area we could use more alcohol, though, is in our competitive sports. That's why you'd be doing yourself and society a favor by organizing a beer Olympics. Beer Olympics can include softball, a three-legged race, and that game where you spin your head on the heel of a baseball bat five times and then try to cross the finish line. Incorporate alcohol into all of that. Not only will it be fun, it'll be educational: you'll see which of your friends has a real tolerance. You can even have a medal ceremony. It's not really drinking, think of it instead as a more challenging way to exercise.

Rest for the Wicked Have a designated puking station, especially for beer dizzy bat.

The Simplest Beer Olympics Game

Pick a word at the beginning of the night. Every time someone says that word . . . DRINK!

OCTOBER 20

Have a One-Night Stand

When sex is good there's nothing better, and when it's bad it's not bad.

—UNKNOWN

There's something enticing about the thought of meeting somebody, having a night of wild passion, and then never having to speak to that person again. Unfortunately you aren't that type of person.

Wait a minute, of course you are. Everybody is that type of person! Sure love and relationships are nice, but every now and then you need to skip all that mushy crap and fast-forward to the fun stuff. And there's nothing wrong with that—as long as your date doesn't extend his or her invitation past one night.

To find your temporary bedmate, belly up to your local bar and scope out the scene. When you spot a potential suitor at your local watering hole, spark up a conversation and keep it casual. Steer the conversation as far away from "relationships" and "intimacy" as possible. You want him or her to think of you purely in-the-moment. When the timing feels right, invite your pick back to your place for "coffee" (the international code word for sexy time). If he or she agrees, you're good to go. You should be able to take it from here . . .

Rest for the Wicked Prepare an exit strategy ahead of time. An early morning meeting or doctor's appointment should get them out the door.

How to Avoid Giving Out Your Number

- "I'm getting my number switched this week, so it wouldn't be worth it to give it out."
- "What's a phone?"
- "I thought I gave it to you already? Sorry, got to go!"

OCTOBER 21

Drop Everything to Fulfill a Life Goal

By working faithfully eight hours a day you may eventually get to be boss and work twelve hours a day.

—Robert Frost

Being employed full-time is quite the accomplishment, but unless you've somehow stumbled across your dream job, chances are you have more meaningful tasks filed under "life plans." So when do you start checking those off your list?

Try now. There aren't many life goals you can achieve while sitting at a desk for nine hours a day. So drop everything and go for it. If your goal is to complete the Appalachian Trail, take a leave of absence and get hiking. If you'd like to write a novel, request all your vacation time in one chunk and get a running start. If you'd like to drive across the country, collect some buddies and hit the road.

Why now? Because as the great Billy Joel once said, "Tomorrow is today." Get going.

Rest for the Wicked Life goals are great, but they don't always pay. Make sure you have a way to make the rent once you're done fulfilling your dreams.

Five People Who've Followed a Dream to Success

- J. K. Rowling
- Oprah
- Bill Gates
- Maya Angelou
- Barack Obama

OCTOBER 22

Cook with Expensive Wine

We owe something to extravagance, for thrift and adventure seldom go hand in hand.

—Jennie Jerome Churchill

There's an old saying when it comes to cooking with wine, "Never cook with anything you wouldn't drink." Well, today you're going to take that adage to the extreme.

If it seems excessive to pour a $100 bottle of cabernet into a smoking skillet, that's because it is. Delightfully, and deliciously excessive.

Whether you're making extravagant coq au vin or a simple chicken with pan sauce recipe you found online, go ahead and grab that vintage bottle you were saving for a special occasion off the shelf. If your wine rack is bare, head to the liquor store and buy the best bottle you can't afford.

Don't bother inviting over anyone over to share in your extravagant meal. This one's all yours.

Rest for the Wicked Be careful when chopping or dicing if you've been sampling the wine while you cook.

Top Five Wine-Producing Countries

1. France
2. Italy
3. Spain
4. United States
5. Argentina

OCTOBER 23

Steal Office Supplies from Work

Organized crime in America takes in over forty billion dollars a year and spends very little on office supplies.

—WOODY ALLEN, COMEDIAN

How many times have you been at home and realized that you desperately need but do not have paper clips, a stapler, envelopes, or all of the above? Somehow office supplies never seem to make it onto your grocery list, so you might as well just quit trying. The solution is simple: steal them from work.

Companies across the country are awash in office supplies, from 3-ring binders to tape dispensers. Supplies are available for employee use, so if you're an employee, help yourself! That's not to say you should cart out whole boxes of stuff, but surely no one will miss a Post-It cube here, or a ruler there.

Don't even think of it as stealing. Instead, consider your little office supplies caper as "utilizing the resources your company provides to the fullest extent." Even HR can't argue with that.

Rest for the Wicked Appropriate your goodies either before or after work to minimize your chances of being caught.

Revenge Is Sweet

A recent OfficeMax survey revealed that 6 in 10 Americans have taken office supplies from work to use at home. Not surprisingly, pens, pencils, and highlighters were the most commonly taken items.

OCTOBER 24

Ignore Oral Hygiene

I told my dentist my teeth are going yellow. He told me to wear a brown tie.

—Rodney Dangerfield

When you were a kid, brushing your teeth seemed like the most vile of punishments, second only to taking a bath or cleaning your room. The daily chore may not seem so terrible as an adult, but maybe your childhood self was onto something.

If you stopped worrying about your teeth, you could chow down on cotton candy, soda, and ice cream to your heart's content. Think of all the real estate you'd free up in your pockets by ditching breath mints and chewing gum. Our ancestors lived without toothpaste for centuries. You can live without it for twenty-four hours.

So leave your floss next to the sink for the day and resist the urge to pick up a toothbrush. Get creative and gargle with soda instead of mouthwash or floss with licorice rope. Sure it may be gross, but thankfully your family and friends are the ones who have to deal with your dragon breath, not you.

Rest for the Wicked Don't bathe either. The smell may mask your day-long morning breath.

Alternative Breath Fresheners

- Cardamom seeds
- Hydrogen peroxide and water
- Parsley leaves
- Cinnamon sticks
- Baking soda

OCTOBER 25

Assume a Fake Identity

We are what we pretend to be, so we must be careful about what we pretend to be.
—KURT VONNEGUT

No matter how comfortable you are with yourself, wouldn't it be fun to be someone else, even if just for a day? Why not go for it?

Buy a wig. Find nonprescription cat's-eye glasses. Style your hair in a brand-new way. Wear red lipstick. Become that guy who dons seersucker suits and carries a cane, or that woman who sports pink wigs and sparkly eye shadow. Adopt an accent. Assume a new name—a fun one—and introduce yourself enthusiastically wherever you go.

After all, this is textbook acting, and there are no limits to the person you can become. You might even like the new you so much that you decide to let your alter ego stick around indefinitely.

Rest for the Wicked Be sure you've carefully internalized your new name so you don't give yourself away by not responding to it.

Fun Alternate-Identity Names

- Veronica
- Beatrix
- Svetlana
- Claude
- Engelbert
- Thor

OCTOBER 26

Buy Something You Don't Need

Buying is a profound pleasure.

—Simone de Beauvoir (French feminist and writer)

Ever since you were a kid people have advised, warned, and nagged you about saving money. You've been told to open a savings account, start a 401K, think of your future, and, above all else, "avoid frivolous purchases."

That's all well and good if you don't want to start having fun until you retire, but what about the here and now? There's a lot to be said for living in the present.

A 70-inch flat-screen TV? A ride-on lawnmower? An indoor cloud maker? Sure they're useless and expensive—and you don't even have a lawn to mow—but that's beside the point.

Think of all the things you've ever hesitated to buy and then make them yours. Don't even take a moment to think about it, just break out your credit card and start swiping. It doesn't even have to be something that will last a lifetime. Splurge on an expensive round of golf or an extravagant meal. The more self-indulgent, the better.

Sure, saving money can be gratifying in the future, but spending it can give you pleasure right now.

Rest for the Wicked Bouncing a check or overdrawing your account will put a damper on your shopping spree. Make sure you have enough money to cover your purchases.

Fun Fact

The phrase, "Keeping up with the Joneses," comes from a comic strip debuting in 1913. The "Joneses" were neighbors of the strip's main characters.

OCTOBER 27

Park Wherever You Want

Politics ain't worrying this country one-tenth as much as where to find a parking space.

—Will Rogers

For some reason, the world's city planners have decreed that all the best places to park would instead be used to house fire hydrants, loading zones, bus stops, and taxi stands. Not exactly convenient when you are late for a lunch meeting.

A better person would drive around aimlessly and hope for the best, but not you. You gave up being a sap months ago. Today you're going to park wherever you want and the cops and meter maids can just deal with it.

Stop praying to the parking space gods and make a beeline for the nearest empty section of curb. Even if there are dozen signs that say "Don't Even Think About Thinking About Parking Here," just pull right up, lock the car, and go about your business.

You can worry about the inevitable parking ticket later. For now, just enjoy your lunch.

Rest for the Wicked Handicapped spaces are still off limits. You're selfish, not heartless.

Most Popular Parking Methods

- Camping – pull over and monitor a single street
- Stalking – follow people to their cars
- Wedging – squeeze into a space that's too small and climb out the window

OCTOBER 28

Hire a Personal Chef for the Day

One cannot think well, love well, sleep well, if one has not dined well.

—Virginia Woolf

Few things are as enjoyable as a homemade meal at the end of a long day. Unfortunately, few things are as stressful as making that meal.

Nothing about cooking dinner is easy or quick. You have to search through thousands of recipes and fight your way through the grocery store—and that's before you even get to the kitchen. Then you have to grapple with complicated instructions and unfamiliar techniques. It's enough to make anyone resort to fast food and microwave dinners.

The solution is as easy as it is perfect: Hire yourself a personal chef. Tonight, you'll see how it feels to sit back and relax while someone else runs around your kitchen. Instead of measuring quantities and prepping vegetables, you'll be measuring jiggers of gin and cracking open a bottle of olives. And while you're sipping at your martini, take a moment to appreciate your clever decision to stay in and order out the chef. You should reward your cleverness by hiring a personal chef for tomorrow, too. And maybe the day after that.

Rest for the Wicked Find a personal chef whose culinary tastes match your own. Love rare hamburgers and buffalo wings? Don't hire a chef who specializes in wheatgrass and silken tofu.

The Best Nights to Hire a Personal Chef

- A first date
- When your in-laws come to visit
- The day before a big meeting
- Your first night back from vacation
- A Tuesday

OCTOBER 29

Bump Up Casual Friday to Monday

Problems are only opportunities in work clothes.

—Henry J. Kaiser, American Industrialist

Four days each week, you suffer an eight-hour stint in scratchy suits and uncomfortable shoes while Casual Friday glimmers at the end of the work-week tunnel. Unfortunately, you can't speed up the calendar—but you can bump up Casual Friday to Monday.

This might seem like laziness or blatant disregard of company policy, but it's nothing of the sort. If anything, it demonstrates how closely you're following the rules.

Just take a look at your job description: It's the same on Mondays as on Fridays, isn't it. Of course it is. So why do you have to be all fancy for the start of the week? Monday isn't any better than Friday. It's not any more important than Friday. And if you've managed to meet company deadlines while decked out in jeans and a T-shirt each Friday, you'll probably be able to do the same on Monday. And even if you're productivity does take a dive, your positivity will make a leap in the opposite direction.

Rest for the Wicked People will take notice of your outfits on Casual Day and no one wants the office nickname of "Jorts" or "Jersey Shore." Be comfortable, but leave the embarrassing cut-offs and Affliction tees at home.

Swiss Neutrality

A forty-four-page dress code manual issued by a Swiss bank included instructions for men to wear ties that "match the bone structure of the face" and for women to wear only skin-colored underwear.

Toilet-Paper a House the Night Before Halloween

Today you can go to a gas station and find the cash register open and the toilets locked. They must think toilet paper is worth more than money.

—Joey Bishop, comedian

When you were young, if a teacher, fellow student, or parent offended your sensibilities, you did the brave thing. You teamed up with your friends, bought sixteen rolls of toilet paper, and anonymously TP'd the offending party's house. The person then knew they had violated some kind of social code and had to hang their head in shame as the neighborhood snickered at them behind their backs.

Get back in touch with your inner child and TP a house this Halloween. You had so much fun doing it as a child. It was a beautiful combination of fear and righteous indignation. Now that you're older and have dignity, the fear factor will be even higher. Plus, the decoration goes well with the holiday. It makes the tree look like it's celebrating along with everyone else. So join in the fun this holiday season, and let the toilet paper fly.

Rest for the Wicked Wear dark clothing and do the TPing at night.

Interactive Theater

At showings of *The Rocky Horror Picture Show,* when the character Dr. Scott enters the lab and the character Brad cries out, "Great Scott!" fans hurl toilet paper into the air as part of the audience participation.

OCTOBER 31

Go Trick-or-Treating

Nothing on Earth is so beautiful as the final haul on Halloween night.

—Steve Almond, American short story writer

As far as children are concerned, Halloween is one of the greatest holidays ever conceived. In a single night, one can accumulate pounds of delicious, tooth-decaying candy simply by donning a funny outfit and ringing doorbells. And the best part, no adults are allowed to join in—except of course to hold said candy when it gets too heavy.

But who is to say you can't join in the fun just this once? After years of dutifully handing out Mars Bars to the neighborhood ankle-biters, you've certainly paid your dues. Besides, it's not like there's not enough candy to go around.

While it helps to have a few children in tow (to blend in), there's nothing stopping you from wrapping up in an old bed sheet and hitting the town solo. If you stick to costumes that conceal your entire body, you might be able to convince the candy givers that you are a new kid in town who just happens to be a few feet tall for his age.

Rest for the Wicked Don't trick-or-treat in your own neighborhood, where you are likely to be recognized.

Cheapest Concealing Costumes

- Robot (refrigerator box)
- Mummy (toilet paper)
- Ghost (bedsheet)
- Kid with a Bag on His Head (paper bag)

NOVEMBER 1

Bake an Entire Cake and Eat Just the Frosting

Y'all can have your cake but that ain't $#%@ without frosting.

—Sam Adams, rapper

Let's face it, everybody eats cake for the sugary, creamy frosting on top. Without it, cake's no better than a breakfast muffin. In fact, if tradition didn't insist otherwise, you'd reverse the cake-to-icing ratio right around.

If you're really being honest, the truth is that you'd skip the cake altogether and just go for a delicious helping of the gooey florets and "Happy Birthday" letters adorned on top.

It's time to give in to the decadence and finally eat cake the way you like it. Whether you're a fan of cake mixes or prefer to bake from scratch, whip up a cake to use as your frosting platform. Don't get too picky because the icing is where the real work comes in. Using a piping bag, squirt tubes, sprinkles, and plenty of frosting tubs, spread on the sugary goodness thick like a Van Gogh. Feel free to be thorough or sloppy in your craft; just make sure you're generous in your adornments.

When your masterpiece is done, grab a fork and skim off as much as you can, gathering only a few crumbs of the layer below. The reward is like, well, icing on the cake.

Rest for the Wicked To prevent nausea or a severe sugar crash, don't attempt on an empty stomach.

Mother of Cake-dom?

Betty Crocker was not a real person. The Washburn Crosby Company of Minneapolis (later merged into General Mills) used the pseudonym to respond to baking questions, adopting an executive's last name and an all-American first name.

Listen to Your Favorite Song on Repeat

Happiness is the longing for repetition.

—Milan Kundera, Czech novelist

Variety may be the spice of life, but that doesn't stop us from eating at the same restaurant every Friday and rewatching the same sappy movie we've seen a hundred times. Perhaps variety is overrated.

Today you are going to take repetition to a whole new level and listen to your favorite song on repeat—a few hundred times. It's your favorite song after all, it's not like you're going to get tired of it.

Whether your tune of choice is a universal classic like "American Pie" or a top-40 train wreck like Britney Spears's "Baby One More Time," cue it up as the first and only song on your playlist. If your music device has speakers, blast it to full volume so as to share your monotony with the rest of the world. If anyone complains, resist the urge to switch to something else and just keep on rocking.

Rest for the Wicked Carry a spare mp3 player to avoid a continuity break in case the battery dies.

Musical Parasites

Psychologist Daniel Levitin coined the term "earworm" to refer to pieces of music that repeat in one's head. Some people are more susceptible to the effect than others.

NOVEMBER 3

Fake Sick to Get Waited Upon

The secret of life is honesty and fair dealing. If you can fake that, you've got it made.
—Groucho Marx

Being moderately sick isn't the worst thing in the world. You get to miss work, you can stay in bed all day watching TV, and most importantly, people call to check on you and see if you're okay. Some may even cook you tomato soup and wait on you hand and foot.

Alas, you're fit as a fiddle and completely undeserving of any special care today. It sure would be nice to get treated like royalty though. Well, like they always say, when in doubt, fake it.

All you have to do is force a few sickly coughs, lick your palms so they're nice and clammy, and put on your best "woe is me" face. If you live with someone, help should arrive shortly. If not, you might need to send some text messages. "Feeling sick, can't talk, very feverish," should get the point across. Suddenly an outpouring of concern is headed your way.

Take full advantage of your crew of get well-wishers, and send them out to get you everything from chicken soup and ginger ale to gossip magazines and DVDs. They won't mind, as long as it helps you along to a speedy recovery.

Just make sure not to give away your ruse, or your lackeys might just give you something to feel sick about.

Rest for the Wicked If anyone is taking your temperature, have a heat lamp nearby to get that temperature into the fever range.

Banking on Sick Time

The International Personnel Management Association says some companies are beginning to incentivize not using sick leave. According to a survey they conducted:

- 58 percent of companies cash out sick leave at retirement
- 45 percent offer cash/pay for unused sick leave
- 33 percent offer sick leave sharing/leave banks
- 11 percent convert sick leave to vacation time
- 9 percent convert sick leave to insurance at retirement

NOVEMBER 4

Make a Selfish Dinner

As a child my family's menu consisted of two choices: take it or leave it.

—Buddy Hackett

Whether it's nixing shellfish for your seafood-averse girlfriend or sticking to buttered pasta and fish sticks for your finicky kids, it might seem the closest you get to cooking something of your choosing is popping a Lean Cuisine into the break room microwave.

So tonight, make dinner all about you. Shrimp-stuffed crab cakes? Why not! Your girlfriend can order a pizza. Squid-ink fettucine with white-wine clam sauce? Sure. Your kids might just like that it looks like worms. Meatballs and mashed potatoes? That works too.

Because if you're the one doing the work, shouldn't the outcome be something you're excited about? And if you simply can't overcome the guilt, it's not too late to throw those frozen fish sticks in the oven.

Rest for the Wicked Make sure whatever you cook doesn't aggravate the food allergies of your significant other, family, or roommates. Sometimes being in the same room as the offending ingredient is all it takes.

Favorite Food

What's the most popular dish in New York, according to Foodspotting.com? The "Shake Burger," sold at Shake Shack kiosks around the city.

NOVEMBER 5

Get Back at Your Childhood Bully

Bullies are always cowards at heart and may be credited with a pretty safe instinct in scenting their prey.

—Anna Julia Cooper, American Teacher and Writer

He stole your lunch money, knocked your books on the ground, made fun of your glasses, and generally made your life a living hell. You may have grown up without any permanent damage, but the years of incessant tormenting simply cannot go unpunished. It's payback time.

Some would argue that by sinking down to the bully's level, you are no better than he was. Well, those people would be wrong. There's only one way to restore the cosmic karma balance, and that's revenge.

Thanks to the wonders of social media, your bully should not be too difficult to find. Once you track him down, unleash a little playground justice in the form of wet willies, Indian burns, and a torrent of childish name-calling. By the time you finish him off with an atomic wedgie (underwear over the head), he'll be begging for your forgiveness.

Rest for the Wicked Try not to enjoy the revenge too much, or you risk becoming a bully yourself.

Bully Survival Tip

- Don't carry more than $.33 in cash
- Never walk home the same way twice
- Pre-cut your underwear elastics, so they rip easier
- If cornered, aim for the genitals and run

NOVEMBER 6

Go Barefoot for the Day

If you scatter thorns, don't go barefoot.

—English proverb

When you get home from work, your feet are begging for relief. They're hot, they're sweaty, they're throbbing from being constrained all day. When you take off your shoes, the feeling of fresh air on your skin is like aloe on a cut.

The next time there's a day with the temperature over 80 degrees, skip that whole masochistic routine and set a new trend. Just go barefoot. Shoes will only hurt you. Not only do they smell bad and pinch your toes, they're dirty. It's no wonder. Name another article of clothing you wear every day. There isn't one. And your feet will smile all day from being free.

How can you walk outside without shoes on? Easy. You just do. Every college had that one person who didn't wear shoes and walked around barefoot every day. That person got by okay. For a day, so will you.

Rest for the Wicked Besides not wearing shoes, look otherwise presentable. You don't want to be mistaken for a hippie.

Best Barefooted Movie Characters

1. John McClane, *Die Hard*
2. Ed Bloom, *Big Fish*
3. Fred Flintstone, *The Flintstones*
4. Willie Scott, *Indiana Jones & the Temple of Doom*
5. Pocahontas, *Pocahontas*

NOVEMBER 7

Skip Laundry Day

It's better to have loved and lost than to have to do forty pounds of laundry a week.

—DR. LAURENCE J. PETER, AMERICAN HIERARCHIOLOGIST

Of all the chores we put off as long as is humanly possible, doing the laundry has got to be the worst repeat offender. It's not that it's particularly challenging or labor-intensive, it's just so hard to get motivated to do it.

As you sit there staring at a mountain of dirty socks and soup-stained shirts, think of all the valuable things you could be doing with your afternoon, like working on your tan or watching the grass grow. Your whites have waited a month already. What's another day?

Dig deep into the dark recesses of your dressers and piece together a hodgepodge outfit. If you can't find anything that even remotely matches, you can always settle for the least soiled contestants from the dirty clothes hamper. Wearing mismatched socks is a small price to pay for another day free from dryer sheets and fabric softener.

Rest for the Wicked Cover any noticeable stains with patriotic flag pins.

Alternatives to Laundry

- Turn clothes inside out
- Walk through a car wash
- Shower in your clothes
- Join a nudist colony

NOVEMBER 8

Toss Your Junk Furniture and Finally Buy Stuff That Matches

Spending is quick, earning is slow.

—Russian Proverb

At a certain point in life, it becomes embarrassing to host a dinner party where the guests sit on folding chairs and your ratty old couch is used as a substitute if more people than expected show up. Sure, your old hand-me-down furniture has sentimental value (that beer pong tournament where the other team had to do a naked lap), but at some point, you just have to grow up.

Translation: toss your old junk and finally, finally buy some furniture that matches. Your house will look better and you'll even feel better knowing that you a) have the means to, and b) care enough to buy yourself some real adult furniture.

True, furniture can be expensive. But if you shop around, you won't have to break the bank. Plus, you've got a way better chance of getting laid if it's on a nice new sofa, rather than the one that's been sitting in your parent's basement since 1982. Just sayin'.

Rest for the Wicked Set a budget before you start furniture shopping. That way you won't even be tempted to overspend.

Fun Furniture Facts

- Al Capone's business card said he was a used furniture dealer
- The IKEA catalogue is distributed to more than 180 million people worldwide
- The first tables referred to as coffee tables were made in Great Britain during the late 1800s

NOVEMBER 9

Take a Mental Health Day

I always arrive late to the office, but I make up for it by leaving early.

—Charles Lamb, English essayist

Monday through Friday, 9 A.M. to 5 P.M. You spend forty hours a week at your job. Chances are you've taken a day off for a dentist appointment or sickness. But do something even crazier: Take the day off for no reason.

All it takes is a one-sentence e-mail: "I'm not coming in today." Don't respond to the seemingly concerned response you'll get—the sender has ulterior motives. All your employers have to know is that you won't be there that day. You've got an appointment with your TiVo and takeout.

It feels good—freeing, even—to still be in your pajamas at 11 A.M. on the day of a presentation or deadline. But you won't know until you do it. Enjoy the day off while your boss worries about you. You'll be back in the office at 9 A.M. the next day, refreshed and with your own little secret.

Rest for the Wicked Don't tell any of your coworkers about your plan to take a mental health day. If you even tell one, word's bound to get out.

What to Do on Your Day Off

- Watch every show on your DVR.
- Order from all of your favorite takeout places.
- Hang out with all of your unemployed friends.
- Go see as many movies as you can fit in the day.
- Don't check your work e-mail. In fact, don't even think about work.

NOVEMBER 10

Watch Saturday Morning Cartoons

Wait a minute, ghosts can't leave fingerprints!

—Daphne, *Scooby-Doo*

Saturday mornings are known for two things: Nursing hangovers, and cartoons. As a kid some of the best times were waking up early on a Saturday morning, making eggs and toast, and sitting down to some cartoons. Of course, since the glory days of *Smurfs, The Incredible Hulk,* and *Alvin and the Chipmunks,* things have changed. That's why for both anthropological and sentimental reasons, you should wake up early and indulge in Saturday morning cartoons.

Do it just like you did as a kid. Wake up at 8 A.M., stay in your pajamas, cook some eggs and toast, pour a big glass of orange juice, and let the entertainment wash over you. Next time you speak with a six- to ten-year-old, you'll have something to talk about. And you'll actually wake up before 1 P.M. on a Saturday, and maybe even accomplish something. And if the current selection of Saturday morning cartoons doesn't live up to your expectations, just throw some *Saved by the Bell* on your Netflix. Technically it's not a cartoon, but the characters are close enough.

Rest for the Wicked For an optimal viewing experience, watch on a comfortable couch, with a light blanket nearby.

Best Saturday Morning Programming of All Time

1. *Soul Train*
2. *The A-Team*
3. *New Scooby-Doo Mysteries*
4. *Road Runner* cartoons
5. *Saved by the Bell*

Order One of Everything

You get fat in the moments between when you should stop and when you do.
—Michael Lipsey

Everyone knows the most difficult part of dining out is not picking a neighborhood, or even a restaurant in which to eat, but something much more critical—selecting your meal. Do you want fish or steak? Pasta or salad? Sometimes the choices are so voluminous that there is only one logical decision: order one of everything.

Your wallet is obviously going to take a hit from an activity such as this, but obvious benefits exist as well. You'll minimize ordering time and maximize eating time. You'll know exactly what you do and don't like on the menu. And you'll obviously have a fridge packed with leftovers once you're able to waddle home.

So go ahead and order it all—from the crab cakes to the chocolate cake. Gluttony is a word usually reserved for Thanksgiving and Fourth of July weekend, but let's be honest—shoveling huge amounts of food into your face twice a year just isn't enough.

Rest for the Wicked Wear stretch pants. Otherwise your jeans are likely to burst open mid-meal.

Offset the Meal Cost By . . .

- Coercing a friend into dining with you
- Slipping a dead bug into your ravioli
- Dining and dashing

NOVEMBER 12

Get an Expensive Haircut

I'm not offended by all the dumb blonde jokes because I know I'm not dumb. I also know I'm not blonde.

—Dolly Parton

Looking back on photos from high school, it's clear that everyone had some horrendous haircuts. Whoever thought that bowlcuts and curled bangs were attractive, anyway? Oh, we did.

Don't you ever wonder if you're walking around with the 2011 version of the mullet—a horrendous haircut that will be held up by future generations as The Worst Haircut of All Time?

We get it. Money's tight and the prices at the mall can't be beat. But remember: You can't put a price on dignity. Go ahead, spring for an expensive haircut.

Just think of what a good haircut did for Jennifer Aniston and Justin Bieber. That's right: instant fame. Before you know it, there will be a haircut dubbed "The Mid-Level Executive" or "The Between Jobs" and you'll have instant celebrity. And even if your new 'do doesn't catch on, you'll have gotten a scalp massage and the confidence that there isn't a rat-tail tickling the nape of your neck.

Rest for the Wicked Never say "yes" to frosted tips or perms. Not today, not tomorrow, not ever.

Famous Haircuts

- Jennifer Aniston's "The Rachel"
- Justin Bieber floppy 'do
- Donald Trump's comb-over
- Sarah Palin's poof
- Farrah Fawcett's feathered flip

NOVEMBER 13

Refuse to Share

There are only two things a child will share willingly—communicable diseases and his mother's age.

—Benjamin Spock, *Dr. Spock's Baby and Child Care*

It's easy to remember the kindergarten lessons that stick with you throughout life. Look both ways before crossing the street, don't bite people you don't like, and above all, share with others. But let's be honest—sometimes you just don't want to share a damn thing.

Lucky for you, it's not kindergarten anymore, so you don't have to. Of course it's the nice, polite thing to do, but everyone deserves a day once in awhile where they keep everything to themselves. So go ahead and hog everything you want, from your favorite orange highlighter to your French fries at lunch.

Don't feel bad about it either—it would be absurd to think that everyone else shares everything all the time. And if people do try to make you feel bad about not sharing, just let out a big sneeze and say "Sorry I'm coming down with something. What were you saying?" Chances are they'll leave you alone.

Rest for the Wicked Avoid ordering movie popcorn on days where you don't plan to share. Otherwise, you could start a riot.

Keep These Items to Yourself

- Used Kleenex
- Ice cream cones
- Nasal spray
- Religious views

NOVEMBER 14

Leave Your Clean Clothes in the Hamper

The laundry has its hands on my dirty shirts, sheets, towels, and tablecloths, and who knows what tales they tell.

—Joseph Smith

Congratulations, you've tackled the layer of dirty clothes covering the bedroom floor and come out victorious. All you have to do is fold up your now-clean laundry and neatly slide everything into its proper place.

If only it were that easy.

After all that sorting, pre-treating, loading, drying, and, of course, waiting, you must be exhausted. You can't possibly be expected to deal with hangers and dresser drawers now. Not only do you need a break, you sure as hell deserve one.

Plunk your hamper down on the floor and let it sit while you pour yourself a drink and kick your feet up. If you need any clean clothes, just rifle through and pick out what you need. There's no reason to put everything away just yet. It's certainly not going anywhere.

Rest for the Wicked Buy a second hamper to use for dirty clothes. Otherwise you will just toss them on the floor and the process will begin anew.

Methods for Minimizing Laundry

- Only wear bathing suits
- Line your pockets with air fresheners
- Walk through the car wash on your way home

NOVEMBER 15

Friends-Only Thanksgiving

Thanksgiving is an emotional holiday. People travel thousands of miles to be with people they only see once a year. And then discover once a year is way too often.

—JOHNNY CARSON

If you ask people what their favorite part about Thanksgiving is, you will probably hear a lot about turkey, gravy, stuffing, and pumpkin pie. What you won't hear is how much they love listening to their grandparents fight over whose arthritis is worse.

If you can't remember the last time you had a Thanksgiving with anyone below the age of seventy, perhaps it's time to invite the people you are really most thankful for: your friends. You've spent every Thanksgiving with your family since before you can remember; they can fend for themselves just this once.

So call up your closest buddies and set the plans in motion for your upcoming Thanksgiving feast. There will be turkey, there will be beer, there will be football, and there will be fun. And for the first time in years, there will not be a Macy's Day Parade.

Rest for the Wicked Make sure someone else in the family can host, otherwise grandma will never let you hear the end of it.

Buffalo Turkey Wings Recipe

4 tablespoons margarine, melted
4 tablespoons hot sauce
2 cooked turkey wings

1. Combine the margarine and hot sauce in a large bowl and stir to combine.
2. Place the turkey wings in the bowl and toss to coat with the sauce.

NOVEMBER 16

Buy Costume Jewelry and Pass It Off as the Real Thing

Maybe I'm paranoid, but in this day and age, I don't want something around my neck that's worth more than my head.

—Rita Rudner

How many times have you gazed longingly at someone else's jewelry, thinking, "If only I could afford that . . . ?" Sadly, most of us don't have a sugar daddy or sugar mama to buy us pretty things, but don't let that stop you from having beautiful jewelry.

Costume jewelry was invented for just this purpose. Although costume jewelry is often tacky and over the top, it's perfectly possible to find pieces that not only look gorgeous, but could pass for the real thing. So whether you've got your eye on a gold-plated watch or a set of pearls, find what you want, buy it, and wear it with pride.

People wear costume jewelry every day to all kinds of functions, so there's nothing to be embarrassed about. Chances are, once you've made and flaunted your purchases, you'll be the one people want to emulate.

Rest for the Wicked When shopping, consulting a jeweler is the best way to make good purchases without breaking the bank.

The Origin of Faux Fashion

Costume jewelry was created in the 1930s as a cheap, disposable accessory meant to compliment a specific outfit.

NOVEMBER 17

Cheat at Game Night

If you know how to cheat, start now.

—EARL WEAVER, MAJOR LEAGUE BASEBALL PLAYER

Sitting around all night playing board games is a rather boring prospect for a Friday night. Throw in the fact that you always seem to lose, and you've got the makings of a downright miserable evening.

Since you aren't about to waste your time perfecting your Connect Four strategy, you really only have one option if you want to end your losing streak.

Cheating.

Regardless of what games you play tonight, you are going to stack the deck in your favor. Both literally and figuratively.

Before you start, distract your friends with some snacks while you offer to set up the game. This is the perfect opportunity to sneak some extra paper money your way or take a peek at some of the trivia answers. Once the game starts, utilize subtle slight of hand to move your pieces closer to the goal.

It may seem a bit drastic and childish for a friendly game night, but it's worth it to avoid watching your buddy's victory dance again.

Rest for the Wicked If you are caught, pretend you didn't know cheating was against the rules.

How to Cheat at Popular Games

- Checkers – Distract your opponent and flip the board around
- Charades – Learn sign language
- Go Fish – Peek at everyone's cards

NOVEMBER 18

Stick It to the Resident Bar Tool

Someone has to pick up the tab when people get out of repaying their own debts.

—CHUCK GRASSLEY, UNITED STATES SENATOR

After a few drinks, everybody becomes a little less polite. You cut the bathroom line or steal the occasional seat at the bar, but nothing crazy. Every now and then though, you encounter someone who takes it to a whole new level.

Every bar has at least one loud, obnoxious patron who is only there to be a jerk. When he's not knocking over your beer or interrupting your conversation, he's trying to pick a fight with everyone at your table.

Although you'd love to crack him in the jaw, it would be far better to hit him where it hurts: his wallet.

Wait for him to initiate an argument (shouldn't take long) and offer to buy him a round to bury the hatchet. Now, promptly inform the bartender that the resident douchebag will be picking up your tab. He'll be so busy signaling the bartender for his free drink, that it will appear he's waving for your check.

Sure he'll be furious when you leave and he's stuck footing the bill, but maybe next time he'll think twice before acting like such a jackass.

Rest for the Wicked Be prepared to avoid your favorite watering hole for at least six months.

Other Revenge Tactics

- Distract him and pour salt in his drink
- Buy a round for everyone but him
- Pay the bartender not to serve him

NOVEMBER 19

Tear Up a Parking Ticket

A real patriot is the fellow who gets a parking ticket and rejoices that the system works.

—Bill Vaughn

After hours of aimless wandering, you've managed to find what looks like the perfect parking space. No fire hydrant, no yellow curb, and not a single "No Parking" sign in sight. Fast forward a few hours and you're stuffing a big, fat parking ticket into your pocket, at a loss for what you could possibly have done wrong.

The right thing to do would be to pony up the cash and try to be more careful next time. It would be infinitely more rewarding, however, to just tear it up and go along your merry way.

You pay taxes, you donate to your local fire department, haven't you given the city enough of your money already?

Take the ticket out of your pocket and unceremoniously rip it into a hundred tiny pieces. Find the nearest meter maid and throw the pieces into the air like confetti. That'll teach him for doing his job.

Rest for the Wicked Once you've made your point, pick up the pieces so you don't get fined for littering.

Methods for Avoiding Tickets

- Ride a bike
- Break the parking meter
- Leave a note ("Getting change, brb.")
- Be a cop

NOVEMBER 20

Let the Garbage Pile Up

Ambition is a poor excuse for not having sense enough to be lazy.

—Milan Kundera

Let's face it—taking out the garbage is gross. Inevitably something reeks in there, and half the time there's some kind of mystery juice from hell seeping out, which you notice only after it's dripped all over your floor. Then you take the lid off the outside garbage can and get hit in the face with a thousand filthy flies that've been feeding off last week's mystery juice. The whole process is dreadful.

So this week, go ahead and skip it. No one's ever died from letting the garbage sit there an extra week, right? It might even be a good time to challenge yourself to cut down on the amount of trash you accumulate. If you have a lawn or garden, throw things like eggshells and coffee grounds into a compost heap. Recycle bottles, paper, and aluminum as usual. Eat more leftovers. And if you're afraid to throw something potentially foul-smelling in there, like shrimp shells or leftover meat, wrap it up in a smaller plastic bag and tie tightly before tossing.

Because taking the garbage out every week isn't a hard-and-fast rule. And the less mystery juice you come into contact with, the better.

Rest for the Wicked Keep trash bins out of eating areas (kitchen, dining room, etc.) so the smell doesn't put a damper on meals.

Biodegradable?

How long does it take a glass bottle to degrade? Some experts estimate the answer at about one million years.

NOVEMBER 21

Adopt Your Neighbor's Cat for a Day

No amount of time can erase the memory of a good cat, and no amount of masking tape can ever totally remove his fur from your couch.

—Leo F. Buscaglia

Cats: You love 'em. But your significant other is allergic. Or your landlord won't allow them. Or you can barely scrape together enough change for Ramen and Kraft singles, let alone cat food. So why not borrow one?

The next time that friendly orange tabby takes a detour through your yard, lean out the back door with a "here, kitty kitty," a saucer of milk, and a dangling ball of yarn. Voilà—cat for a day! Drag that ball of yarn around the house until you're both exhausted. Curl up together in a sliver of sun for a long nap. Crack open a can of tuna and go crazy. Since your guest for the day is an outdoor cat, chances are his owners won't even miss him.

When evening falls, thank your new feline friend for his company and point him toward home. Consider it a vacation for you both—and your cat fix satisfied.

Rest for the Wicked If your borrowed kitty appears frightened or distressed, set him free and wait for a more suitable four-legged candidate.

Project Acoustic Kitty

In the 1960s, the CIA outfitted a cat with advanced bugging equipment as an espionage tool. Dubbed Acoustic Kitty, the project came to a halt when the cat was run over by a taxi during its inaugural mission.

NOVEMBER 22

Bid and Bail

If you must play, decide upon three things at the start: the rules of the game, the stakes, and the quitting time.

—CHINESE PROVERB

The rush of an auction house is something so few people actually get to experience. You'd love to up the ante on an iconic Lichtenstein painting or a Michael Jackson glove, but all those zeros lined up in the bidding price make it a little beyond your budget.

What no one thinks to ask is, who says you have to buy when you bid? At the next big auction, you don't and you won't.

Check the local papers for a chance to get your auction thrill. When the day arrives, put on your most sophisticated, "I have money" outfit and arrive early to scope out the competition. With bid card in hand, watch the big players as the auction begins and follow their lead. Really spice things up as the price climbs by waiting to bid until the very last minute and throwing in an exorbitant ante. Applause will break out when you finally win, at which point you can slyly duck out and bolt down the street. Now that's a thrill that money can't buy.

Rest for the Wicked To avoid getting caught, use an alias and face mask, à la Phantom of the Opera.

Best Auction "Wins"

- Vintage BMW
- A Picasso
- Madonna's cone bra

NOVEMBER 23

Ignore Price Tags

I buy expensive suits. They just look cheap on me.

—Warren Buffett

This must be how the wealthy live—or at least those with unlimited credit cards. Take yourself out shopping for the day and pay no mind to the number on the price tag. In fact, don't even look at the price tags. When the girl rings you up at the register, tell her you'd rather not know the total. Just swipe your card and worry about the money later.

When you're not worrying about money, the shopping experience is all about the look and feel of the clothes. Try on elegant ball gowns or sharply cut suits. That cashmere sweater sure does feel nice to the touch. Why not buy two? A different pair of fancy underwear for every day of the year? Sure! When money is no object, no object is off limits.

Rest for the Wicked Become familiar with the store's return policy and save all receipts so you can make any necessary returns once the inevitable buyer's remorse sets in.

Making Extra Cash to Pay Off Your Credit Card

- Babysit your neighbors' kids
- Donate sperm/eggs
- Sell old books and clothes
- Get a second job bartending at night
- Have a garage sale

NOVEMBER 24

Become a Parking Meter Vigilante

The early bird gets a parking spot and the next guy gets a ticket . . . that's how it works for us, unfortunately.

—GARY CUNNINGHAM, COLLEGE BASKETBALL COACH

Sometimes it seems like everyone's out to get you when you're driving a car. If it's not a disgruntled cop ticketing you for disobeying the speed limit, it's a cyclist cutting you off or a pedestrian playing Frogger outside of a crosswalk. But the worst of all are meter maids. They have one goal and one goal only: to ruin a driver's day. Why not save them the pleasure and put money in your fellow drivers' expired meters?

If possible, wait until a meter maid is approaching. Lean nonchalantly against an expired meter, and when the villain whips out a ticketing pad, watch that smug smile fade away as you slip a quarter into the meter. Sure, you'll have made one enemy, but your fellow drivers will consider you a superhero.

Not only are you preventing someone's day from being ruined, you're making someone's day. A quarter is worth much more than twenty-five cents when it saves someone a $25 ticket.

Rest for the Wicked The ticket is recorded the second the maid's pen hits the paper, so make sure to get there before that happens.

Potential Superhero Names (Every Vigilante Needs One)

- The Meter Maiden
- The Ticket Taker
- The Defender of the Fender
- The Parking Protector
- The Driver Defender

NOVEMBER 25

Pimp Your Ride

When buying a used car, punch the buttons on the radio. If all the stations are rock and roll, there's a good chance the transmission is shot.

—Larry Lujack, disc jockey

What you drive says a lot about you. And your silver four-door Honda sedan with a dent on the side isn't sending the right message. The time has come to do as Xzibit says and pimp your ride.

Never mind that you'll spend thousands of dollars on a car that's probably worth a fraction of that. That's the point. First, of course, you'll need a brand new interior. Get some decals on the side, some fire coming out of rocket launchers would work well. Of course you need a new speaker system and those subwoofers that make your front two tires bounce up and down like you're in a Dr. Dre video. In addition, you'll need high-def TV screens in the backs of the headrests, two PlayStation 3 systems for each TV set, and a home theatre system in your trunk. And, of course, a popcorn machine for when you're watching movies out of your trunk.

Even if you can't live the pimp life, you can pretend.

Rest for the Wicked While you're at it, get state-of-the-art airbags, perhaps made of cashmere.

Rejected "Pimp My . . . " ideas before MTV settled on "Pimp My Ride"

- Pimp My Toilet
- Pimp My Family Photo Albums
- Pimp My Pet
- Pimp Eye for the Lame Guy

NOVEMBER 26

Have Sex on Your Boss' Desk

If you think your boss is stupid, remember: you wouldn't have a job if he was any smarter.

—John Gotti

Perhaps it's part of their DNA, or maybe it's thanks to something in their coffee, but there is one universal fact that every boss in the world shares—they're all assholes. Each and every one of them.

Just once, you're going to stick it to your horrible troll of a boss and pay her back for that time she made you stay late on Friday to organize her collection of antique cookie jars. And what better way to do that than to invite your partner over for a late night rendezvous and violate your boss's desk?

Wait until the rest of your coworkers are gone and check the office and surrounding area for surveillance cameras. Once you are certain it's just you, your partner, and the wall, it's time to scurry into the boss' office and get your revenge on. Make it quick, but make sure you take the time roll around all over the antique mahogany.

Now every time she calls you into her office to chew you out, you can take comfort in the knowledge that your bare butt once rested in the same place she keeps her "Best Boss" coffee mug.

Rest for the Wicked Resist the urge to chronicle your exploits with a digital camera. It's bound to make its way onto the Internet somehow.

Other Revenge Options

- Pour laxative in her coffee
- Fill her office with packing peanuts
- Change the default language on her computer to Chinese

NOVEMBER 27

Commission a Self-Portrait

Few persons who have ever sat for a portrait can have felt anything but inferior while the process is going on.

—ANTHONY POWELL, NOVELIST

After searching for weeks, you still haven't been able to find a piece of artwork that looks perfect above your fireplace. Everything is too small, too ugly, or too weird. What's a person to do?

Commission a self-portrait, of course! Once reserved exclusively for the rich and famous, self-portraits are a fabulous way to both decorate your home and serve your ego in one fell swoop. Whether you mimic Demi Moore's infamous naked-while-pregnant portrait, or go for something a little more traditional, you're sure to wow family, friends, and yourself every single day with your stunning artwork.

At first, hanging a large portrait of yourself in your home might seem a little weird. But remember that most people have photos of themselves, their spouses, their kids and their dogs all over their homes. You're doing the same thing—just in a more expensive, larger way. Guaranteed that once you have a self-portrait, all of your friends will want one too.

Rest for the Wicked Don't commission a friend to paint your portrait—if it turns out badly, your friendship may be ruined.

Self-Portrait Poses to Consider

- The Thinker
- The Captain Morgan
- The Mr. Clean
- The Superman

Rock Out in the Shower

There's no half-singing in the shower. You're either a rock star or an opera diva.
—Josh Groban, American singer and songwriter

Singing out loud can be fun and therapeutic, but most of us would rather die than hum a few bars in public. Luckily there's one place where everyone can sing like a rock star without feeling self-conscious: the bathroom.

You may lack the confidence to perform on stage, but you should be able to handle an audience of shampoo bottles and body wash.

Invest in some waterproof speakers and cue up your favorite guilty pleasure song. You're all alone anyway, so nobody's going to judge your taste in music. Grab a loofah microphone and put on the performance of your life. Butcher the lyrics and mangle the high notes.

If anybody does overhear, just ignore the bangs on the door and pleas to quiet down. A true star stops rocking for no one.

Rest for the Wicked Resist the urge to break into a choreographed dance in your tub.

Soundproofing Your Shower

- Close all windows
- Turn on the fan to create white noise
- Stuff towels underneath the door
- Set the water to the highest (read: loudest) setting

NOVEMBER 29

Buy Shoes for Every Occasion

Always wear expensive shoes. People notice.

—BRIAN KOSLOW, AMERICAN AUTHOR

According to a 2007 poll by Consumer Reports, the average woman only owns nineteen pairs of shoes. If you think the use of the word "only" is inappropriate, then you are clearly reading the wrong book.

Whether you're a man or woman, nineteen pairs of shoes is barely enough to cover the basics. You may be able to handle job interviews and going to the gym, but good luck if you get invited to a traditional Swedish clog-dancing festival. Unlike the rest of the under-prepared savages out there, perhaps you should invest more in the future of your feet.

Head straight to your local shoe emporium and start combing the aisles in search of the perfect shoes for every situation. Stock up on enough dress shoes, sneakers, slippers, sandals, boots, and cleats to last a lifetime. It doesn't matter if you have to rent out a storage unit to house them all. You'll never be caught without the appropriate footwear again.

Rest for the Wicked If the perfect shoe doesn't fit, just suck it up and squeeze in. Pain is beauty.

Best Shoes for the Occasion

- Wedding: Polished black loafers (men); Pumps with a modest heel (women)
- First date: Brown oxfords (men); Open-toed slingbacks with a kitten heel (women)
- Rain forest hike: Hip waders (both)

Send Back a Mediocre Meal

The food here is terrible, and the portions are too small.

—Woody Allen

Everyone knows what it's like to sit anxiously in a restaurant, gazing at every plate that passes by, wondering, "Is it mine?" Anticipation mounts as the server finally places your plat du jour on the table. You dig in, excited for your prize, until after one bite you realize your food kind of sucks.

Usually you would just eat it anyway, muttering under your breath about sliding restaurant standards. But alas, no more. Today you are going to finally grow the cojones for something you've been aching to do for years—send it back!

So summon both your courage and the waiter. Kindly explain that the meal does not meet your standards—whether the steak is undercooked or the broccoli is overcooked. Make sure you are overflowing with politeness and ask them to fix it—you should have a delicious plate in front of you in no time. After all, you're paying for this, so you have every right to get what you want.

Rest for the Wicked Never signal a waiter by snapping your fingers—unless you want a few surprises in your food.

Foolproof at Any Restaurant

- Water
- Bread
- Ice cream

DECEMBER 1

Have a Little-Kid Birthday Party

No matter how desperate we are that a better self will emerge, with each flicker on the cake, we know it's not to be. And for the rest of our sad, wretched, pathetic lives, this is who we are to the bitter end. Inevitably, irrevocably. Happy birthday? No such thing.

—JERRY SEINFELD

After you hit the big 2-1, birthdays became a little anticlimactic. Unless you're counting down the days to declare your presidential plans, you probably view the anniversary of yourself with a mixture of dread and antipathy.

You can't turn the clock around, but you can bring some fun of single-digits birthday parties into your twenties and thirties.

The first step in a little kid birthday party is buying some fill-in-the-blank stationery and inviting all your closest pals to celebrate your special day. Make sure they know that presents are expected. The evening will start at McDonald's (a birthday toast over orange soda, anyone?) and end with a bowling party—bumper bowling, that is. It's your birthday, after all, and there will be no zero-point frames for you. During downtime between games, open your presents in front of everyone and enjoy the entertainment of Bubbles the Clown and his balloon animals. Finally, even if everything is going your way, feel free to a throw a temper tantrum or two. After all, it's your birthday and you'll cry if you want to.

Rest for the Wicked Avoid any possible charges of pedophilia. Make this an adults-only party and steer clear of any families.

Make the Most of the Party

- Exchange your orange soda for "suicides" (a mix of every single fountain soda available)
- Ask Bubbles to make "adult" balloon animals
- Include a gift registry with your invitations
- Don't send thank-you cards (your mom will be so mad!)
- Hand out goodie bags stuffed with booze and condoms

DECEMBER 2

Hire an Assistant

Happy is the man with a wife to tell him what to do and a secretary to do it.
—Benjamin Mancroft, House of Lords

Somehow there's never enough time in the day to finish everything you need to do. Those pesky little tasks like doing your laundry and paying your bills just seem to pile up, adding even more stress to your already busy life. Not. Worth. It.

To minimize task-time and maximize play-time, hire an assistant. Whether it's a recent college grad desperate to get some work experience or your fifteen-year-old sister who just wants to escape your parents, you can absolutely find and train someone to do all those little things you hate. Never again will you miss the deadline for paying rent, or fail to iron your favorite blouse before an important meeting.

Just think how much happier, easier, and more stress-free your life will be with an assistant to handle the mundane. If it's good enough for corporate America, it's good enough for you.

Rest for the Wicked Pay your assistant under the table to escape any sort of IRS intrusion.

The Least They Can Do

Use Administrative Professionals Day to recognize your assistant for everything he or she does. This floating holiday, which used to be called Secretaries Day, falls in the last full week of April.

DECEMBER 3

Tell Off Your Boss by Anonymous E-mail

Accomplishing the impossible means only that the boss will add it to your regular duties.

—Doug Larson

Your boss is kind of a jerk sometimes. Your boss makes you do work, corrects your so-called mistakes, makes more money than you, and sits in a bigger office. What a jerk. You tell people about it over drinks after work and with your friends at dinner. But it's high time you tell your boss directly.

Of course you don't have the cojones or the financial capital to afford that. The obvious solution is to send an anonymous e-mail. Set up a fake e-mail account that wouldn't ever be linked to you, write out everything you ever wanted to tell your boss, and edit it for expletives. If you don't do it, your boss will never stop being a jerk. He'll never correct his little habit of clicking his cheek when he's done asking you for a favor. And he'll never stop leaning back in his chair with his legs crossed like a smug jerk. So do the courageous thing: anonymously send an e-mail detailing all your boss's shortcomings. You'll be an office hero, even if no one can ever know it.

Rest for the Wicked Use a public computer for everything so the IP address can't be traced back to you.

Most Annoying Workplace Habits

- Keeping the office kitchen a mess
- Listening to your radio without earphones
- Leaving the toilet seat wet and unusable
- Eating a lunch that smells up the whole office
- Humming/singing

DECEMBER 4

Slide Down the Banister

As you slide down the banister of life, may the splinters never point the wrong way.

—OLD IRISH BLESSING

Bart Simpson was hardly the first fictional person to slide down the banister, but he certainly made it fashionable and opened the practice up to a wider audience. But instead of ending your journey with a loud, off-screen thud like Bart, a successful slide down the banister ends like a gymnastics routine—with a graceful landing. That's why it's important to not be carrying bulky, cumbersome items while sliding. They could compromise the entire endeavor.

There are any number of reasons to slide down the banister. In this modern world where time is a luxury, sliding down the banister is a quicker way to get from point A to point B. Maybe there's a subway train about to depart that you need to catch. Or you're running from a predator. Maybe you don't want to touch the disease-ridden banister with the same hands you feed yourself with. Or maybe you're just trying to impress a passing stranger. Either way, it's a great way to travel in style. And it's damn fun.

Rest for the Wicked Before you decide to slide, make sure the banister ends with a smooth curve down and not with a pointy knob or engraved figurine.

Banister-Sliding Hall of Fame

Mary Poppins may be the all-time greatest banister slider. In addition to traveling by umbrella and jumping into sidewalk paintings, Mary has the ability to slide *up* banisters.

DECEMBER 5

Go on a "Supermarket Sweep" at the Grocery Store

They don't have a decent piece of fruit at the supermarket. The apples are mealy, the oranges are dry. I don't know what's going on with the papayas!

—MICHAEL RICHARDS, *SEINFELD*

There's no need to concern yourself with such delicate and time-consuming aisles like the produce department or the deli counter when doing a "Supermarket Sweep." No. The point here is to race through the grocery store as fast as possible while filling your shopping cart as much as possible. Have a friend time you, putting two minutes on the stop watch and counting down across the PA system when you have only ten seconds to go.

On the show, the best part was always the cereal aisle. The contestant would fly past the shelves, scooping row upon row of boxes into their cart as they went. Follow suit by stocking up on packaged desserts, pasta sauce, olives—whatever you pass by belongs in the cart. Canned corn? You'll take twenty. Pickles? You'll need at least fifteen. It's not like you have a shopping list, so there's really nothing to forget. Changes are you'll never actually be on a game so, so now's the time to indulge your fantasy.

Rest for the Wicked Since money is no object here, make sure you have enough in your account to cover your purchases. Also helpful is a car big enough to get all those boxes of cereal home.

Trivia

The original *Supermarket Sweep* game show first aired in 1965 on ABC and was hosted by Bill Malone.

Upgrade to First Class

Airline travel is hours of boredom interrupted by moments of stark terror.

—Al Boliska, Canadian radio personality

Once the novelty of featherless flight wears off, the experience of traveling in an airplane is pretty abysmal. Dozens of sweaty, smelly passengers crammed into miniature seats with nothing but a bag of peanuts and uncomfortable headphones to distract them. Unless, of course, you fly first class.

Sadly, first class is expensive, unnecessary, and elitist. But then again, who cares? What's a few extra bucks when your personal comfort is at stake? If it means you can trade in the screaming infants and Salisbury steak for fuzzy slippers and a decent meal, then it's worth it.

If you have a vacation planned, now's the time to give your travel agent a call and work some magic. You might even be able to use some frequent flyer miles to get the first class bump. If there aren't any trips in your immediate future, then book yourself a short first-class jaunt. You'll feel like a jet-setting movie star, if only for a few hours.

Rest for the Wicked Book a seat as close to the front as possible. You'll be farther away from the peasants sitting in coach.

Transform Coach Into First Class

- Mix seltzer and orange juice into makeshift mimosas
- Bring your own bag of macadamia nuts to replace peanuts
- Arrange pillows on your chair for a more comfortable seat

DECEMBER 7

Take a Vacation by Yourself

A vacation frequently means that the family goes away for a rest, accompanied by a mother who sees that the others get it.

—Marcelene Cox

Few aspects of life create as much excitement and anticipation as the beautiful word loved by eighth graders and eighty-year-olds alike: vacation. Sure they sound great on paper, but let's get real—vacations mean headaches, stress, and annoyances, usually caused by one's traveling companions.

So this year, avoid all of that nonsense by doing something so simple you'll wish you'd thought of it years ago—take a vacation by yourself. Whether you want a spa weekend in the Caribbean or a ski vacation in Colorado, you will finally get the peace and quiet you deserve.

Not to mention, there won't be any fights about where to eat dinner or which souvenir T-shirt to buy, ensuring that your familial relationships will be securely intact when you get home. There's always your annual summer trip to Florida to open that can of worms.

Rest for the Wicked If needed, invent a plausible excuse so the kids won't want to go with you. A knitting convention comes to mind.

For a Kid-Free Vacation, Avoid . . .

- Disney World
- Disneyland
- EuroDisney
- Pretty much anything Disney

DECEMBER 8

Walk Around in a Bathrobe All Day

I don't want to look like a weirdo. I'll just go with the muumuu.

—HOMER SIMPSON

You may have yourself convinced your work clothes are perfectly comfortable, but let's face it, your comfiest suit doesn't even hold a candle to your bathrobe.

It seems kind of silly that you only wear your most luxurious garment for a few minutes each day. Just this once, you're going to get a little more use out of it.

When you get out of the shower, reach for your cushiest bathrobe and wrap yourself in its warm, soothing embrace. Instead of treating it as a piece of transition clothing, wear it around and go about your life as normal. Walk the dog, run errands, head to yoga class—all in the comfort and style of a robe.

Better yet, go to dinner and/or drinks in the robe, ignoring any protests by front-of-house staff. Smoke cigars and read the paper as you see fit.

If anyone asks why you're wearing a bathrobe in public, just roll your eyes and keep on strutting. Haters gonna hate.

Rest for the Wicked Secure your robe tightly or risk flashing the entire restaurant.

Notorious Robe Wearers

- Hugh Hefner
- Monks
- Freelancers
- Hogwarts students
- The elderly

DECEMBER 9

Bum a Ride Off Your Bud

A good friend is someone who thinks you are a good egg although he knows you're slightly cracked.

—Bernard Meltzer, Radio Host

Though most people can drive, not everyone likes doing it. It's hard finding pleasure in coasting along the same route to work, home, and the grocery store. In fact, it can be so "pleasure-less" that using deception to get out of driving feels rather shameless.

The next time you plan on driving to meet your pals, force them to come get you. You deserve a break, and it wouldn't hurt to save a little gas. Tell your pals that your car is in the shop and that your bike just won't cut it. Make sure to park your vehicle up the street so your friends won't see it when they pick you up.

If your friends give you any trouble, promise to pick them up next time. Buy them a drink or two but make sure they don't overdo it. They are your automatic designated drivers tonight, after all.

Rest for the Wicked Make sure to come up with a "car problem" to bitch about at the bar. It will make your situation more believable.

Viable Car Issues

- "The starter died."
- "I forgot to get the oil changed."
- "The A/C won't work and it's hot out, bro."

DECEMBER 10

Eat Only at Four-Star Restaurants All Day

Nouvelle cuisine, roughly translated, means: I can't believe I paid ninety-six dollars and I'm still hungry.

—Mike Kalin

If you're like the rest of us, you eat at four-star restaurants once every ten years or so. You then proceed to live off the glory of that one meal for the remaining decade, dreamily sharing the decadent thrill of that tuna tartare and those braised sweetbreads to anyone who happens to sit by you during a meal.

But why should the best foods in the world be reserved for the fat cats who can't possibly appreciate them? This is America, dammit, and if you want to splurge on a crispy pavé of Kurobuta pork belly at every meal, then you can. So take a day and treat yourself to four-star meals at three different sittings. That's right—four-star breakfast, four-star lunch, four-star dinner. Gastronomically speaking, it doesn't get any better than that.

Because if one incredible meal can keep you satisfied for a decade, think of the mileage you'll get out of three.

Rest for the Wicked Don't forget to make reservations well ahead of time, even for breakfast.

The Sandwich of Kings

Think a sandwich can't be high-class? Try the von Essen Platinum Club Sandwich in Taplow, Berkshire, available for just short of two hundred dollars.

DECEMBER 11

Run Home for a Nooner

Women need a reason to have sex. Men just need a place.

—Billy Crystal

You are trying your best to concentrate on spreadsheets, but for some reason you just can't seem to focus. Perhaps it's because you came into the office to prepare for a 9:00 A.M. meeting instead of fitting in that morning quickie with your significant other.

And now you're stuck waiting until quitting time before you have another chance at sexy time.

Or are you?

You came in early this morning, after all. It's not like the office would fall apart if you slipped out for a long lunch—and perhaps a little dessert?

Call up your significant other and see if you can arrange for a little lunchtime loving. If home is too inconvenient, now is the perfect time to explore the halfway point between your respective jobs. If you can't find a hotel close by, park in a secluded lot and get busy before anyone realizes what's going on. When you get back to work, the rest of the day should fly by as you revel in your secret little rendezvous.

Rest for the Wicked Try to keep your clothes off the floor during your noontime getaway. Wrinkles are a dead giveaway.

Secluded Nooner Locales

- Skeezy hourly hotel
- Restaurant bathroom
- Empty conference room

DECEMBER 12

Skip the Morning Shower

Don't shave, don't shower, don't care. Be really stinky and wear the same clothes every day. I think what makes a man sexy is not being self-aware. That's what's really cute to me.

—Gwen Stefani

Of all the elements of our morning routine, the daily shower is by far the most time-consuming. If it weren't for our irrational need to soap up each morning, we could pretty much roll straight out of bed and into our car.

Now there's an idea.

Sure you may smell a little funky at your morning meeting, but that's a small price to pay for an extra fifteen minutes of sleep. Besides, our ancestors didn't take a high-pressure shower before heading out to work in the fields, and they survived just fine.

Since you won't be taking a shower this morning, you can take your time and ease into the workday for a change. Make yourself a hot breakfast and grab the morning paper. Don't even bother combing your hair, just leave it in its natural "bedhead" configuration and you're good to go.

Rest for the Wicked Carry plenty of cologne or perfume to mask your natural musk.

Old Wives' Tale

Tomato juice does not remove foul odors such as skunk spray. It merely masks the smell. A combination of baking soda and hydrogen peroxide will neutralize many offensive smells.

DECEMBER 13

Film Your Friend Getting Hurt

I hope life isn't a big joke, because I don't get it.

—JACK HANDEY

There are moments in life that stand out more than others. When people express true, deep emotions in real time, those are rare and memorable. That's why sports games always show the reaction shots, whether it be success or failure. That's what gets them the big bucks.

It's time for you to capture some reaction shots of your own. Tell your best friend you have something important to tell him. Bring him over, sit him down, and hide the camera in the corner. Tell him that before he starting dating his significant other, that you two had a one-night stand. If that's not enough to get them going, start going into details. Let him sit and suffer and react, and keep the ruse up as long as you can without getting physically attacked. Keep pushing it. Include details. Love letters, sext-messages. Then when you can't contain yourself any more, tell him you're just kidding. Then exploit your friend for potential Internet fame by posting the video on YouTube. You may not talk to each other for several weeks, but in twenty years you'll be laughing about it.

Rest for the Wicked Make sure you hit the record button, so your friend only gets hurt once.

Most Commonly Posted Videos by Amateurs to YouTube

1. Sex right up until nudity happens
2. Footage of people watching other people have sex
3. Personal diaries
4. Movie reviews
5. A person filming themselves playing guitar in their room

DECEMBER 14

Pass a Forgery Off as an Original Painting

Bad artists copy. Good artists steal.

—Pablo Picasso

When you see a famous painting hanging on someone's wall, you can't help but admire their sense of good taste and envy their ability to afford such indulgences. It certainly makes you wish you could trade in your family portraits for something a little more classy.

But just because you can't afford expensive art doesn't mean you don't deserve a nicely decorated wall. Instead of waiting to save up thousands of dollars to purchase an original, perhaps you can settle for the next best thing: a clever forgery. For a fraction of the price of an authentic painting, you can purchase a respectable recreation online.

Once you get it home, you can create an elaborate story to explain its presence in your humble home. Perhaps your great-uncle was an art dealer. Maybe your parents found it beneath the floorboards in their attic. If you invest in an expensive frame and stick to your story, nobody will ever know your sinful secret.

Rest for the Wicked Pick relatively obscure artists to display. People are less likely to spot the forgery if the painting isn't famous.

Alternative Options

- Finger painting (modern art)
- Newspaper collage (contemporary art)
- Empty frame (existential art)

DECEMBER 15

Buy a Round for the Bar (On Someone Else)

I feel sorry for people who don't drink. When they wake up in the morning, that's as good as they're going to feel all day.

—Frank Sinatra

After you've kicked back a few, it's only natural to want to share your newfound euphoria with the rest of the bar in the form of a round of drinks. Sadly, the contents of your wallet—two singles and a coupon for free coffee—just aren't going to cut it. Desperate times call for desperate measures and if you want to be the hero of the bar, you'll have to outsource the financial responsibility.

Walk up to the bar and proudly order a round of drinks for everyone. Inform the bartender that the creepy guy in the corner offered to pick up the tab (let's call him Seabass). Give old Seabass a reassuring wave, and when he responds in kind he will have unwittingly agreed to pay for everyone's booze.

Sure it's juvenile and dishonest, but it's not like Seabass is actually going to be held accountable. He'll sort everything out with the bartender later, but not before everyone has already consumed the evidence and you're miles out of reach of any potential backlash.

Rest for the Wicked Don't pull this stunt at a bar you would like to revisit in the future.

Why Your Bartender Hates You

- You order complicated drinks
- You tip with spare change
- You snap your fingers to get attention
- You pay with a credit card
- You don't know what you want

Test Drive an Expensive Car

Car designers are just going to have to come up with an automobile that outlasts the payments.

—Erma Bombeck, American humorist

If you've never experienced the raw power and hairpin handling of a hyper-expensive car, you're missing out. But not everybody has $150,000 to drop on a new Lamborghini.

But who says you can't get a little taste of the experience for free? While it's true you have no intention of buying a fancy new car, the salesman at the car dealership doesn't need to know that.

Put on your most expensive suit and call up a local dealership to schedule a test drive. You'll be playing the part of a successful businessman with money to burn, so complete your ruse with some expensive jewelry and a smug air of self-importance.

Once you get behind the wheel, let her rip. Roll down the windows and let the wind blow through your hair. Enjoy yourself, because who knows when you'll have another opportunity to drive something worth more than your house.

Rest for the Wicked Try to keep it below 100 mph until you are comfortable with the car.

Most Expensive Cars of 2011

- Bugatti Veyron Super Sport: $2.6 million
- Koenigsegg Agera: $ 1.5 million
- Maybach Landaulet: $1.4 million
- Hennessey Venom GT: $895,000
- Leblanc Mirabeau: $728,000

DECEMBER 17

Leave the Dishes for Tomorrow

Best way to get rid of kitchen odors: eat out.

—Phyllis Diller

After slaving away to make dinner yet again, you've enjoyed a leisurely meal complete with an overindulgence in your favorite adult beverage. You clear the table post-feast, only to be abruptly reminded of the complete and utter mess lurking in your kitchen.

Instead of breaking down and reaching for the closest sponge to attack that glaring mound of dirty dishes, just turn around and walk away. Surely your best stainless steel pot won't be ruined by an extra twenty-four hours of mashed potato residue. Nor will that once-delicious-but-now-disgusting-looking caramelized barbeque sauce leave a permanent scar on your grandmother's frying pan.

It's been a long day, so treat yourself to a mini-marathon of ESPN programming, or pull out the latest issue of *USWeekly* that's stashed in your nightstand. You've done enough dishes in your life to know that sometimes, the mess can just wait. And anyway, it's your significant other's turn to wash the dishes, isn't it?

Rest for the Wicked Turn off the kitchen lights to make the mess disappear.

How to Permanently Escape Dish Duty

- Hire a maid
- Only use paper plates
- Eat nothing but TV dinners

DECEMBER 18

Unleash Your Inner Road Rage

Road rage is the expression of the amateur sociopath in all of us, cured by running into a professional.

—Robert Brault, author

On the road, there are obstacles in every direction. Bikers who swerve into the street, a double-parked car that's blocking the lane, jaywalking pedestrians. Considering you're driving something that's capable of decapitating someone with the slightest mistake, it can be pretty stressful.

Typically you vent your frustrations by directing a small honk in the offending pedestrian's direction or just muttering under your breath as your hairs fall out one by one. But now the time has come to let your inner road rage out. Lay on that horn. Scream out the window. Swerve close to hitting the person. Feel free to even get out of your car and get in their face. This is the only way drivers will ever get the voice they have for so long been lacking. And your doctor says its better to express yourself than keep your feelings bottled in. It's healthy, it's good for society, and you'll feel great when you're done.

Rest for the Wicked Avoid Hells Angels motorcyclists.

America's Most Courteous Drivers

An AutoVantage Road Rage survey found the following cities had the most courteous drivers:

1. Portland, OR
2. Pittsburgh
3. Seattle/Tacoma
4. St. Louis
5. Dallas/Fort Worth

DECEMBER 19

Leave Your Ex's Number on the Bathroom Wall

There's nothing wrong with revenge—it's the best way to get even!

—ARCHIE BUNKER, *ALL IN THE FAMILY*

Being dumped is about the worst feeling a human being can experience. But once you get over the loss of self-esteem and the unfathomable loneliness, there's only one desire that remains: Revenge.

There are a number of ways you can vent your frustration, unfortunately most of them require a blunt object and a general disregard for personal property. You need an outlet that won't land you in prison.

Etching your ex's name and number on a bathroom wall may not seem like much, but it's embarrassing enough to cause damage without resorting to violence. Best of all, it gives you plausable deniability. Hundreds of people have your ex's digits . . . it could have been anybody.

Grab a marker and hit up every public bathroom within a five-mile radius. Since you are limited in the number you can hit, commission a friend of the opposite gender to ensure full coverage. You may be childish, but you're still thorough.

If you start to feel bad, just power through it and keep writing. Your ex always wanted to make new friends. This is just an odd way of making that a reality.

Rest for the Wicked Disguise your handwriting in the off chance your ex sees it.

Best Graffiti Options

- Classic – "For a good time, call . . . "
- Backhanded Burn – "[name here] is pretty good in bed. For a dead fish."
- Childish – "[name here] is a dumb dumb poopy head."

DECEMBER 20

Resurrect Your Bad Habits

Motivation is what gets you started. Habit is what keeps you going.

—Jim Rohn, American author

It took years of intense aversion therapy, but you are finally free of all your nasty, irritating habits. While you may be more pleasant to be around, are you sure it was really worth it?

You're at least ten times more strung out and irritable now that you can't bite your nails or crack your knuckles to relieve tension. On top of that, you won't even scratch an itch on your nose for fear you might start picking it.

Let's face it, you were happier when you just did what you wanted regardless of what people thought. Perhaps it's time for a relapse.

Don't ignore your natural urges to crack, pick, bite, and scratch—embrace them. Throw out your subliminal tapes and bitter apple nail polish and embrace your inner OCD. Go ahead and hum while you work, and don't hesitate to snap your gum while you do it. These habits make you the person you are. Don't hide them, flaunt them.

Rest for the Wicked Just don't grind your teeth. It's bad for your enamel.

Go Ahead and Crack

Recent studies show there is no link between cracking one's knuckles and arthritis.

DECEMBER 21

Ditch the Company Holiday Party

You moon the wrong person at an office party and suddenly you're not "professional" any more.

—Jeff Foxworthy

The holidays should be a time for family togetherness and general good cheer. There's no reason to spend them awkwardly chatting with coworkers around a bowl of stale chips.

No matter how much fun your company insists this year's party will be, rest assured it will be a miserable experience. All the streamers and holiday-themed cookies in the world can't hide the fact that you're partying in the office.

This year, instead of donning your frumpy holiday sweater and biting the bullet, just go home. Nobody's going to cancel the party just because you're not there.

When your coworkers start shuffling toward the designated party room, grab your stuff and prepare to make your escape. As you head for the nearest exit, steer clear of anyone wearing fake reindeer antlers or drinking egg nog—they might force you to join the "fun."

Rest for the Wicked Only worry about saving yourself. Don't be a hero and try to liberate any of your work friends.

Boss's Holiday Party Checklist

- Tray of rock-hard sugar cookies
- Powdered fruit punch (alongside optional jug of vodka)
- Non-denominational holiday music
- Noise makers you'll regret buying

DECEMBER 22

Follow an Ambulance Through Traffic

I stop and look at traffic accidents. I won't hang around, but when I hear something is terrible, as bad as it is, I've gotta look at it.

—Norman Lear

Drive at night one time and you'll notice something strange. The commute is a little smoother and quicker. There aren't as many cars on the road. You're not cursing out the window or at yourself as much. Traffic, it seems, doesn't exist.

It's a lovely sight, in contrast to your rush-hour commute when it takes an hour to move a mile.

But there are certain cars that are granted the privilege to pass through traffic whenever they want. They're called ambulances and all they have to do is turn on their signal and cars get out of their way, no matter how crowded the streets are. It's high time you take advantage of this, and just follow the ambulance through traffic. Nobody is going to be later because of it, and the cars behind you will have one less car to worry about, since you'll be zooming up ahead of the pack.

It might get you some honks and dirty looks, but at least you'll get home in time to watch the *Law & Order: SVU* marathon.

Rest for the Wicked Stay close to the ambulance or risk getting stuck back in traffic.

Traffic Adds Up

In 2003, according to the Texas Transportation Institute, congestion in eighty-five urban areas it studied added up to 3.7 billion hours of delay, or an annual delay per person of forty-three hours.

DECEMBER 23

Eat Frozen Pizza with Your Most Expensive Silverware

It is impossible to overdo luxury.

—French Proverb

Tucked in the far reaches of your forks and knives drawer lies the fancy silverware for "special occasions." The closest you've actually come to such an occasion is the time your friends came over for the latest HBO finale and you ate dinner around the coffee table.

Tucked in the far reaches of your freezer you happen to have a delicious meat lover's pizza just waiting to be eaten.

Why not bring them both out of hiding?

Create your own special occasion with your favorite frozen entree. While you warm up the oven, pull out the expensive utensils and give them a quick polish. Lay down a tablecloth with your best professional flick and light a candle for an extra flourish. For the place setting, grab a cloth napkin and arrange the silverware in proper fashion. Once the pizza is cooked to perfection and on the table, you're ready to dig in and eat like a king or queen. Royalty never had it this good.

Rest for the Wicked To keep the silverware intact for when you finally throw a dinner party, don't forget to hand wash.

Get Fancy with Frozen Food

- Bean burrito – fresh herb garnish
- Bagel bites – assorted toothpicks
- Stir-fry in a bag – porcelain chopsticks
- Ice cream – china bowl

DECEMBER 24

Draw All Over Your Walls

Art is the only way to run away without leaving home.

—Twyla Tharp

Turn your apartment into one big canvas. As a kid, you always dreamed about what it would be like if you could draw all over your walls and not get in trouble for it. Well, your parents don't make the rules anymore. There's no one stopping you. You pay the rent, so you get to decide how to decorate.

Exercise your inner Van Gogh by drawing and painting all over the walls. Feeling extra artsy? Keep going and take that masterpiece across the ceiling. Replicate "The Creation of Adam" from the Sistine Chapel. Michelangelo had nothing on you.

Don't worry about what the landlord will say—you can always paint over it later. Better yet, convince him it's a priceless piece of art from an up-and-comer just about to hit it big. New York art galleries have been buzzing with talk about this new star of the art world. Sell him the piece at a handsome price. Spend your money on more art supplies.

Rest for the Wicked Include your roommates in on the fun, or at least run it by them first. Nothing says "you're a terrible roommate" like a surprise mural all over the kitchen ceiling.

What's Your Medium of Choice?

- Paint
- Crayons
- Markers
- Charcoal
- Pen

DECEMBER 25

Give Junk as Christmas Gifts

I once bought my kids a set of batteries for Christmas with a note on it saying, toys not included.

—Bernard Manning, English comedian

Christmas may be a time for charity, family togetherness, and good cheer, but it's also pretty bloody expensive. Whoever said, "'Tis better to give than to receive," clearly never maxed out his credit card buying overpriced gifts from the local shopping mall.

Perhaps your loved ones could use a reminder that there's more to the holiday spirit than dollar signs. And if you get a little creative with your presents this year, they might just get the message.

Sure second-hand gifts are unconventional, but so are big-screen TVs and video games. It's not like the three wise men stopped into their local Best Buy on their way to the manger. Rest assured, your niece's Christmas won't be ruined just because she got a used deck of cards in her stocking instead of a Barbie Doll.

Before you drive over to meet your family, gather up all your gifts and return them to the store. Instead, wrap up a few stray items you have lying around the house. A few coasters, an old toaster oven, that uneaten chocolate bunny from last Easter.

It may be old junk to you, but it will be new junk to them!

Rest for the Wicked Include hand-written gift receipts so recipients don't know you spent $0 on their present.

Deceptive Junk Gifts

- Expired gift cards
- Wine bottles filled with grape juice
- Stray cat/dog
- Donation to a fake charity
- Empty DVD cases

Get a Body Piercing

I think men who have a pierced ear are better prepared for marriage. They've experienced pain and bought jewelry.

—Rita Rudner

Of all the acts of teenage rebellion—smoking cigarettes, staying out late, flunking trigonometry—getting a body piercing is by far the most badass. When you stick a giant needle through your nose just to give the proverbial middle finger to someone, you really have to mean it.

You may be all grown up now, but buried deep down dwells that same uncontrollable angst you flaunted as a teenager. Well, it's time to let it back out.

Sure nobody is forcing you to be home by 10:00 sharp anymore, but there's still plenty to rebel against. An obnoxious boss, a hyper-critical spouse, or even overbearing in-laws. Just picture the look on their faces when you show up with a shiny new tongue stud.

Seek out your local mall and head straight to Hot Topic to pick out your new body bling. If you have trouble finding it, just follow anyone dressed in black wearing a spiked dog collar. Once you've settled on a location for your piercing, it's just a simple matter of gritting your teeth and holding still. That last part being especially important . . .

Rest for the Wicked Whatever you do, don't watch as they do it.

What Your Piercing Says about You

- Lip – secretly wants to be a fish
- Eyebrow – looked up "edgy" in the dictionary
- Tongue – thinks they're good in bed
- Genitals – knows they're good in bed

DECEMBER 27

Get a Manicure and Pedicure

You're the toast of the town. Finish your salad and I'll take you for a little mani-pedi-botox.

—SAMANTHA, *SEX AND THE CITY*

Whether your little piggies are heading to market or going "wee wee wee" all the way home, they better be clean and shiny. The same goes for your mitts. But why do for yourself what someone can do for you?

Going to a spa for a manicure and pedicure might seem like an indulgence, but it makes perfect sense. Unless you've gone through beauty school, it's practically impossible to paint your own nails. Most times, they end up so smudged that you have to claim that your five-year-old niece painted them.

Stop battling with your own ineptitude and take yourself over to the nearest spa for a manicure and pedicure. Once you're there, get off those stompers and put your feet up. Lean back as someone scrubs at your legs and makes the skin feel soft as a baby's bottom. Don't lift a finger except to sip from a refreshing cucumber water or flip through the pages of a magazine. Your digits will look so good you'll find reasons to talk with your hands and might even feel compelled to start gesturing with your toes.

Rest for the Wicked Skip jet-black polish in favor of shades actually within the color spectrum. Unless your clothes are from Hot Topic. In which case, go for it.

Conversation Starters Not to Use at the Spa

- "How much do you get paid, anyway?"
- "So you didn't go to college, huh?"
- "My feet have been so itchy lately!"
- "What gym do you go to? There was just an outbreak of athlete's foot at mine."

DECEMBER 28

Mail Things from Work

Mail your packages early so the post office can lose them in time for Christmas.
—Johnny Carson

Work is good for a few things. One, it gives you something to complain about. Two, it allows you to live. Three, it provides you with essential materials that you can use to complete your everyday errands. In no area is this more clear than in mailing things.

You have two options when you're mailing things. You could either take time out of your non-work schedule to go to the post office (either on a Saturday or during your lunch break, since it's conveniently only open from 9 A.M. to 5 P.M., when everyone has free time apparently) and pay for everything yourself. Or you can take ten minutes of work time to get an envelope and stamp, mail everything you need, and not pay for anything. You're a rational human being; do the right thing.

And when the holiday season comes around, use it as a center to send out your holiday greetings. It is, after all, the season of giving. Your company can afford you some extra perks.

Rest for the Wicked For bulk mailings, slowly accumulate the materials you'll need over time so as to avoid raising suspicion.

Most Useful Office Supplies for Personal Use

- Stamps, to mail things
- Rubber bands, to make a rubber band ball
- Paper clips, to make paper clip figurines
- Paper, to make paper airplanes, fortune tellers, and to learn origami
- Internet, to bid on items on eBay

Go to a Bar Without Money

Pretty women make us BUY beer. Ugly women make us DRINK beer.

—Al Bundy, *Married with Children*

There are few things more fun than hitting the town with a few friends, placing a credit card on the bar, and ordering up round after round of liquid confidence. Of course this is immediately followed by the miserable task of paying the tab at the end of the night. Lucky for you, tonight you won't be the one left holding the check.

Just this once, leave your wallet at home and rely on your good looks and irresistible charm to score free drinks. Sure you could afford to buy your own, but you have better things to spend your money on than Jager bombs.

Belly up to the bar and make yourself look approachable. When a hopeful suitor does buy you a drink, be polite and chat for awhile, but not too long. You're here to have fun, not leech off the same person all night. Who knows, along with a few free drinks, you might even score a few new friends in the process.

Rest for the Wicked Always get your drinks directly from the bartender, and never leave a drink unattended.

What Your Drink Says about You

- Cosmopolitan – fun, yet sophisticated
- Light beer – still in college
- Single-malt scotch, Neat – tough as nails
- Mojito – high maintenance
- Tequila – you mean business

DECEMBER 30

Construct a Fortress of Solitude

Solitude would be ideal if you could pick the people to avoid.

—Karl Kraus, Austrian Journalist

You may love your family more than anything in the world, but everyone needs some alone time here and there. Which can be hard to come by when you all share the same roof.

What you need is a space to call your own. A room that's off limits to whining kids, nosy in-laws, nagging spouses, and even the needy golden retriever. A veritable fortress of solitude.

Your house must have at least one unused guest room or a secluded basement, and today you're going to claim it as your own. Pimp it out with a pool table and dart board, or keep it minimalistic with a yoga mat and some workout equipment. Since this is your cave, you can furnish it however you want.

Finish off your new hideaway with a homemade "No Trespassing" sign and you're good to go. It'll be just like that secret club from your childhood, except this time you'll actually get in.

Rest for the Wicked Never let anybody else see inside your secret hideaway, or else they might want to come hang out.

Names for Your Cave

- The Awesome Room
- Area 52
- The Bat Cave
- Super Secret Club House

DECEMBER 31

Celebrate New Year's Early

New Year's Resolution: To tolerate fools more gladly, provided this does not encourage them to take up more of my time.

—JAMES AGATE, BRITISH CRITIC

Every year it's the same. You wait all night for the ball to drop so you can drink champagne, but then you only get a few sips before everybody drinks it all—or spills it on the floor.

Of course, you could just celebrate early and have an entire bottle to yourself. You've spent the whole year being completely selfish. Why stop now?

Just before midnight, quietly excuse yourself and snag an unattended bottle of bubbly from the fridge. Find a nice secluded area, set your watch forward a few minutes and start your own personal countdown.

5 . . . 4 . . . 3 . . . 2 . . . 1 . . . Drink!

Down the whole bottle and hide the evidence before returning to the party for round two.

Rest for the Wicked Chase the stolen bottle with a mint to mask any champagne odor that might give you away.

What's in a Name?

True champagne is made from grapes grown in the Champagne region of France. Otherwise that bubbly you're drinking should be referred to as sparkling wine.

Index

Accent, adopting an, Feb 20
Adams, Douglas, May 2
Adams, Jessi Lane, Jun 30
Adams, Sam, Nov 1
Adrenaline rushes, Mar 29
Affection, public displays of, Aug 18
Agate, James, Dec 31
Age, lying about, Sep 24
Aggression outlets, Mar 27
Air conditioners, Aug 4
Ali, Muhammad, Jun 7
Allen, Fred, Feb 14
Allen, Woody, May 23, Oct 23, Nov 30
All-nighter, Jun 8
All-you-can-eat buffet, all day at, Jun 15
Almond, Steve, Oct 31
Alone time at home, Feb 17, Jun 12
Amusement park lines, cutting, Sep 17
Apartment, renting a clean, Jun 24
Art, drawing on the walls, Dec 24
Asimov, Isaac, Apr 14
Assistant, hire an, Dec 2
Auctions, Nov 22
Austin, Mary, Mar 17
Avoid traffic tickets, lying to, Feb 26
Azmi, Lubina, Aug 21
Azrari, Aug 4

Babysitter, TV as, Sep 27
Back scratchers, May 22
Baker, Josephine, Feb 18
Bald head, Jan 28
Ball pits, Jun 2
Banister-sliding, Dec 4
Barr, Roseanne, Apr19
Barry, Dave, Jan 16, Jul 11, Jul 20
Barrymore, John, Mar 25
Bathrobes, Dec 8
Bathroom scale, adjusting down, Jul 9
Bathroom usage, Apr 28
BBQs, crashing, May 28
Beauvoir, Simone de, Oct 26
Bed, staying in, Apr 22
Beecher, Henry Ward, May 13, Jun 22, Oct 15
Beer Olympics, Oct 19
Being naked, Mar 7
Bellack, Dan, Sep 14
Bergman, Ingrid, Aug 18
Berra, Yogi, May 31
Bills, not paying, Sep 1
Birnbach, Lisa, Jul 14
Birthday, a pretend, Jul 24
Birthday party, Dec 1
Bishop, Joey, Oct 30
Blake, William, Jul 10
Boating, Jul 11
Body piercings, Dec 26
Boliska, Al, Dec 6
Bombeck, Erma, Mar 31, Apr 8, Jun 2, Aug 29, Sep 12, Dec 16
Bookstore-as-library, May 13
Bookstore bathroom, Jun 25
Borges, Jorge Luis, Jul 31
Boynton, Sandra, Oct 9
Bradbury, Ray, Oct 11
Brando, Marlon, Jun 28
Brault, Robert, Dec 18
Brent, David, Sep 11
Brilliant, Ashleigh, May 30
Broken items, returning, Sep 23
Broun, Heywood C., Oct 4
Bruce, Lenny, Jul 17
Bruxton, Charles, Mar 19
Bubble gum, Apr 13
Bueller, Ferris, Oct 7

Buffett, Warren, Jun 9, Nov 23
Bukowski, Charles, Jul 30
Bullock, Sandra, May 5
Bullying, Nov 5
Bumming rides, Dec 9
Bumstead, Dagwood ("Blondie"), Apr 22
Bundy, Al, Dec 29
Bungee jumping, Oct 11
Bunker, Archie, Dec 19
Burgundy, Ron, Jul 18
Burke, Billie, Sep 24
Buscaglia, Leo F., Nov 21
Bush, George H. W., Jul 5
Bush, George W., Apr 1
Butler, Samuel, Apr 12, Aug 31
Butlers, Jun 27
BYOB to a bar, Feb 25

Cable, stealing, Jul 6
Cake frosting, Nov 1
Calorie count, Aug 2
Calvino, Italo, Mar 11
Camping, May 19
Camus, Albert, Oct 2
Candy, office hiding places, Oct 9
Candy, stealing from a baby, Jul 16
Capone, Al, Nov 8
Cappuccino maker, Jun 18
Carlin, George, May 19, Sep 29, Oct 14
Carpool lanes, Feb 6
Carrey, Jim, Jul 22
Cars, expensive, Dec 16
Carson, Johnny, Nov 15, Dec 28
Carter, Lillian, Jan 14
Cartoons, Saturday morning, Nov 10
Casual Monday, Oct 29
Cat for a day, Nov 21
Celebrations, Apr 18
Charities, Jan 17, Mar 5
Chavez, Cesar, May 28
Chef, hire a personal, Oct 28
Child, Julia, Sep 18
Chocolate, Jan 23
Chores, neighborhood kids and, Apr 8
Christmas gifts, give junk as, Dec 25
Churchill, Jennie Jerome, Oct 22
Churchill, Winston, Sep 20
Claiming an empty office, Jun 20
Clarke, Arthur C., Jul 9
Cleaning services, house parties and, Oct 8
Cleaning techniques, Apr 27
Cliff's notes, Aug 11
Clinton, Hillary, Jan 28
Clothes, wear once, Apr 12
Clothing, custom-made, Sep 22
Clothing store fashion show, Apr 24
Cloud gazing/observatories, Aug 5
Coffee
  booze added to, Sep 6
  consumption, May 9
  shops, Mar 15
  vocabulary, Jun 18
Cohen, Vanya, Apr 15
College days, reliving, Jan 30
Colton, Charles Caleb, May 3
Coltrane, Robbie, Apr 4
Community gardens, Aug 20
Company credit cards, using, Oct 5
Company holiday party, ditching, Dec 21
Company time, use of, Jun 6
Concerts, private, Jan 6
Concerts, sneaking into, Oct 6
Continental breakfast, stealing a, Jan 15
Converting cubicle into an office, Jun 14
Cookie, the last one, Aug 25
Cookies, eating the whole batch, Mar 11
Coolio, Jan 7
Cooper, Anna Julia, Nov 5
Cooper, Tommy, Jun 5
Coppola, Francis Ford, May 20
Couch, sleeping on, Jun 26

Couch forts, Jun 7
Country clubs, Mar 2
Couples, Fred, Aug 7
Cowman, C. E., Aug 28
Coworker's lunch, stealing, Feb 19
Cox, Marcelene, Dec 7
Creditors, avoiding, Sep 1
Crystal, Billy, Dec 11
Cummings, E. E., Aug 24
Cunningham, Gary, Nov 24

Dance party, subway, Oct 13
Dangerfield, Rodney, Oct 24
Dauten, Dale, Oct 16
Davis, Marvin, Sep 26
Debauchery, Jan 1
Deep-frying, Jan 10
Delany, Dana, Aug 15
Denby, Edwin, Oct 13
Depp, Johnny, Sep 2
Derek, Bo, May 1
Diaries, May 11
Dieting, Jun 28
Diller, Phyllis, Apr 9, Dec 17
Dining out, not paying and, Jun 19
Dining out, super size everything, Jul 19
Dinner, desert first, May 16
Dinner out, no leftovers, Aug 10
Dinner reservations, stealing, Jul 7
Dinner with in-laws, Jul 22
Diran, Richard, Aug 20
Dishwashing, Dec 17
Disorganization, Apr 27
Doctor's appointment, fake, Jun 11
Dogma, Aug 4
Drinking
  away sorrows, Feb 1
  before noon, Oct 3
  on other's money, Dec 15
  twenty-one shots and, Jan 3
  without money, Dec 29
Driving slow, Mar 6
Dryer sheets uses, Jan 25
Durocher, Leo, Mar 21

Earworm, Nov 2
Eating without utensils, May 4
Edwards, Bob, Mar 24
Einstein, Albert, Feb 13, May 24, Sep 15
Electronics, eliminating, Feb 13
Elevators, Jan 5
Eliot, T. S., Feb 2
E-mail, anonymous, Dec 3
E-mail, ignoring, Mar 12
Emerson, Ralph Waldo, Feb 20, Jun 11, Aug 12
Empty coffee pot, Feb 2
Eno, Brian, Mar 12
Erickson, Lou, Aug 1
Ewing, Sam, May 7, Jul 8
Expense accounts (per diem), Jul 29
Expensive painting, buy, Apr 26

Farting, May 21, Oct 1
The Fast and the Furious, Jun 23
Fast foods, Jan 2, Aug 2
Fields, W. C., May 26
Financial planning, May 1
Fireworks, illegal, Jul 4
First date dining, Feb 4
Flowers, sending, Feb 14
Flowers, stealing, Jun 22
Flying, buying entire row of seats, Jan 16
Flying first class, Dec 6
Food. *See also* Coffee; Pizza
  all-you-can-eat buffet and, Aug 30
  cookies and, Mar 11, Aug 25
  cooking with wine, Oct 22
  dessert only, Sep 12
  eating best part, Jul 5
  eating frosting only, Nov 1
  fast, Jan 2, Aug 2

fights, Apr 30
five-course lunch and, Sep 3
five-second rule and, Sep 29
four-star restaurants, Dec10
hire a personal chef, Oct 28
homemade/store-bought, Sep 18
junk, Aug 16
kid's meals and, Jan 2
Krispy Kreme doughnuts and, Feb 23
meat and, Aug 13
mediocre meal and, Nov 30
ordering everything on menu and, Nov 11
religious services and, Sep 16
a selfish dinner and, Nov 4
takeout, May 30
wasting, Aug 29
Ford, Gerald R., Apr 25
Ford, Henry, Jun 10
Fortress of solitude, Dec 30
Foxworthy, Jeff, Dec 21
Franklin, Benjamin, Jun 1, Jun 8
Fraser, Dawn, Oct 19
Frost, Robert, Mar 30, Oct 21
Fry, Christopher, Jun 24
Furniture, Nov 8

Gabor, Zsa Zsa, Jun 26
Gadgets, useless, Aug 9
Gambling, bet black, Sep 15
Game night, cheating at, Nov 17
Garbage, Nov 20
Gardening, Aug 1
Gates, Bill, Mar 15
Gibbons, Anne, Oct 8
Gibbons, Peter, Jun 6, Jun 14
Global warming, Aug 4
Goethe, Johann Wolfgang Von, Jun 27
Going barefoot, Nov 6
Golfing, Jan 31, Jul 20
Gore, Al, Jan 9
Gotti, John, Nov 26
Gould, Glenn, Jan 6
Graham, Billy, Apr 29
Grassley, Chuck, Nov 18
Groban, Josh, Nov 28
Groceries, online ordering, Jun 17
Grocery store express lines, Jan 29
Guillemets, Terri, Apr 10, Oct 10
Gump, Forrest, Aug 27
Gunther, John, Jan 15

Habits, resurrect bad, Dec 20
Hackett, Buddy, Nov 4
Hagen, Walter, Mar 6
Haircut, expensive, Nov 12
Hamilton, Steve, Apr 30
Hammock lounging, Jan 11
Handey, Jack, Dec 13
Hand washing, Oct 14
Hannah, Daryl, Mar 7
Harrison, George, Jul 24
Hazing at the office, Mar 28
Headaches, faking, May 27
Hedberg, Mitch, May 12
Heirlooms/antiques, Apr 29
Helmets, biking and, Sep 21
Hemingway, Ernest, Oct 3
Hendrix, Jimi, Aug 3
Hepburn, Audrey, Jun 12
Hepburn, Katharine, Jan 23
Hill, Gene, May 18
Hitchcock, Alfred, Oct 12
Hitchhiking, May 2
Hobbies, Jun 1
Hollywood walk of fame, Aug 23
Hotel couches, sleeping on, May 12
Hotels, five star, Jul 23
Hotel swimming pools, May 5
Hot tubs, Feb 24
House cleaning, Apr 19

Household chores, ignoring, Jul 15
Howe, Edgar Watson, Jan 21
Hubbard, Kin, Aug 14
Hunt, Leigh, Jun 16

Ice cream
in bed, Jun 13
for breakfast, Jan 13
sample all flavors, Jun 30
the ultimate sundae, Oct 4
Identity, assume a fake, Oct 25
International Pole Championship, Sep 19
Internet, Jan 9, Mar 3
IRS criminal investigation data, Apr 15
Izzard, Eddie, Mar 27

Jaeger-bomb, Jan 3
Jaffe, Charles, Jul 29
James, Kevin, Mar 22
Jardin, Xeni, Jul 28
Jefferies, Jim, Mar 1
Jet-setting, Aug 14
Jewelry, costume, Nov 16
Jewelry, trying on, Apr 21
Johnson, Samuel, Jan 4
Jones, Franklin P., Feb 8
Jordan, Barbara, Aug 25
Judge, Mike, Feb 12
Junk, throwing out, Sep 13
Junk food, Aug 16

Kaiser, Henry J., Oct 29
Kalin, Mike, Dec 10
Kant, Immanuel, Jul 21
Kardong, Don, Jun 13
Kennedy, John F., May 14
Kidder, Margot, Mar 23
Kids, chauffer for, Apr 11
Kid's meals, Jan 2
Kid's toys, playing with, Apr 6
Kinsey, Alfred C., Aug 8
Kissing a stranger, Jun 16
Knowles, John, Mar 28
Kocsis, Natalie, Jun 29
Koslom, Brian, Nov 29
Kraus, Karl, Dec 30
Krispy Kreme doughnuts, Feb 23
Kundera, Milan, Nov 2, Nov 20

Lamb, Charles, Nov 9
Lapoce, Michael, Jul 25
Larson, Doug, Feb 3, Dec 3
Laryngitis, Jan 20
Laundry, Nov 14
Laundry day, skipping, Nov 7
Leaf piles, jumping into, Oct 2
Lear, Norman, Dec 22
Lebowitz, Fran, May 8, Aug 13
Lennon, John, Oct 6
Leno, Jay, Aug 23
Letterman, David, May 9, Jul 4
Levitin, Daniel, Nov 2
Lewis, David, Feb 27
Lewis, Joe E., Feb 1
Library, sex and the, Jul 31
Library collection, personal, Feb 15
Library of Congress, Feb 15
Liebman, Wendy, Sep 30
Life, faking an impressive, Apr 7
Life goal, fulfilling a, Oct 21
Lights, turning on all, Jan 14
Limousine, Feb 10
Line cutting, Feb 21
Lipsey, Michael, Nov 11
Littering, Aug 30
Living dangerously, Sep 21
Living room, as a theater, Sep 28
Lobsters, Jul 2
Lottery, playing the, May 8
Lounging in underwear, Feb 18
Lujack, Larry, Nov 25

Lunch, three hour, Apr 25
Lunch breaks, Mar 14
Lunch meeting, crashing a, May 17
Lunch room, cool-kids table and, Jul 12

Magazines, stealing, Mar 13
Mail, using company resources, Dec 28
Malcolm, Andrew H., Jun 10
Mancroft, Benjamin, Dec 2
Manicure/pedicure, Dec 27
Manning, Bernard, Dec 25
Marathon, the last mile, Mar 4
Marquis, Don, Jul 1
Martin, Demetri, Jul 16
Martin, Steve, Sep 28
Marx, Groucho, Mar 2, Nov 3
Massage, full body, Oct 18
McCarthy, Jenny, Oct 1
McLaughlin, Mignon, Apr 24
Mean Girls, Jul 12
Meat, eating, Aug 13
Meetings, Oct 18
Meltzer, Bernard, Dec 9
Mencken, Henry Louis, Mar 26, Sep 9
Mental health day, Nov 9
Milkshake flavors, Jan 18
Milne, A. A., Jan 31
Mirrors, avoiding, Feb 11
Miss Piggy, Jan 2
Miyamoto, Shigeru, May 6
Molko, Brian, Feb 9
Mother's Day, May 7
Movie alarm clocks, Apr 16
Movies
  buying all the seats, Aug 26
  going to the, Feb 12
  horror films and, Oct 12
  sneaking in food, Mar 16
  watching all day, May 20
  at work, Mar 30
Mud, playing in, Jun 3
Music, blasting in traffic, Mar 26

Nakedness, Mar 7
Napping at work, Aug 17
Nash, Ogden, Apr 11, May 22, Jul 13
Nastase, Ilie, Oct 5
Newspaper, stealing neighbor's, Mar 20
Newton-John, Olivia, Oct 18
New Year's Eve, celebrating, Dec 31
New Year's resolutions, Jan 1
Nielsen, Leslie, Apr 2
Nietzsche, Friedrich, Jan 8, Apr 6, Jul 3, Sep 17, Sep 21
Nude beach with clothes, Aug 19
Nugent, Ted, Aug 2

Office chairs, Jul 13
Office jerks, Aug 6
Office supplies, stealing, Oct 23
100 miles per hour, Apr 23
One-night stands, Oct 20
Online dating, Sep 30
Oogling, Apr 14
Open relationships, Mar 9
Oral hygiene, ignore, Oct 24
Original painting, forgery as, Dec 14
O'Rourke, P. J., May 29
Osborne, John, Feb 11
Oswalt, Patton, Mar 16
Overdressing, Feb 9

Palahniuk, Chuck, Sep 4
Parker, Dorothy, Mar 10
Parking, illegal, Oct 27
Parking space, executive, Jul 25
Parking tickets, Jun 5, Nov 19
Parties, May 29
Parton, Dolly, Nov 12
Party venues, Jul 28
Pausch, Randy, Mar 18
Personal trainers, May 25

Peter, Laurence J., Apr 27, Nov 7
Pets, May 18, Jul 21
Philanthropy, Jan 17
Picabia, Francis, Aug 9
Picasso, Pablo, Apr 7, Dec 14
Pillow fight, public, Sep 10
Pimping your ride, Nov 25
Piro, Stephanie, Jun 18
Pizza
    eating alone, May 31
    expensive silverware and, Dec 23
    sharing, Mar 22
Plato, Jan 29
Playground games, Jun 29
Pool cleaner, Aug 15
Potlucks, Mar 18, Sep 18
Powell, Anthony, Nov 27
Powell, John Enoch, May 11
Powers, Steve, Jan 12
Prank calling, Apr 10
Pranking, Apr 1
Prohibition slang, Jul 1
Protest, create a, Jul 8
Proust, Marcel, Apr17
Proverbs, Jan 11, Jun 19, Jun 21, Sep 5, Nov 6, Nov 8, Nov 22, Dec 23
Proxmire, William, Feb 10
Public fountains, jumping into, Jul 10
Public peeing, Aug 27
Puddle jumping, Apr 5
Pulp Fiction, Jan 18
Punctuality, Feb 8
Pyle, Andrew, Jun 15

Quitting a job, Apr 20

Racing for pink slips, Jun 23
Radner, Gilda, Sep 22
Rainy day fund, spending, Aug 24
Rather, Dan, Feb 6
Reality TV, Jan 12
Refills, free, May 15
Religious holidays, Jan 24
Religious services, free food and, Sep 16
Rental cars, Aug 22
Reservoir Dogs, Jun 4
Restaurant deliveries, Feb 5
Resumes, embellishing, Sep 5
Revenge, Nov 5, Nov 18, Nov 26, Dec 19
Revenge/humiliation, May 3
Richards, Michael, Dec 5
Richter, Andy, Feb 5, Jan 27
Rivers, Joan, Jul 19
Road rage, Dec 18
Robotic vacuums, Jan 22
Rodman, Denis, Jul 26
Rogers, Will, Oct 27
Rohn, Jim, Dec 20
Romans, Ben, Sep 10
Romantic dinners, Feb 16
Rose color meanings, Jun 22
Rothko, Mark, Apr 26
Royko, Mike, Mar 4
Rudner, Rita, May 25, Aug 22, Nov 16, Dec 26
Russell, Bertrand, Jan 26, Feb 28

Saavedra, Miguel de Cervantes, Apr 16
Samuels, Jim, Apr 23
Sand, George, Mar 5
Sandburg, Carl, Jun 3
Sandcastles, Aug 3
Sartre, Jean-Paul, Jan 17
Savings account, cashing out a, May 24
Scenic drives, Mar 6
Scooby Doo (Daphne), Nov 10
Second job, on company time, Mar 19
Seinfeld, Jerry, Mar 20, Jun 25, Sep 25, Dec 1
Self-portrait, commission a, Nov 27
Seuss, Dr., Mar 13
Sex, Mar 25, Dec 11

on boss' desk, Nov 26
in elevator, Aug 8
library and, Jul 31
make-up, May 23
records, Apr 3
Sexting, Jan 27
Sexy lingerie, Jul 26
Share, refusing to, Nov 13
Shaw, George Bernard, Jul 23, Sep 3
Sheets, luxurious, Mar 10
Shoes, Nov 29
Shopping, ignore price tags, Nov 23
Shower
hour long, Jun 21
singing in, Nov 28
skipping morning, Dec 12
Sickness, faking a, Nov 3
Significant other, inventing a, Oct 15
Simpson, Bart, May 21, Dec 4
Simpson, Homer, Jul 6, Sep 6, Dec 8
Sinatra, Frank, Dec 15
Single day, taking a, May 10
Sites, Internet, Mar 3
Skinny dipping, Jun 9
Skydiving, Mar 29
Sleep aids, Jan 21
Sleeping, Jan 21
Smiley, Jane, Feb 24
Smith, Joseph, Nov 14
Smith, Patti, Sep 16
"Smoke" breaks at work, Jan 26
Smoking, Oct 17
S'Mores, May 19
Snooze buttons, Apr 16
Snow, Carrie, Aug 17
Snowball fights, Feb 3
Snow day, taking a, Feb 22
Soco and lime, Jan 3
Song, on repeat mode, Nov 2
Southey, Robert, Jan 3
Sowell, Thomas, May 17
Spacing out at work, Apr 2
Spa treatments, Apr 9
Speakeasy, opening a, Jul 1
Spending money senselessly, Oct 26
Spiking the punch, Mar 1
Spock, Benjamin, Nov 13
Sports, watching at work, May 14
Stefani, Gwen, Dec 12
Stein, Gertrude, May 10
Story stealing, Oct 10
Stowe, Harriet Beecher, Jul 27
Strip clubs, Sep 19
Strip poker, Mar 17
Student discounts, Feb 7
Styling team, personal, Sep 7
Subway etiquette, Mar 8
Sunday drives, Jun 10
Supermarket Sweep, Dec 5
Surprise party, create own, Mar 24
Swearing/vulgarities, Jul 17
Swimming pools, Jul 3, Jul 18, Jul 30

Tabloids, supermarket, Mar 23
Takeout food, May 30
Tanning, Jul 14
Tattoos, Sep 2
Taxes, cheating on, Apr 15
Taxi cabs, Aug 12
Telemarketers, Aug 7
Telephone use, Jan 4
Temperature control, office, Jan 19
Temper tantrums, Feb 27
Tennyson, Alfred Lord, Mar 9
Thanksgiving, friends only, Nov 15
Tharp, Twyla, Dec 24
Thoreau, Henry David, Jan 10
Three wise men, Jan 3
Tipping, Jun 4
Toilet-paper a house, Oct 30
Toys, buying cool, Sep 26
Traffic, driving the shoulder, Sep 14

Traffic, following an ambulance, Dec 22
Traffic laws, Mar 21
Trash/recycling, Sep 4
Trick-or-treating, Oct 31
Trillin, Calvin, Jul 7, Aug 10
Trivia, cheating at, Apr 4
Turnstiles, jumping, Aug 21
TV remote, controlling, Sep 25
Twain, Mark, Jan 5, Feb 15, Feb 26, Jun 20, Aug 19
Twenty-one shots, drinking, Jan 3
Tyler, Anne, Jun 17

Ulmer, Ernestine, May 16
Underwear, Feb 18

Vacations, going alone, Dec 7
Vacations, inventing, Apr 17
Vaughn, Bill, Nov 19
Vega, Vincent, Jan 18
Video games, cheating at, May 6
Video gaming, Jan 7
Videos, hurtful, Dec 13
Vigilante, parking meter, Nov 24
Vodka-infused pineapple, Jan 8
Voltaire, Jan 13
Volunteering, Jan 1
Vonnegut, Kurt, Jan 20, Oct 25

Wardrobe, buying a new, Aug 31
Warhol, Andy, Feb 16, Sep 27
Warner, Charles Dudley, Jan 1
Watterson, Bill, Feb 17, Feb 22
Weaver, Earl, Nov 17
Wedding crashing, Sep 9
Welles, Orson, Mar 14
Werkheiser, Devon, Jul 15
West, Mae, Apr 21
Wieners, Gretchen, Jul 12
WiFi, stealing, Jan 9
Wilde, Oscar, Jan 25, Apr 20, May 4, Sep 1, Sep 7, Sep 8, Sep23, Oct 17
Williams, Bern, Mar 3
Williams, David, Feb 21
Wine, May 26
Wine, cooking with, Oct 22
Winter into summer, Jan 8
Winters, Shelley, Sep 19
Wood, David, Jan 30
Woods, Alan, Aug 6
Woods, Tiger, Feb 5
Woolf, Virginia, Oct 28
Work, arrive late, Sep 11
Work, skipping, Oct 7, Nov 9
Working at home, Feb 28
Workplace habits, annoying, Dec 3
World Wide Web, Jan 9
Wreaking havoc, Sep 20
Wright, Stephen, Aug 11

Yard, cleaning a, Aug 28
Young, Edward, Aug 5
Youngman, Henny, Jan 24, Mar 29, Jul 22, Aug 30

About the Author

Eric Grzymkowski is a humor writer and unapologetic sinner. He hopes someday to earn enough money writing so he can relax in bed all day drinking milkshakes made from imported Belgian chocolate out of stolen artisanal goblets. When not writing he can be found flipping off unsuspecting motorists, cutting in line at the supermarket, and talking on his cell phone at the movies. He resides in Somerville, MA, where his self-centered nature generally goes unnoticed.